Leaving The Crowds Behind

A Guide To Backcountry Camping
In Rocky Mountain National Park

By

John E. Heasley

RAS Publishing, Fort Collins, Colorado

RAS Publishing, 2917 Eagle Drive, Fort Collins, CO 80526

Printed in the United States of America

Photos and maps by the author

Book design by Resource Analysis Systems, Ft. Collins, CO

970 - 226- 2311   www.resourceanalysis.com

06 05 04 03 02   54321

Library of Congress Control Number: 2002091943

ISBN: 0-9671040-1-7

Disclaimer

This book contains information gathered from many sources. Every effort has been made to ensure the accuracy of this information. This book is published for general reference and not as a substitute for independent verification by users when circumstances warrant. The publisher and author will not be held responsible for any inconvenience or injury resulting from the use or misuse of the maps, diagrams, or text of this book.

Contents

About The Author

John Heasley has been hiking, camping, and fishing in Colorado for over 20 years. Since he received his PhD in ecology in 1978, John has been actively involved in the application of technologies to natural resource problems. He has worked for Colorado State University, the US Fish and Wildlife Service, and the US Forest Service. He founded Resource Analysis Systems in 1988. RAS is dedicated to the development and application of new technologies for the collection and analysis of information concerning our use of the natural environment. These technologies include: computer simulation models of ecological systems, visual analysis software, information systems and decision support systems for use in environmental assessments, and digital mapping software.

In 1994, John developed software for the generation of 3D trail maps for several wilderness areas in northern Colorado and Rocky Mountain National Park. These maps help the hiker to better visualize the terrain and the lay of the land. A lot of information has been collected about natural resources that is not readily available to people who love the outdoors. John hopes to change that by using technology to bring you truly useful information through the publication of books, maps, CD's, development of outdoor recreation kiosks, and making detailed information about Colorado's outdoor resources available on-line (www.resourceanalysis.com). John has also written "Colorado Campgrounds: Volume 1", a book providing detailed descriptions of northern Colorado campgrounds and "Colorado's Indian Peaks Wilderness -- A Guide to Trails and Lakes". John hopes to publish a CD covering all of the trails in Rocky Mountain National Park some time in the summer of 2002.

Acknowledgment

I would like to thank all of the backcountry campers and Park personnel that I met, while collecting the data for this book, for sharing their impressions and experiences of backcountry camping in the Park. A special thanks goes to Barry Sweet of the RMNP backcountry office for providing me with campsite data and usage statistics. Ron Thomas, geographic information specialist for the Park, provided digital map data on trails and cross country zones. My friend and fellow outdoor writer and photographer John Messineo expertly composed the author's photo and provided valuable feedback on the manuscript. Wayne Crownhart of Vison Graphics provided very helpful advise on the printing aspects of the book.

A special thanks goes to my wife Linda for reviewing the manuscript, and without whose support this book would not have been possible.

Introduction

Rocky Mountain National Park (RMNP or the Park) is one of the most spectacular and beautiful places in Colorado. This jewel of our National Parks encompasses over 415 square miles of majestic granite peaks, windswept alpine tundra, pristine forests, icy blue lakes, and rushing streams. The Park is divided into east and west sides by the Continental Divide. The east side is characterized by steep cliffs and U-shaped valleys and receives about 15 inches of precipitation a year. On the west side of the Park the mountains gradually recede into the Kawuneeche Valley. Here the precipitation averages about 20 inches per year with deeper snows. The landscape of RMNP is made up of approximately 60% forest, 13% alpine tundra, 18% exposed rock, and a 9% mixture of vegetation types. Vegetation types characterize the elevation zones of the Park and consist of: ponderosa pine and grass/shrubland from 7,800 to 8,500 feet, lodgepole pine from 8,500 to 9,500 feet, spruce and subalpine fir from 9,500 to 11,500 feet, and alpine tundra over 11,500 feet. The highest elevations are primarily rock.

Rocky Mountain National Park is home to the headwaters of four major river systems: the North Fork of the Colorado River, the Big Thompson River, the Cache La Poudre River, and the North Fork of St Vrain Creek. The Colorado River flows west while the other three flow to the east. There are 147 lakes and about 473 miles of stream within the park. Only 51 of the lakes contain populations of trout. Over the past few decades the Park Service has had an on going effort to restore native trout populations (Greenback Cutthroat and Colorado Cutthroat) to the lakes and streams of RMNP. Many of these water bodies are designated catch and release only. Some of the waters are closed to fishing.

The Park is one of America's premier destinations for wildlife watching, providing opportunities offering great potential for seeing elk, bighorn sheep, mule deer, moose, coyotes, and a myriad of small mammals and birds. Rocky Mountain National Park has a large variety of wildlife including 66 species of mammals, 260 species of birds, 11 species of fish, 5 species of amphibians, and one species of reptile. Elk, deer,

moose, and bighorn sheep are the large ungulates found in the Park. Moose are primarily seen in and around the Kawuneeche Valley on the west side. Elk bugling in September is a very popular attraction for wildlife watching visitors to RMNP. Some of the more

The beautiful pine grossbeak is a rare treat for backcountry bird watchers.

common bird species found in the Park include the American robin, red-tailed hawk, Stellar's jay, broad-tailed hummingbird, gray jay, Clark's nutcracker, pine siskin, mountain chickadee, and dark-eyed junco.

The number of visitors to the Park has increased significantly over the last 40 years. Since 1994, the yearly number of visitors has topped three million. Most of those people confined their visits to areas immediately adjacent to Trail Ridge Road and Bear Lake Road. Visitation at Rocky Mountain National Park is about the same as Yellowstone National Park. However, RMNP is one eighth the size of Yellowstone. Although recent statistics have not been compiled, a study in 1977 reported that over 700,000 hikers took to the 350 miles of trails in Rocky Mountain National Park that year.

In the midst of this ever-increasing pressure how does one find a wilderness experience among a sea of humanity? The areas around the roads provide only a limited picture of the true beauty of Rocky Mountain National Park. Viewing the Park from here is much like viewing animals in a zoo. The only way to truly appreciate the beauty and grandeur of this area is to get out in it. The National Park Service has recently completed a wilderness management plan whose goal

The Bear Lake area is one of the most crowded areas in Rocky Mountain National Park.

is to provide means for visitors to experience the unique wilderness quality of the Park and at the same time preserve the character that makes this land wild.

There are over 110 maintained trails that provide access to most areas in the Park. Popular areas (e.g. Bear Lake, Longs Peak), though less crowded than the roads, may not offer the solitude needed by many visitors to truly appreciate the beauty and uniqueness of this jewel of the National Park System. Popular trails sometimes seem like an endless conveyor of hikers. Backcountry camping, for many, is the best way to enjoy the wilderness character of Rocky Mountain National Park. It allows you to experience the Park at its most magical times, early morning and late evening. Staying overnight in the backcountry allows you to experience a high altitude view of the stars. Unencumbered by city lights, you'll experience a sky full of stars that you never knew existed. Gone are the day-hikers along with the inhibitions of secretive wildlife. Your chances of observing wildlife are greater without the presence of the multitudes.

The National Park Service has done a commendable job in managing the backcountry of the Park to give you the most enjoyable wilderness experience possible. Backcountry campsites are designed to minimize your impact on this high altitude ecosystem. Most are hidden from the traffic of daytime seekers of a wilderness experience. At the same time, they provide a level of convenience for those less experienced in the rigors of backcountry camping. Cross-country zones are available to those who wish even more solitude and are more experienced in cross-country travel and primitive camping. Taking your trip at less popular times (spring, fall, midweek) and

visiting less used campsites will improve your wilderness experience.

This book is not a "how to" book on backcountry camping. There are a plethora of good books on that subject. Some of these include: *Backpacking One Step At A Time* by Harvey Manning, *Walking Softly In The Wilderness* by John Hart, and *Hiking and Backpacking* by Karen Berger. Anyone wishing to experience backcountry camping in Rocky Mountain National Park would do well to read some of these books. This book is a guide to opportunities in Rocky Mountain National Park for a high altitude wilderness experience through camping in the backcountry. Its purpose is to provide you, the perspective backcountry

The snowshoe hare is a rare sight more likely seen by back-country travelers.

camper, with detailed information on what various sections of the Park are like, what activities are available near each campsite, what camping facilities are available, and how to get to your chosen camping location. Information is also provided on the popularity of each camping location. Statistics on the percentage of the primary camping season (June through September) that a camping location has been occupied are presented. Except for basic rules, winter camping areas and climbers bivouac areas are not covered in this book. Information on trail mileages, elevations and elevation changes, travel times, and campsite positions were computed from Park Service Geographic Information System data, USGS Digital Elevation data, and data collected by the author. It is hoped that the information contained in this volume will encourage users of the Rocky Mountain National Park backcountry to explore less popular areas of the Park and thus even out our impact on this precious resource.

Camping In The High Country

Camping in the backcountry of Rocky Mountain National Park presents campers with unique challenges, especially for those who normally live at lower elevations. The most significant of these challenges are the altitude and the weather. Many visitors to RMNP live in areas of much lower elevation. The backcountry campsites are located at elevations ranging from 8,100 to 12,760 feet above sea level. Fourteen

High country camping in Rocky Mountain National Park offers beauty as well as solitude.

campsite locations are between 8,000 and 9,000 feet, fifty are between 9,000 and 10,000 feet, fifty are between 10,000 and 11,000 feet, five are between 11,000 and 12,000 feet, and one campsite location is above 12,000 feet. The air at these elevations is generally drier and contains less oxygen than at lower elevations. If not properly acclimated, backcountry campers can develop altitude sickness. Symptoms include headaches, shortness of breath, loss of appetite, nausea, and lethargy. Give yourself a few days to acclimate to the elevations and drink often even though you don't feel thirsty. You can become dehydrated very quickly as you lose significant water through your lungs and via sweating. Take your time getting to your camping destinations. It is a good idea to make your first day easy and to camp at a lower elevation. If you do experience symptoms, move to a lower elevation and rest. Only continue to climb after the symptoms have gone away. Different people react differently to the thin air at high elevations. It has nothing to do with how physically fit you are. Minor symptoms will generally subside with a rest day. If you ignore them and push on, you may contract acute mountain sickness. That can be fatal!

It has been said that the only certainty about the weather in Rocky Mountain National Park is that you'll have some. Forecasters frequently miss the mark when trying to predict mountain weather. The weather can change very rapidly in the high country. You may encounter hot and sunny weather one moment and rain or snow the next. Always be prepared for the worst. Practice layering when it comes to clothing. Hypothermia is the most common threat to safety that backcountry travelers face in RMNP. Too often hikers or backpackers venture into the high country without adequate equipment or the knowledge to use it. Hypothermia can sneak up on you without warning. High winds above treeline can make becoming hypothermic even easier. Afternoon thunderstorms are common during the summer in RMNP. Lightning is particularly dangerous above treeline. Plan to avoid the alpine tundra during summer afternoons and know what to do if caught in the open by a sudden thunderstorm. Avoid ledges on steep inclines, taking shelter under an overhang or in a cave, or sitting in a depression. These areas attract lightning that travels along the ground. Always carry good rain gear to avoid

Weather in Rocky Mountain National Park can be unpredictable. Afternoon thunderstorms are common in summer.

getting wet with the possibility of becoming hypothermic.

Dehydration can be a problem when camping in the high country. Drink plenty of water even when you don't feel thirsty. The days of pure mountain water are long gone. Always boil or filter water before drinking. The parasite Giardia is present in the waters of Rocky Mountain National Park and can cause severe intestinal illness if ingested.

High altitude ecosystems are more fragile and less resilient than those in less extreme climates. Vegetation of the alpine tundra is hardy but cannot withstand repeated trampling. It may take a hundred years for plants to recover from damage caused by thoughtless hikers and campers. Walk single file on maintained trails where they exist and spread out when walking over tundra where there are no trails. As backcountry

The alpine tundra is a fragile environment. Take care to minimize your impact when crossing it.

areas receive heavier use, it becomes increasingly important that you leave no evidence of your having been there. Learn and practice Leave No Trace camping techniques. The principles of no trace camping are simple: Pack out what you pack in, clean up your mess, and leave the campsite better than you found it. Some things that you can do to minimize your impact on the wilderness and to help preserve it for others to enjoy include:

- Plan ahead and prepare for your wilderness trip. Be knowledgeable of the area, have good maps, and know what to expect. Plan meals and repackage foods in reusable containers. Have the proper gear for expected weather and trail conditions. Plan your trip so as to minimize your impact.

- Stay on trails in heavily used areas and stick to durable surfaces where possible. Do not create new trails to avoid wet or muddy areas. Travel in single file on heavily used trails. Spread out when traveling cross-country in remote areas.

- Camp in designated or previously used campsites in high use areas. Camp on durable surfaces (sand, dry grass, rock,

etc.). Move camp often in remote areas. Leave your site better than the way you found it.

- Avoid building campfires whenever possible. If necessary, use existing fire rings. Use only dead wood found on the ground. Make sure fires are completely out and cool to the touch.

- Don't use soap around any lakes or streams.

- Pack out what you pack in. Leave no trash or garbage in the wilderness. Burying or burning garbage are inefficient methods of disposal.

- Bury all human waste 6 - 8 inches at least 200 feet from all lakes, streams, and wet areas as well as camping areas. Use toilet paper sparingly and pack it out.

- Avoid damaging plants and trees. Don't hammer nails into trees or cut branches for bedding. Don't build permanent structures such as cairns.

- Respect the privacy of others. Keep noise to a minimum.

- Packstock are easily spooked. Avoid a dangerous mishap by stepping to the downhill side of trails and speaking softly until all stock have passed.

- Do not pick wildflowers or disturb wildlife.

Besides the solitude, one of the joys of backcountry camping is being able to observe wildlife in their natural habitat. These animals, though accustomed to people, are wild and should not be approached or fed. While camping, keep all food stuffs and any scent producing items (toothpaste, soap, etc.) out of the reach of wildlife. Do not keep food in your tent. Packs left unattended with food in them may fall victim to the teeth of hungry critters accustomed to handouts. Put food in bear boxes where provided or hang food in a container from a branch 10' high and 4' from the trunk of a tree.

Permits, Reservations, and Rules

The National Park Service instituted a permit and reservation system at RMNP to minimize the impacts of overnight use in the backcountry. A permit is required for all overnight trips into the backcountry all year round. One permit is required per party per trip. Individuals are allowed to obtain a permit for up to 7 nights during the summer months (June through September) and an additional 14 nights the rest of the year (October through May) for a total of 21 nights per calendar year. An administrative fee (currently $15) is charged from May through October only. This fee is nonrefundable, nonexchangeable, and does not include the Park entrance fee. Permits may be obtained year round at the Backcountry Offices near the Beaver Meadows and Kawuneeche visitor centers. In the summer, permits are also issued at the Longs Peak, Corral Creek, and Wild Basin Ranger Stations as well as the CSU Pingree Park Campus. In winter, self-registration permits may be picked up at self-registration boxes located at the Beaver Meadows and Fall River entrance stations and the Wild Basin, Sandbeach Lake, Longs Peak, and Dunraven trailheads. The permit must be displayed on the outside of your pack while hiking to and from your campsite and on the outside of your tent while in camp. A vehicle dash tag will be issued for each vehicle that is parked overnight at a trailhead. The tag lists your last name, vehicle license plate, trailhead where parked, and a code for the date when you should be out of the backcountry.

In order for campers to plan ahead, a reservation system has been established. All backcountry camping areas are available for reservation. Unreserved permits may also be obtained on the day of the trip on a first come first served basis. Reservations can only be made for the current calendar year. The following is the current reservation schedule for RMNP:

- January 1 - February 28: Reservations by phone, mail, or walk-in (for January or February only)

- March 1 - May 15: Reservations by phone, mail, or walk-in

- May 16 - September 30: Reservations by mail or walk-in only

- October 1 - December 31: Reservations by phone, mail, or walk-in

Reserved permits may be picked up no sooner than 30 days prior to the day of the trip. They must be picked up by 10:00 AM on the first day of the trip (May through October) or they will be cancelled in their entirety and offered to other campers.

There are five types of camping permitted in the backcountry of RMNP. These are: designated sites, stock sites, cross-country areas, bivouac areas, and winter areas. The following rules apply to each type:

Designated Sites (individual and group):

- Camp must be established within 15 feet of the metal arrowhead and post marking the site or on designated tent pads.

- Camp stoves only. Fires are prohibited, except in sites specified for wood fires with a visible metal fire ring (use down and dead wood only).

- Party size is limited to 7 at individual sites and 12 at group sites.

- Groups that split up must camp in campsites at least one mile apart.

- If a site has more than 4 inches of snow, follow the winter area rules.

Stock Sites (individual and group):

- Camps must be established in stock camps only.

- Party size is limited to 6 individuals and 8 stock at individual stock sites.

- Party size is limited to 12 people and 16 stock at group stock sites.

- Camp stoves only. Fires are prohibited, except in sites specified for wood fires with a visible metal fire ring (use down and dead wood only).

- Grazing is prohibited. Certified weed-free feed is required.

- Use hitchrails that are provided. Highlining, hobbling and loose herding is prohibited.

Cross-country Areas:

- Camp must be:
  - Established within the cross-country zone
  - At least 200' (70 adult steps) from water.
  - Out of sight and sound of trails and other campers.
  - Below treeline and out of meadows.
  - Moved at least 1 mile each night.

- No more than 2 nights in 1 cross-country zone.

- Party size is limited to 7 people.

- Camp stoves only. Fires prohibited.

- Stock prohibited.

Bivouac Areas:

- A bivouac is defined as a temporary, open-air encampment.

- Permits are issued only to technical climbers.

- The climb must be 4 or more technical pitches and 3.5 or more miles from the trailhead.

- Party size is limited to 4 people (all must be climbing).

- A bivouac must be established:
  - Within the designated bivouac area, or at the base or on the face of the climb.
  - At least 200' (70 adult steps) from water.
  - With camp set up at dusk and taken down before dawn.
  - Without the use of erected type shelters, tents or supported tarps.
  - On rock or snow only, not on vegetation or in meadows.

- Camp stoves only. Fires prohibited.

- Stock prohibited.

Winter Areas:

- Camp at least 200' (70 adult steps) away from designated sites if more than 4 inches of snow.

- Party size is limited to 12 people.

- Camps must be established:
  - Within the designated winter area.
  - At least one mile from the trailhead.
  - At least 200' (70 adult steps) from water.
  - On snow or rock only (never on vegetation or in meadows).
  - Out of sight and sound of other campers, trails, or winter travel areas.

- Camp stoves only. Fires prohibited.

To further minimize impacts on the backcountry the following are prohibited everywhere in the backcountry:

- Pets, weapons, and vehicles (incl. bicycles)

- Fires (except at sites with metal fire rings)

- Hunting, feeding, approaching or disturbing wildlife

- Removing or disturbing natural features

- Trenching around tents and camps

- Shortcuts between trail switchbacks

- Littering or leaving trash in sites or pit toilets

- Washing dishes or bathing within 200' (70 adult steps) of water

All persons 16 years of age or older must have a valid Colorado fishing license to fish in RMNP. Only one rod or line may be used. Artificial flies or lures only may be used with the exception that children under 12 may use worms or fish eggs in open park waters. No bait is allowed in catch-and-release waters. See website (www.nps.gov/romo/fishing.htm) or Park Service personnel for special regulations and possession limits.

Backcountry Campsites

There are 219 campsites at 120 locations in the backcountry of Rocky Mountain National Park. These locations are grouped into camping areas representing a general area of the Park. These areas include: Bear Lake Area, East Inlet Area, Gorge Lakes Area, Hague Creek Area, Mummy Range, Longs Peak Area, Never Summer Range, North Fork Area, North Inlet Area, Timber Lake Area, Tonahutu Area, and Wild Basin Area. Of the 219 campsites in the Park, 197 are designated as individual sites and 22 are classified as group sites. Individual campsites permit 1 to 7 campers per site. Most will accommodate 1 to 2 tents (2 or 3 man). Some have room for 3 or 4 tents. The majority of individual sites are well shaded with plenty of vegetation for privacy. They are generally located well off the hiking trails. Group campsites are designed to accommodate 8 to 12 campers. Group sites have a much larger area for pitching your tents. Most will accommodate 4 to 8 tents. Group campsites may not

Group campsites such as this one at the July campsite location are much larger than individual campsites.

Individual campsite at Lost Lake.

be reserved for less than eight people unless within five days of your trip. At this time any available group sites will be released to parties of less than eight campers. Groups that split up and use individual sites must camp at sites at least a mile apart. This is to discourage the creation of social trails. Most of the campsites have easily identifiable bare areas for pitching your tent. Use these bare areas to minimize the impact on vegetation.

There are also campsites that are suitable for camping with stock (horses, burros, mules, llama). These sites are just like the others but also have facilities (hitchracks or tethering posts) for confining stock overnight. There are thirteen campsites suitable for

camping with stock.

Although aesthetically pleasing, campfires cause considerable impact on the backcountry. They also have the potential for getting out of control. For this reason campfires are allowed in only eighteen of the 120 campsite locations available. These sites include: Boundary Creek, Silvanmere, Halfway, Aspen Meadow

Hitchracks are provided at stock sites suitable for horses.

Group, Happily Lost, Lost Falls, McGregor Mountain, Bighorn Mountain, Sprague Lake Handicamp, East Meadow, Gray Jay Group, Summerland Park, North Inlet Group, Footbridge, Porcupine, Tonahutu Group, Flatiron, and Mummy Pass Creek. Where allowed, metal fire grates/rings are provided and must be used. Firewood is not provided. Campers are encouraged to pack in wood or gather wood (wrist size) from a wide area around their camp. Use nothing but dead and down wood. Do not burn noncombustible items such as foil, glass, or plastic. Never leave a fire unattended.

Toilet facilities in the form of pit toilets, outhouses, compost toilets, and solar toilets are

The fire ring at Bighorn Mountain Group campsite.

provided at over half of the camping locations in the Park. Although, to some, the presence of toilet facilities intrude upon the wilderness setting, they are necessary to minimize the degree of human waste impacts in areas of high use. Sixty five of the camping locations in the park have toilet facilities available. Most group campsites are equipped with pit toilets or outhouses. Privacy walls are provided in high use areas and where there is little natural vegetative screening. In camping locations where toilets are not provided, campers should use either the pack-it-out method or the cat hole system.

Water is generally available at each campsite from nearby streams or lakes. A few campsites may require

Typical pit toilet provided in high use areas.

packing in water during the driest times of the year (July, August, September). As Giardia is always a potential problem in the waters of Rocky Mountain National Park, always purify the water that you collect before using it. Methods acceptable for this task include:

- Use a water filter that eliminates Giardia
- Use water purifying tablets that eliminate Giardia
- Boil water for ten minutes

Backcountry campers are required to secure food and other scented items such as toothpaste or deodorant from wildlife when not being immediately used. Using a portable food storage container or hanging items from a tree ten feet from the ground and four feet from the trunk horizontally are recommended. Food boxes or "bear" boxes (metal ammunition containers) are provided in areas where unacceptable conflicts between campers and wildlife occur or the potential for problems is high. These are brown containers with a yellow top.

Food containers (bear boxes) are provided in some camping locations.

Campsites are marked by wooden signs, red plastic arrowheads, and silver arrowheads. The access trails leading to each campsite are prominently marked by a wooden sign on the nearest hiking trail. Many of these access trails, but not all, are marked with red plastic arrowheads attached to trees along the path. In some cases, the access trails are lined with logs or rocks. Each campsite is marked with a silver arrowhead on a metal post. Campers must

Campsite marker.

camp within fifteen feet of this arrowhead or on established tent pads.

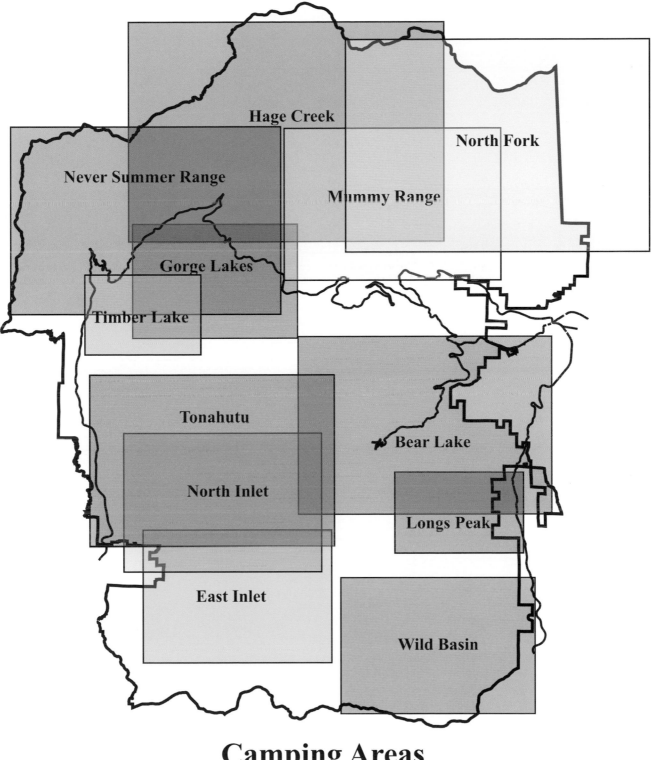

Hage Creek

North Fork

Never Summer Range

Mummy Range

Gorge Lakes

Timber Lake

Tonahutu

Bear Lake

North Inlet

Longs Peak

East Inlet

Wild Basin

Camping Areas

Bear Lake Area Campsites

Campsite	No. of sites	Wood Fires	Elevation	Privy	Nearest Trailhead	Distance	Elevation Change	Travel Time	Stock	Use
Andrews Creek	1	stoves only	10,560 ft	yes	Glacier Gorge Junction	3.5 mi	1,474 ft	2.5 - 3 hr	no	100%
Arch Rock	1	stoves only	8,240 ft	no	Fern Lake	1.2 mi	314 ft	45 min	no	82%
Boulder Brook	2 / 1grp	stoves only	10,200 ft	yes	Storm Pass	2.5 mi	1,508 ft	2 hr	no	62%
Cub Creek	2	stoves only	8,600 ft	yes	Cub Lake	1.9 mi	687 ft	1.5 - 2 hr	no	67%
Fern Lake	4 / 1grp	stoves only	9,530 ft	yes	Fern Lake	3.5 mi	1,536 ft	3 hr	no	83%
Glacier Gorge	1	stoves only	10,100 ft	yes	Glacier Gorge Junction	3.4 mi	1,035 ft	2.5 - 3 hr	no	100%
Mill Creek Basin	2	stoves only	9,026 ft	yes	Hollowell Park	1.8 mi	671 ft	1 - 1.5 hr	no	63%
Odessa Lake	2	stoves only	10,020 ft	yes	Bear Lake	3.6 mi	1,820 ft	3.5 - 4 hr	no	89%
Old Forest Inn	2	stoves only	8,400 ft	yes	Fern Lake	1.7 mi	488 ft	1 hr	no	91%
Over The Hill	1	stoves only	8,870 ft	yes	East Portal	1.3 mi	569 ft	45 min	no	38%
Sourdough	1	stoves only	10,600 ft	yes	Bear Lake	2.4 mi	1,045 ft	2 - 3 hr	no	100%
Sprague Lake Handicamp	1	yes	8,820 ft	yes	Sprague Lake	.5 mi	20 ft	20-30 min	no	14%
Spruce Lake	2	stoves only	9,670 ft	yes	Fern Lake	4.4 mi	1,752 ft	4 hr	no	52%
Upper Mill Creek	2	stoves only	9,150 ft	yes	Hollowell Park	1.9 mi	743 ft	1 - 1.5 hr	no	64%
Upper Wind River	2	stoves only	8,980 ft	yes	East Portal	1.5 mi	568 ft	1 - 1.5 hr	no	75%
Ute Meadow	1	stoves only	9,415 ft	no	Up. Beaver Meadows	2.7 mi	1,261 ft	2 hr	llama	36%
Wind River Bluff	1	stoves only	8,720 ft	yes	East Portal	.6 mi	301 ft	45 min	no	60%

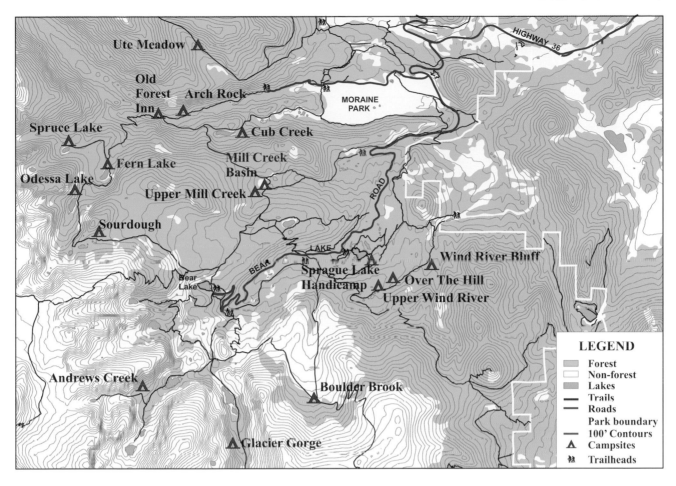

Bear Lake Area

The Bear Lake area is one of the most popular sections of the Park for day hikers. There are over 35 trails in this area. The most popular areas, however,

The Bear Lake area encompases over 60 square miles of the Park.

are not close to the backcountry campsites. There are 17 camping locations within this area containing 30 campsites. Two of these sites are group sites and one permits the use of llamas. Sprague Lake is the only handicamp site in the Park. Fifteen of the sites have toilet facilities. The Sprague Lake Handicamp is the only site to permit the use of wood fires. All of the sites are located in forested areas. Some are more shaded than others. Elevations range from 8,240 feet at Arch Rock to 10,600 feet at the Sourdough campsite.

Most of the campsites offer easy access to stream or lake fishing. Look for signs indicating catch and release fishing only on many of the waters in the Park. Check with Park personnel to be sure. Numerous peaks are found in this area. Some of these include: Hallett Peak (12,713'), Taylor Peak (13,153'), Powell Peak (13,208'), and McHenrys Peak (13,327').

Trailheads providing access to campsites in this area include: Bear Lake, Glacier Gorge Junction, Sprague Lake, East Portal, Hollowell Park, Cub Lake, Fern Lake, and Upper Beaver Meadows. The distance from a trailhead to campsites ranges from .5 miles to 4.4 miles with hiking times ranging from 45 minutes to 4 hours. Topographic maps that cover the area include the McHenrys Peak and Longs Peak quads.

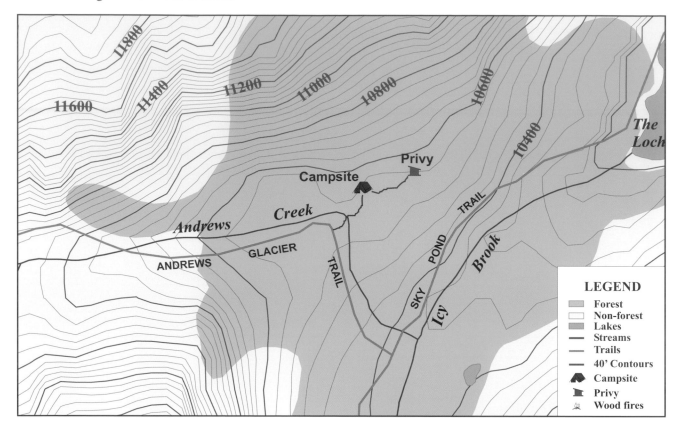

Andrews Creek

Description:

The Andrews Creek campsite is located northeast of the Andrews Glacier Trail in a stand of spruce and fir trees. The path to the site is marked with red arrows on the trees. It crosses a stream over a log bridge and travels a few hundred yards to the site. There are two distinct tent sites with room for 2 to 3 tents. The site is in an area with a lot of downed trees that resulted from an avalanche that occurred in the winter of 1985-1986. Fires are not permitted here, use camp stoves only. There is a pit toilet (no walls) a little farther to the northeast from the site. Water may be obtained from Andrews Creek or a slow-moving stream closer to the site. The site is located at an elevation of 10,560 feet, an elevation gain of about 1380 feet from the trailhead. This campsite is one of the most popular sites in the Park.

Activities:

Fishing: The Loch, Lake of Glass, Sky Pond

Hiking: Andrews Glacier Trail, Sky Pond Trail

Peaks nearby: Hallett Peak, Taylor Peak, Otis Peak, The Sharkstooth

Scenic Features: Andrews Glacier, Tyndall Glacier, Timberline Falls

Andrews Creek campsite.

Directions:

Take the Bear Lake Road about 8 miles to the Glacier Gorge Junction Trailhead and parking area. The Loch Vale trail begins across the road. If this lot is full, park in the Bear Lake parking area and hike down the Glacier Gorge Trail (about .75 miles) to the Loch Vale Trail. Take the Loch Vale Trail about 2.7 miles to the Sky Pond Trail. It is about .55 miles to Andrews Creek. Take the Andrews Glacier Trail on the south side of the creek and travel about .2 miles to the sign directing you to the campsite. It takes about 2.5 to 3 hours to hike 3.5 miles over trails of moderate difficulty to reach the site.

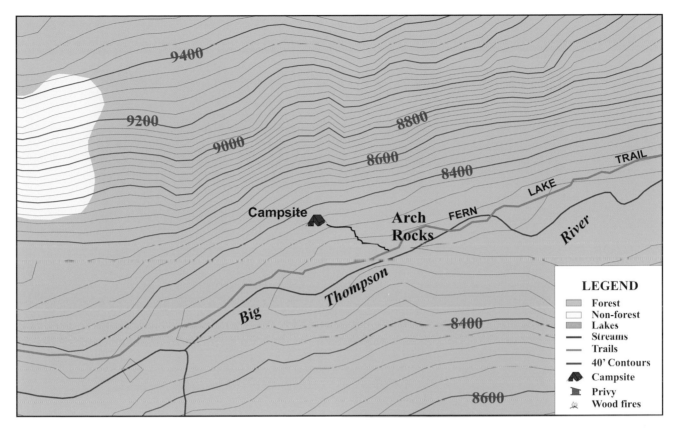

Arch Rock

Description:

The Arch Rock campsite is located on a rise above the Fern Lake Trail just north of the Big Thompson River. The path to the site makes a short climb to the northwest. The site is situated at an elevation of 8,240 feet. It is well shaded by young spruce trees. There is  one tent pad that lies below a large rock in a stand of young spruce trees. It is level and well marked. There is room for one or two tents. Fires are not permitted at this site. Use camp stoves only. There are no toilet facilities near the campsite. Water is available from the Big Thompson River just below the Fern Lake Trail. There is a bear box located about 60 feet east of the site. This is a popular campsite having an 82% occupancy rate.

Activities:

Fishing: Big Thompson River, Fern Creek (catch and release)

Hiking: Fern Lake Trail, Cub Lake Trail

Scenic Features: The Pool, Fern Falls, Arch Rocks, Cub Lake

Arch Rock campsite.

Directions:

The nearest trailhead is the Fern Lake Trailhead. Take the Bear Lake Road to Moraine Park and the Moraine Park Campground turnoff. Follow the road for about a half-mile to the turnoff to the Fern Lake Trailhead. Turn left and take this road to its end at the Fern LakeTrailhead. From here is about 1.2 miles to the campsite. The trail is easy to hike but is somewhat undulating in that it climbs about 200 feet and descends about 100 feet over its course. The net change in elevation is about an 80 to 100 foot gain. It takes about 45 minutes to hike to the campsite.

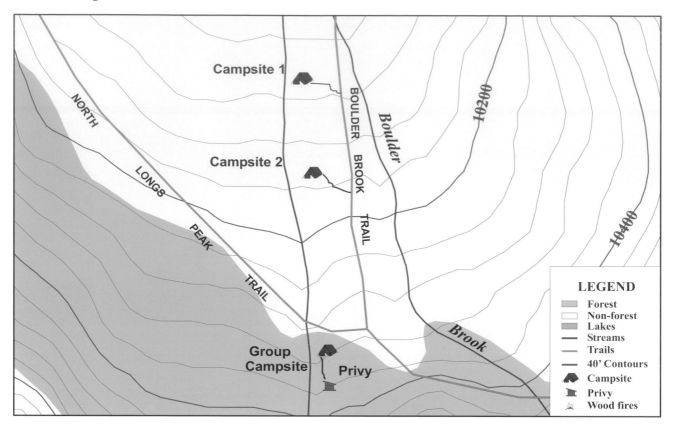

Boulder Brook

Description:

The Boulder Brook campsites are located near the south end of the Boulder Brook Trail at 10,200 feet. There are two individual campsites and one group campsite. The individual sites are north of the North Longs Peak Trail and west of the Boulder Brook Trail. The group site is located just south of the North Longs Peak Trail. The individual sites are situated in a sparse stand of young spruce and pines. The young trees do not provide much shade. The ground is smooth in both campsites but more level in campsite 2. Campsite 1 has room for more tents (about 4) than campsite 2. The group site is about 30 yards south of the intersection of the Boulder Brook and North Longs Peak trails under a canopy of large spruce trees. There are five distinct tent pads. Water is available from Boulder Brook. A pit toilet privy (two walls) is located south of the group site. Bear boxes are provided, across the stream from the individual sites and along the path to the privy near the group site. Wood or charcoal fires are not permitted at this site. Use stoves only. These sites are used 62% of the time.

Activities:

Hiking: North Longs Peak Trail, Loch Vale Trail, Boulder Brook Trail

Boulder Brook campsite 2.

Peaks nearby: Longs Peak, Storm Peak, Mt. Lady Washington, Half Mountain

Directions:

Take the Bear Lake Road for about 6.5 miles to the Storm Pass Trailhead. This is a very small parking area (3 cars) on the right side of the road. The Bierstadt Lake parking area is a short distance to the west. Take the Storm Pass Trail about .6 miles to the Boulder Brook Trail. Follow the Boulder Brook Trail about 2 miles to the campsites. The trail is fairly steep for the first mile but gets easier the farther you climb. The distance from the Bear Lake Road is about 2.5 miles. It takes about two hours to hike to the campsites.

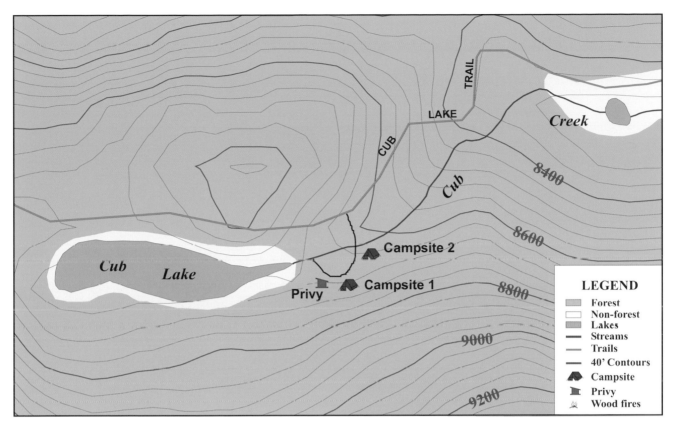

Cub Creek

Description:

The Cub Creek campsites are located below the east end of Cub Lake in a stand of mixed conifer trees on the south side of Cub Creek. There are two individual sites and a pit toilet (two walls). Red arrowheads mark the path from the sign on the Cub Lake Trail to the sites. Water is available from Cub

Creek or Cub Lake. A bear box is located between the two sites near the split in the path to the sites. The forest is fairly dense here offering plenty of shade. The campsites are situated at an elevation of 8,600 feet. Wood or charcoal fires are not permitted at this site. Use camp stoves only. The Cub Creek campsites are utilized about 67% of the time.

Activities:

Hiking: Cub Lake Trail, Fern Lake Trail, Mill Creek - Cub LakeTrail

Peaks nearby: Steep Mountain

Scenic Features: The Pool, Fern Falls, Cub Lake

Cub Creek campsite 2.

Directions:

Take the Bear Lake Road to the Moraine Park Campground turnoff. Turn right on this road and then bear left on the road toward the Fern Lake Trailhead. Travel this road for about 1.2 miles to the Cub Lake Trailhead on the left side of the road. This is a popular area and parking may be scarce. There is another parking area down the road a short distance. Take the Cub Lake Trail for about 1.9 miles to the campsites. The trail is fairly easy to hike with steeper sections closer to the campsites. It takes about 1.5 to 2 hours to hike to the campsites.

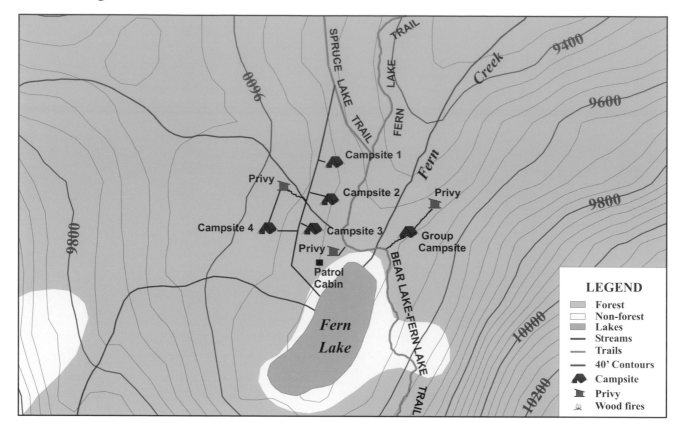

Fern Lake

Description:

The Fern Lake campsites are located both northwest and northeast of Fern Lake. There are four individual sites and one group site. The individual sites are located northwest of Fern Lake just off a path leading south from the Spruce Lake Trail. Take the Spruce Lake Trail just north of Fern Lake a short distance to the path. The sites are situated in a spruce forest on both sides of the path. The group site is located northeast of Fern Lake. There are three privies near Fern Lake: one near the individual sites, one near the group site, and one near the Park Service patrol cabin. Water is best collected from inlet streams to Fern Lake. There are three bear boxes near the sites. One box is located about 10 yards west of site 1, another is 10 yards up the privy trail from sites 2 and 3 near four boulders, and one between site 4 and the privy trail. There is a bear pole on a path behind the group site. Wood or charcoal fires are not permitted at the Fern Lake campsites. Use camp stoves only.

Activities:

Fishing: Fern Lake and Fern Creek (catch and release)

Hiking: Fern Lake Trail, Spruce Lake Trail, Bear Lake - Fern Lake Trail

Fern Lake campsite 1.

Peaks nearby: Gabletop Mtn., Little Matterhorn, Notchtop Mtn.

Scenic features: The Pool, Fern Lake, Fern Falls

Directions:

The nearest trailhead is the Fern Lake Trailhead. Take the Bear Lake Road to Moraine Park and the Moraine Park Campground turnoff. Follow the road for about a half-mile to the turnoff to the Fern Lake Trailhead. Turn left and take this road to its end at the Fern LakeTrailhead. From here is about 3.5 miles to Fern Lake. The trail is easy to hike to The Pool. From there it is a moderate to steep 1.8 mile hike to the lake. It takes about 3 hours to reach these campsites.

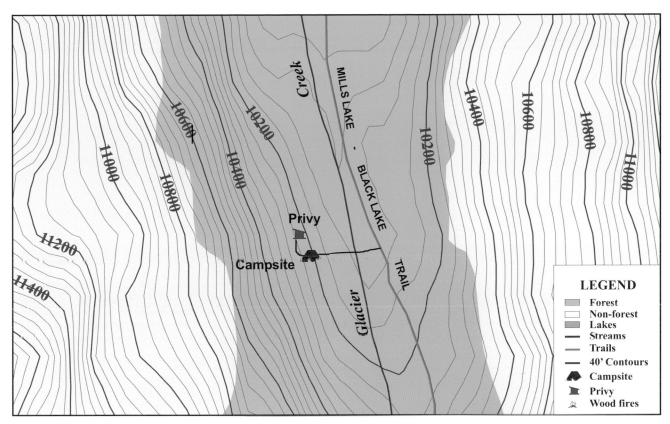

Glacier Gorge

Description:

The Glacier Gorge campsite is situated in a dense stand of spruce trees just west of Glacier Creek and south of Jewel Lake. It has one tent pad that sits on a flat area above the creek. The elevation here is about 10,100 feet. There is room for one or two small tents. You must cross Glacier Creek over a log bridge and make a short climb to the site. There is a pit toilet (no  walls) north of the campsite. Water is available from Glacier Creek just below the campsite. Wood or charcoal fires are not permitted at this site. Use camp stoves only. This campsite is one of the two most popular in the Park. It generally is 100% occupied.

Activities:

Fishing: Mills Lake, Jewel Lake, Black Lake

Hiking: Loch Vale Trail, Mills Lake - Black Lake Trail

Peaks nearby: Half Mountain, Powell Peak, McHenrys Peak, The Spearhead

Scenic features: Mills Lake, Black Lake, Ribbon Falls

Glacier Gorge campsite.

Directions:

The closest trailhead is the Glacier Gorge Junction Trailhead. Take the Bear Lake Road about 8 miles to the Glacier Gorge Junction Trailhead and parking area. The Loch Vale trail begins across the road. If this lot is full, park in the Bear Lake parking area and hike down the Glacier Gorge Trail (about .75 miles) to the Loch Vale Trail. Take the Loch Vale Trail about two miles to the Mills Lake - Black Lake Trail. It is about a 1.4 mile hike to the campsite. It takes about 2.5 to 3 hours to hike to the campsite via this moderately difficult trail.

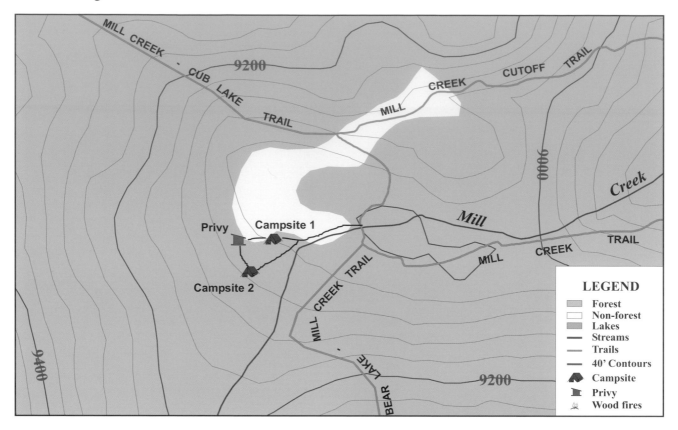

Mill Creek Basin

Description:

The Mill Creek Basin campsites are located at the south end of Mill Creek Basin (large meadow with scattered aspens) in a stand of spruce and aspen. The campsites are situated at an elevation of 9,026 feet. There are two individual campsites with a compost privy (no walls) between them. There is ample shade at these campsites as the forest is fairly dense. Campsite 1 is located just inside the forest near the edge of a large meadow. It has a flat tent pad with room for 1 to 2 tents. The path to campsite 2 winds through the forest to the south and is much farther away from the meadow. This site is larger than campsite 1 and will accommodate 3 to 4 tents. Water is available from Mill Creek. Bear boxes are located south of campsite 2 along the water trail and north along the privy trail of campsite 1. Wood and charcoal fires are not permitted here. Use camp stoves only.

Activities:
Hiking: Mill Creek Trail, Mill Creek-Cub Lake Trail, Bear Lake - Mill Creek Trail
Scenic features: Cub Lake, Bierstadt Lake

Mill Creek Basin campsite 2.

Directions:

The nearest trailhead is the Hollowell Park Trailhead. Take the Bear Lake Road for 3.5 miles to Hollowell Park. There is room for 12 to 15 vehicles. Take the Mill Creek Trail for about 1.8 miles to its junction with the Bear Lake - Mill Creek and Mill Creek - Cub Lake trails. Take the Mill Creek - Cub Lake Trail across Mill Creek then head west along the edge of the meadow to the campsites. The Mill Creek Trail is fairly easy to hike with a few moderate climbs along the way. This site can also be reached via the Bear Lake Trailhead and the Bear Lake - Mill Creek Trail. It takes about 1 to 1.5 hours to hike to the campsite.

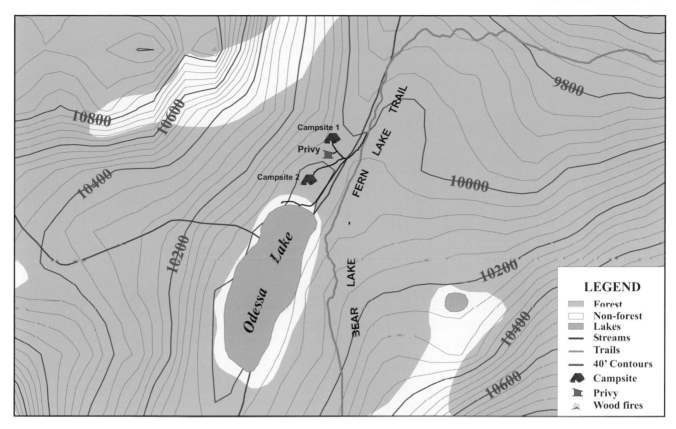

Odessa Lake

Description:

The Odessa Lake campsites are located just north of Odessa Lake in a subalpine fir and spruce forest. There are two individual campsites and a pit toilet privy (1 wall). The campsites are situated at an elevation of 10,020 feet. Campsite 1 and the privy are to the right after crossing Fern Creek. This campsite has room for one tent. Campsite 2 is closer to the lake and sits on a low rise just above the north end of the lake. This campsite has room for 2 to 3 tents and is more open than campsite 1. Water is best obtained from the inlet on the west side of Odessa Lake. There is a bear box to the left of campsite 1 and another along the trail to campsite 2. Wood and charcoal fires are not permitted here. Use camp stoves only.

Activities:

Fishing: Odessa Lake (catch and release), Fern Lake and Fern Creek (catch and release)

Hiking: Fern Lake Trail, Bear Lake - Fern Lake Trail

Peaks nearby: Gabletop Mtn., Little Matterhorn, Notchtop Mtn.

Scenic features: Odessa Lake, Fern Lake, Two Rivers Lake

Odessa Lake campsite 2.

Directions:

The Bear Lake Trailhead is the nearest trailhead to the campsite. Take the Bear Lake Road to its end at the Bear Lake Trailhead. The Bear Lake - Fern Lake Trail begins at the north side of Bear Lake. The trail makes a steady climb for 2.6 miles to Two Rivers Lake. From here it descends for a mile to Odessa Lake. The path to the lake leaves the trail and travels south along Fern Creek. The paths to the campsites leave the lake path just after crossing Fern Creek. Follow the red arrowheads to the campsites. It takes about 3.5 to 4 hours to hike to the campsite.

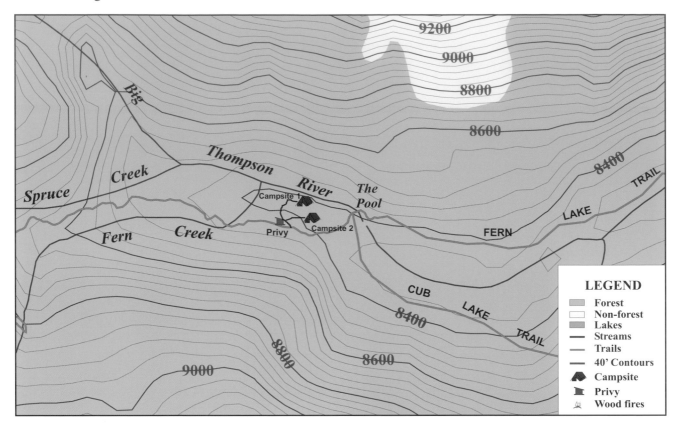

Old Forest Inn

Description:

The Old Forest Inn campsites are located in a stand of spruce and fir on a hill overlooking the Big Thompson River. There are two campsites and a fully enclosed outhouse. The campsites are situated at an elevation of 8,400 feet. Campsite 1 lies under a dense canopy of spruce trees making it well shaded. It has room for 1 to 2 tents. Campsite 2 is more open and

also has room for 1 to 2 tents. The roar of the Big Thompson River will lull you to sleep here at night. Water is available from Fern Creek (a short distance down the Fern Lake Trail). There is a bear box about 45 feet northeast of campsite 1 and one about 70 feet north of campsite 2. Wood and charcoal fires are not permitted here. Use camp stoves only. The Old Forest Inn campsites are very popular with a 91% occupancy rate.

Activities:

Fishing: Big Thompson River, Fern Creek (catch and release)

Hiking: Fern Lake Trail, Cub Lake Trail

Old Forest Inn campsite 1.

Scenic Features: The Pool, Fern Falls, Arch Rocks, Cub Lake

Directions:

The nearest trailhead is the Fern Lake Trailhead. Take the Bear Lake Road to Moraine Park and the Moraine Park Campground turnoff. Follow the road for about a half-mile to the turnoff to the Fern Lake Trailhead. Turn left and take this road to its end at the Fern LakeTrailhead. From here is about 1.7 miles to the campsite. It is an easy hike to The Pool. From here it is a short climb to the campsite. It takes about an hour to hike to this campsite.

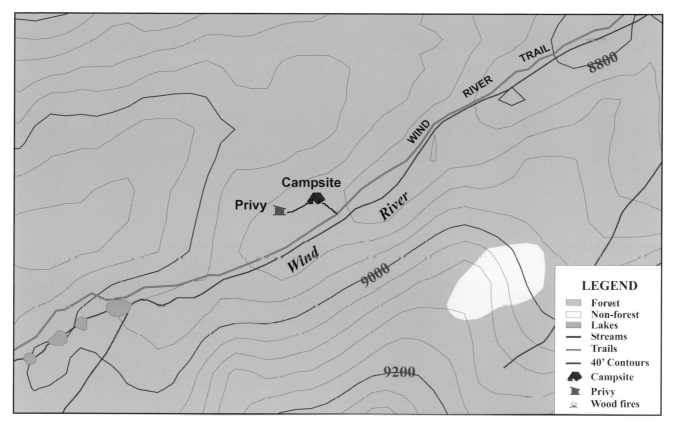

Over The Hill

Description:

The Over The Hill campsite is located in an open lodgepole pine forest at an elevation of 8,870 feet, just west of the Wind River Trail. The campsite is situated on the back side of a small rise west of the trail. The site sits on sandy soil nestled amongst fairly dense lodgepole pine. It will accommodate one tent. There is a pit toilet privy (no walls) just to the south of the

campsite. Water is available from Wind River. Wood and charcoal fires are not permitted here. Use camp stoves only. With just a 38% occupancy rate, this campsite is usually available.

Activities:

Fishing: Sprague Lake

Hiking: Wind River Trail, Storm Pass Trail, Glacier Creek Trail

Scenic features: Sprague Lake, Estes Cone, Emerald Mountain

Over The Hill campsite.

Directions:

The nearest trailhead is the East Portal Trailhead. Take Highway 36 to Highway 66 and 698 toward the YMCA. Travel past the YMCA to the end of the road (about 2.2 miles). Park on the dam near the Adams Tunnel gaging station. There is a small holding pond below. Hike along the road on the west side of the pond to the trailhead. Hike south on the Wind River Trail for about 1.3 miles to the turnoff to the campsite. Turn right at the sign and climb over the rise to the campsite. It takes about 45 minutes to hike to the campsite.

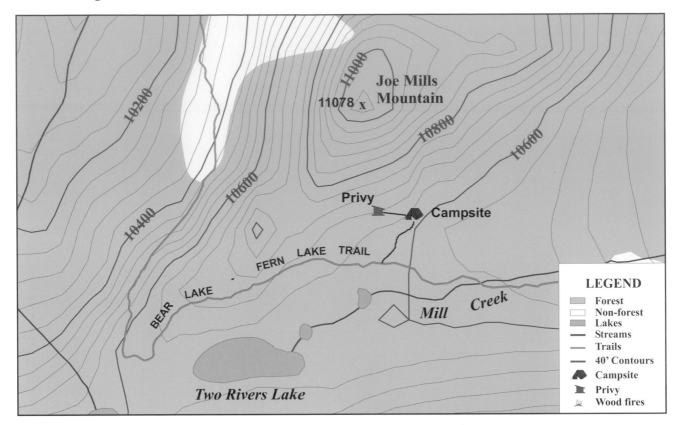

Sourdough

Description:

The Sourdough campsite is located on the south side of Joe Mills Mountain north of the Bear Lake - Fern Lake Trail. The path to the campsite makes a steep climb for 100 to 150 yards to the north. The campsite sits in a small clearing amongst some spruce trees at an elevation of 10,600 feet. There is a large,

level tent pad that will accommodate one tent. A pit toilet privy (no walls) lies about 50 to 75 yards west of the campsite. This site is well shaded and away from the trail. Water is available in some ponds below the Bear Lake - Fern Lake Trail and from Two Rivers Lake. Water can also be obtained from the North Fork of Mill Creek in spring to midsummer. Wood or charcoal fires are not permitted here. Use camp stoves only. This is a very popular campsite. It is occupied just about every night of the camping season.

Activities:

Hiking: Bear Lake - Fern Lake Trail, Flattop Mtn Trail, Bear Lake - Mill Creek Trail

Sourdough campsite.

Peaks nearby: Notchtop Mtn, Flattop Mtn, Hallett Peak, Little Matterhorn

Scenic features: Odessa Lake, Fern Lake, Two Rivers Lake, Bierstadt Lake

Directions:

The Bear Lake Trailhead is the nearest trailhead to the campsite. Take the Bear Lake Road to its end at the Bear Lake Trailhead. The Bear Lake - Fern Lake Trail begins at the north side of Bear Lake. The trail makes a steady climb for 2.4 miles to the path to the campsite. The trail to this point is of moderate difficulty. It takes about 2 to 3 hours to hike to the campsite.

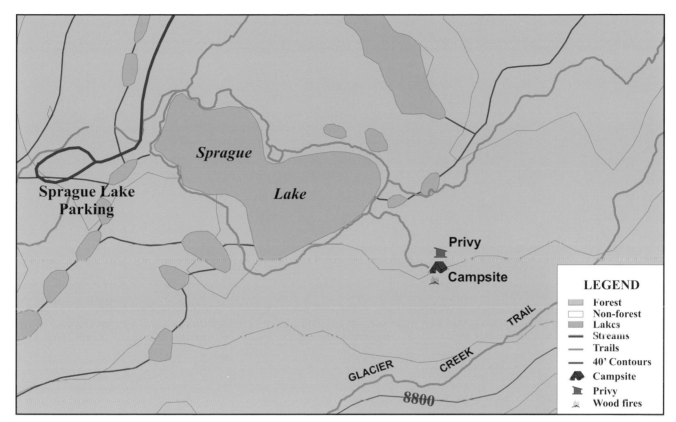

Sprague Lake Handicamp campsite.

Sprague Lake Handicamp

Description:

The Sprague Lake Handicamp is the only backcountry campsite in the Park that is designed for disabled persons. This campsite is located about 300 to 400 yards east of Sprague Lake in a stand of aspen and lodgepole pine. It is situated at an elevation of 8,820 feet. The path to the campsite and paths within the campsite are wheelchair accessible. There are two tent pads that will accommodate up to 12 people including a maximum of six wheel chair users. Persons that are hearing or sight impaired may be accompanied by a certified assistance dog. There are also two storage boxes and two picnic tables. The picnic tables have benches on just one side to accommodate wheelchairs. The site has a fully enclosed outhouse. Wood or charcoal fires are permitted at this site. There is a grill on a pedestal as well as a metal fire ring. Wood must be packed in as wood gathering is prohibited at this campsite. Water can be obtained from the Sprague Lake inlet. Occupancy rate is about 14%.

Activities:

Fishing: Sprague Lake

Hiking: Sprague Lake Five Senses Trail

Scenic features: Sprague Lake

Directions:

Take the Bear Lake Road for about 4.9 miles to the Sprague Lake parking area. Follow the Sprague

Lake Five Senses Nature Trail around the south side of Sprague Lake. The trail to the campsite leaves the nature trail just before you get to a bridge across an outlet stream. It makes a winding path through lodgepole pine and aspens for about 300 to 400 yards before reaching the campsite. It is an easy half-mile walk to the campsite.

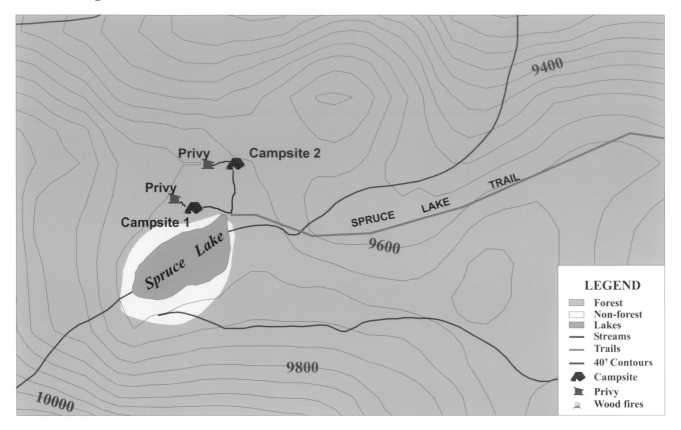

Spruce Lake

Description:

The Spruce Lake campsites are located in a spruce-fir forest on the northwest side of the lake at an elevation of 9,670 feet. There are two campsites, each with its own pit toilet privy. Campsite 1 is off to the left, closer to the lake, and will accommodate 1 to 2 tents. The privy is up in the rocks to the west of the campsite. Campsite 2 is off to the right, situated on a small knoll. It has a level tent pad with a fine gravel bottom. This site is well shaded but farther away from the lake. The privy for campsite 2 is located west of the site at the bottom of a hill. Water is available from Spruce Lake or the inlet stream. Wood and charcoal fires are not permitted here. Use camp stoves only. These campsites have a 52% occupancy rate.

Activities:

Fishing: Spruce Lake (catch and release), Loomis Lake (catch and release), Fern Lake and Creek (catch and release)

Hiking: Spruce Lake Trail, Fern Lake Trail, Bear Lake - Fern Lake Trail

Peaks nearby: Gabletop Mtn., Little Matterhorn, Notchtop Mtn.

Scenic features: Spruce, Loomis, and Fern Lakes

Spruce Lake campsite 2.

Directions:

The nearest trailhead is the Fern Lake Trailhead. Take the Bear Lake Road to Moraine Park and the Moraine Park Campground turnoff. Follow the road for about a half-mile to the turnoff to the Fern Lake Trailhead. Turn left and take this road to its end at the Fern LakeTrailhead. From here is about 4.4 miles to Spruce Lake. The trail is easy to hike to The Pool. From there it is a moderate to steep 1.8 mile hike to the Fern Lake. The Spruce Lake Trail leaves the Fern Lake Trail near the horse hitchracks. This trail is an unimproved trail and is fairly rough as it passes through an area of large rocks. It is about .8 miles from the Fern Lake Trail to the campsites.

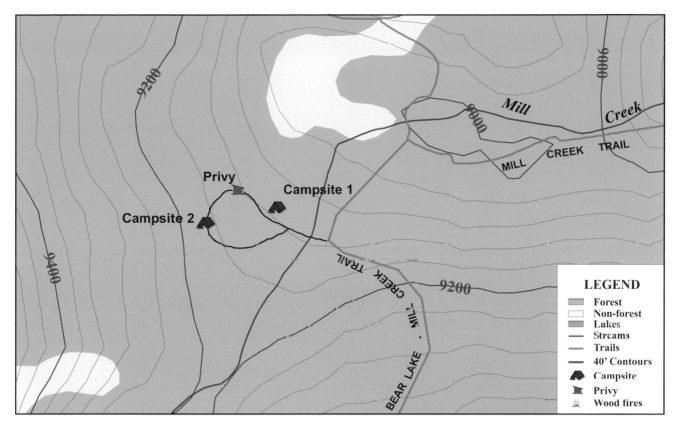

Upper Mill Creek

Description:

The Upper Mill Creek campsites are located in a lodgepole pine forest northwest of the Bear Lake - Mill Creek Trail on the other side of Mill Creek. There are two sites situated at an elevation of 9,150 feet. The forest here is fairly open, almost park like. Campsite 1 is off to the right of some signs. It has a nice flat area that will accommodate 2 to 3 tents. Campsite 2 is off to the left of the signs about 200 yards. Here the forest is less dense than near campsite 1. This site is larger than site 1 and would probably accommodate 3 to 4 tents. There is a pit toilet privy (2 walls) on a faint path between the two sites. Water is available from Mill Creek. Wood and charcoal fires are not permitted here. Use camp stoves only. The Upper Mill Creek campsites are occupied about 64% of the time.

Activities:

Hiking: Mill Creek Trail, Mill Creek-Cub Lake Trail, Bear Lake - Mill Creek Trail

Scenic features: Cub Lake, Bierstadt Lake

Directions:

The nearest trailhead is the Hollowell Park Trailhead. Take the Bear Lake Road for 3.5 miles to Hollowell Park. There is room for 12 to 15 vehicles.

Upper Mill Creek campsite 1.

Take the Mill Creek Trail for about 1.8 miles to its junction with the Bear Lake - Mill Creek and Mill Creek - Cub Lake trails. Take the Bear Lake - Mill Creek Trail southwest for about .1 miles to where it makes a 90 degree turn to the left. Turn right and cross Mill Creek and follow the path to the campsites. The Mill Creek Trail is fairly easy to hike with a few moderate climbs along the way. This site can also be reached via the Bear Lake Trailhead and the Bear Lake - Mill Creek Trail. It takes about 1 to 1.5 hours to hike to the campsite.

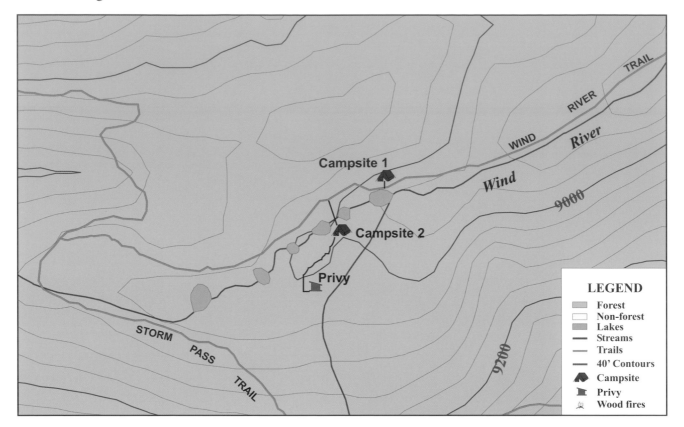

Upper Wind River

Description:

The Upper Wind River campsites are located in a lodgepole pine forest near some beaver ponds at the south end of the Wind River Trail. There are two sites here at an elevation of 8,980 feet. Campsite 1 lies about 50 feet west of the trail on a bench above a meadow. This site will accommodate one tent. The path to campsite 2 is a few hundred yards beyond the

path to campsite 1. It crosses Wind River and travels up into the lodgepole pine forest, about 150 yards east of the trail. There is a pit toilet privy (no walls) about a 100 yards beyond campsite 2. Water is available from Wind River. Wood and charcoal fires are not permitted here. Use camp stoves only. The Upper Wind River campsites are popular and are occupied 75% of the time.

Activities:

Fishing: Sprague Lake

Hiking: Wind River Trail, Storm Pass Trail, Glacier Creek Trail

Scenic features: Sprague Lake, Estes Cone, Emerald Mountain

Upper Wind River campsite 1.

Directions:

The nearest trailhead is the East Portal Trailhead. Take Highway 36 to Highway 66 and 698 toward the YMCA. Travel past the YMCA to the end of the road (about 2.2 miles). Park on the dam near the Adams Tunnel gaging station. There is a small holding pond below. Hike along the road on the west side of the pond to the trailhead. Hike south on the Wind River Trail for about 1.5 miles to the turnoff to the campsite. Turn right at the sign to get to campsite 1. The path to campsite 2 is a few hundreds yards farther down the trail. It takes about 1 to 1.5 hours to hike to the campsite.

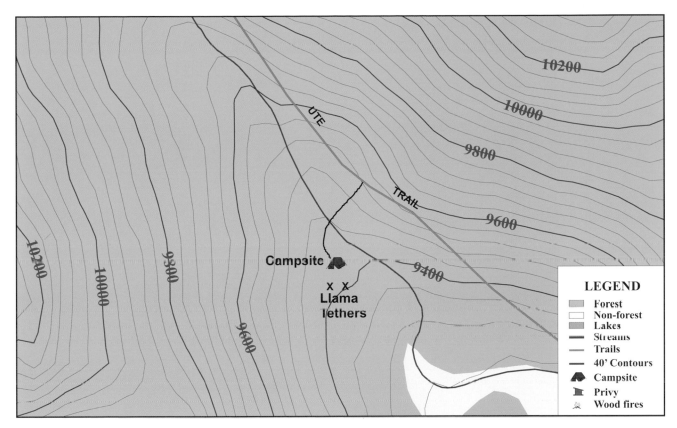

Ute Meadow

Description:

The Ute Meadow campsite is located in a dry, sandy area south of the Ute Trail near Ute Meadow. It is situated at an elevation of 9,415 feet. The path to the site travels through a young white pine-spruce-fir stand south of the trail for about 200 to 300 yards to the site. You must cross a small stream along the way.

It has a level tent site with room for 1 to 2 tents. Llama are permitted at this site. Two tethers are provided just southeast of the site. Water is available from the small stream. There are no toilet facilities near this campsite. Wood or charcoal fires are not permitted at this site. Use camp stoves only.

The Ute Meadow campsite is not heavily used at an occupancy rate of 36%.

Activities:

Hiking: Ute Trail, Beaver Mountain Trail

Peaks nearby: Beaver Mountain

Ute Meadow campsite.

Directions:

The nearest trailhead is the Upper Beaver Meadows Trailhead. Drive west from the Beaver Meadows Entrance Station for about a mile (half mile past the Bear Lake Road). Turn left on a gravel road toward Upper Beaver Meadows. Continue for about 1.5 miles to the end of the road and the Upper Beaver Meadows Trailhead. Take the Beaver Mountain Trail South and then west to the Ute Trail. Hike another 1.2 miles on the Ute Trail to the sign pointing the way to the campsite. It takes about two hours to hike to the campsite.

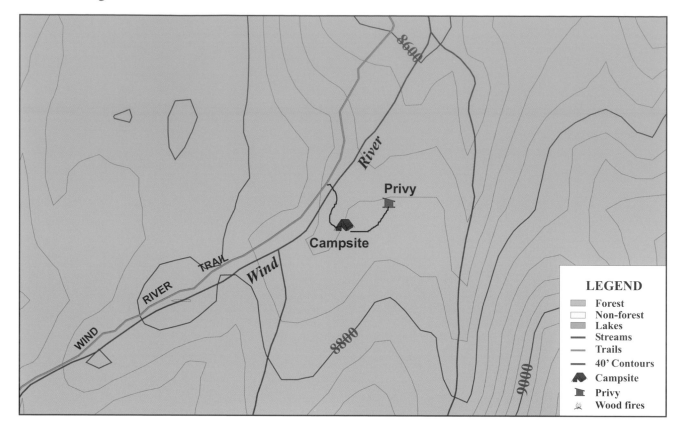

Wind River Bluff

Description:

The Wind River Bluff campsite is located in an open lodgepole pine forest on a bluff above an old beaver pond on the Wind River. The elevation at this location is 8,720 feet. The path to the campsite crosses Wind River over a log foot bridge and climbs the bluff, traveling about 300 to 400 yards to the site. The campsite is a large level area that will accommodate 3 to 4

tents. There is a pit toilet privy (no walls) about 100 yards beyond the campsite. Water is available from Wind River. Wood and charcoal fires are not permitted here. Use camp stoves only. The Wind River Bluff campsite is occupied 60% of the time.

Activities:
Fishing: Sprague Lake
Hiking: Wind River Trail, Storm Pass Trail, Glacier Creek Trail
Peaks Nearby: Emerald Mountain
Scenic features: Sprague Lake, Estes Cone, Emerald Mountain

Wind River Bluff campsite.

Directions:

The nearest trailhead is the East Portal Trailhead. Take Highway 36 to Highway 66 and 698 toward the YMCA. Travel past the YMCA to the end of the road (about 2.2 miles). Park on the dam near the Adams Tunnel gaging station. There is a small holding pond below. Hike along the road on the west side of the pond to the trailhead. Hike south on the Wind River Trail for about .6 miles to the turnoff to the campsite. Turn right at the sign and climb over the rise to the campsite. It takes about 45 minutes to hike to the campsite.

Beautiful Fern Lake has four individual sites and one group site for your camping enjoyment.

Alberta Falls is a major attraction in the Bear Lake area.

East Inlet Area Campsites

Campsite	No. of sites	Wood Fires	Elevation	Privy	Nearest Trailhead	Distance	Elevation Change	Travel Time	Stock	Use
Cats Lair	3	stoves only	9,100 ft	no	East Inlet	3.5 mi	1,600 ft	2 -2.5 hr	no	41%
East Meadow	2	yes	8,550 ft	no	East Inlet	1.5 mi	425 ft	1 hr	no	54%
Gray Jay Group	1grp	yes	9,770 ft	yes	East Inlet	4.4 mi	2,190 ft	4 hr	no	58%
Lake Verna	1	stoves only	10,200 ft	no	East Inlet	6.1 mi	2,690 ft	4 - 5 hr	no	72%
Lower East Inlet	2	stoves only	8,575 ft	no	East Inlet	2.2 mi	590 ft	1 - 1.5 hr	no	34%
Slickrock	1	stoves only	9,950 ft	no	East Inlet	5.0 mi	2,370 ft	3 - 4 hr	no	60%
Solitaire	1	stoves only	10,120 ft	no	East Inlet	5.2 mi	2,520 ft	3 - 4 hr	no	47%
Upper East Inlet	1	stoves only	10,200 ft	no	East Inlet	5.9 mi	2,670 ft	4 - 4.5 hr	no	58%

You get a good view of Grand Lake from the East Inlet Trail.

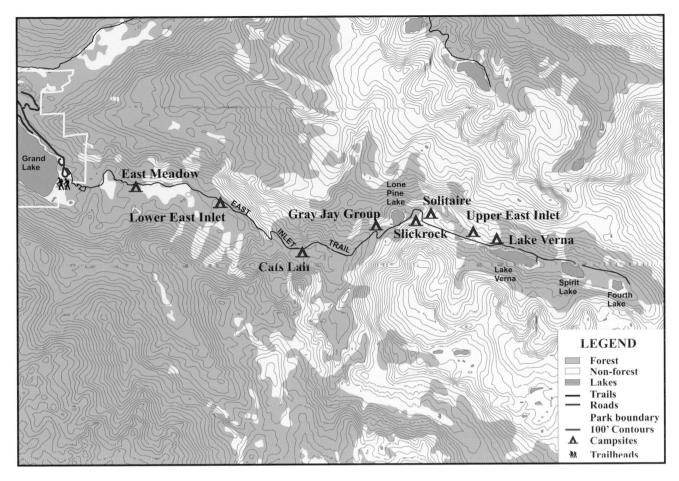

East Inlet Area

The East Inlet area contains campsites that lie along the path of the 7.7 mile East Inlet Trail. This trail is located in the southwest section of the Park

Beautiful Lake Verna lies below the last campsite in the East Inlet area.

and begins near the east shore of Grand Lake. There are eight camping locations and 12 campsites in the East Inlet area. None of the sites are suitable for camping with livestock. Eleven sites are individual campsites and one is designated for groups of 8 to 12 people. A wide range of elevations is found in this

area. Elevations range from 8,550 feet at the East Meadow campsite to 10,200 feet at the Upper East Inlet and Lake Verna campsites. All of the

campsites are located in forested areas. Some have more trees than others. Two sites permit the use of wood fires. Only one site has toilet facilities.

Most of the campsites offer easy access to stream or lake fishing. Fishing is available in East Inlet Creek, Lake Verna, Lone Pine Lake, Spirit Lake, and Fourth Lake. Check with Park personnel for any special restrictions. Peaks in the area include: Mount Craig (12,007'), Andrews Peak (12,565'), The Cleaver, Isolation Peak (13,318'), Mahana Peak, Tanima Peak (12,420'), and Mount Westcott (10,421').

Access to the campsites is via the East Inlet Trailhead and Trail. The distance from the trailhead to campsites ranges from 1.5 miles to 6.1 miles with hiking times ranging from 1 hour to 5 hours. Topographic maps that cover the area include the Grand Lake and Isolation Peak quads.

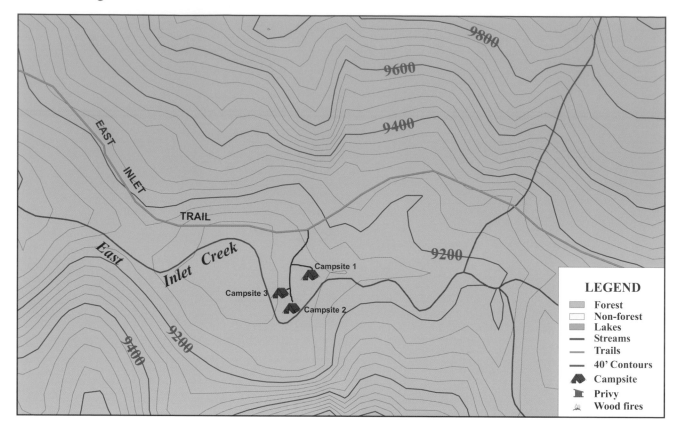

Cat's Lair

Description:

The Cat's Lair campsites are located south of the East Inlet Trail in an area of granite outcrops just above a bend in East Inlet Creek. The area is well shaded by spruce and fir trees and is situated at an elevation of 9,100 feet. There are three individual campsites here. The paths to these sites are not well marked and may be difficult to follow because of the rocks. Campsite 1 is off to the left as you travel toward the creek. It is probably the least level of the sites but is more private. There is room for one tent. Campsite 2 is the largest of the sites and is closest to the creek. It has room for 2 to 3 tents. Campsite 3 is on the other side of some rocks to the northwest of campsite 2. It has room for 1 or 2 tents. Water is available from East Inlet Creek. There are no toilet facilities near this campsite. Wood or charcoal fires are not permitted at this site. Use stoves only. The Cats Lair campsites are occupied 41% of the time.

Activities:
Fishing: East Inlet Creek, Lone Pine Lake
Hiking: East Inlet Trail
Peaks nearby: Mount Westcott
Scenic features: Adams Falls, East Meadow

Cats Lair campsite 3.

Directions:

Take Trail Ridge Road to the west entrance to the Park. Continue south to the road leading into Grand Lake. Turn left toward Grand Lake and then bear left at Tunnel Road across from the Mountain Food Market, just past the stables. Continue on Tunnel Road to the East Inlet Trailhead at its end. There is room for about 30 vehicles at the trailhead. There are restroom facilities at the trailhead. This trailhead is popular for day hikers to Adams Falls. Hike the East Inlet Trail for about 3.5 miles to the Cat's Lair sign on the right. It takes about 2 to 2.5 hours to reach the site. The first 2.2 miles are easy to hike. From there it is a moderate to steep climb.

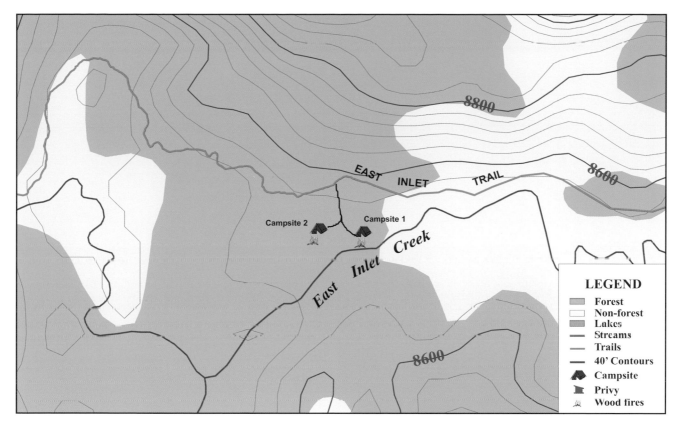

East Meadow

Description:

The East Meadow campsites are located in a stand of lodgepole pines near the east edge of the meadow about 100 feet from East Inlet Creek. There are two individual sites situated at an elevation of 8,550 feet. Campsite 1 is more or less straight ahead on the path from the trail. It has a nice level site with room for 1 to 2 tents. Campsite 2 is off to the right in a more grassy area. It also has room for 1 to 2 tents. Both sites are well shaded. Water is available from East Inlet Creek, a short distance away. There are no toilet facilities near this campsite. Wood fires are permitted at this campsite. Metal fire grates are provided at each site. Fires can only be built within these grates. Do not place rocks in or around your fire. Use only dead and down wood. This is a favorite area for moose. Don't be surprised to see one near camp. These beautiful campsites have a 54% occupancy rate.

Activities:

Fishing: East Inlet Creek
Hiking: East Inlet Trail
Scenic Features: Adams Falls, East Meadow

East Meadow campsite 1.

Directions:

Take Trail Ridge Road to the west entrance to the Park. Continue south to the road leading into Grand Lake. Turn left toward Grand Lake and then bear left at Tunnel Road across from the Mountain Food Market, just past the stables. Continue on Tunnel Road to the East Inlet Trailhead at its end. There is room for about 30 vehicles at the trailhead. There are restroom facilities at the trailhead. This trailhead is popular for day hikers to Adams Falls. Hike the East Inlet Trail for about 1.5 miles to the small East Meadow sign on the right. It takes about an hour of easy hiking to reach the site.

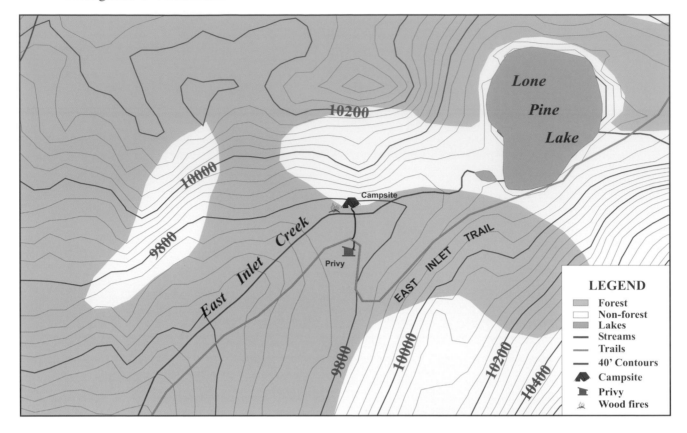

Gray Jay Group

Description:

The Gray Jay Group campsite is located in a stand of spruce trees north of the East Inlet Trail near a small pond. This site, situated at an elevation of 9,770 feet, is well shaded but a little rocky. There is room for 3 to 4 tents. In the spring, when the creek is high, the site becomes an island. Caution should be used in crossing the foot bridge. There is a pit toilet privy (3 walls) to the right of the trail near the campsite sign. Water is

 available from East Inlet Creek. Wood fires are permitted at this campsite. Metal fire grates are provided at each site. Fires can only be built within these grates. Do not place rocks in or around your fire. Use only dead and down wood. This group campsite is occupied about 58% of the time.

Activities:

Fishing: East Inlet Creek, Lone Pine Lake
Hiking: East Inlet Trail
Peaks nearby: Mount Westcott, Mount Craig
Scenic features: Adams Falls, East Meadow, Lone Pine Lake

Gray Jay Group campsite.

Directions:

Take Trail Ridge Road to the west entrance to the Park. Continue south to the road leading into Grand Lake. Turn left toward Grand Lake and then bear left at Tunnel Road across from the Mountain Food Market, just past the stables. Continue on Tunnel Road to the East Inlet Trailhead at its end. There is room for about 30 vehicles at the trailhead. There are restroom facilities at the trailhead. This trailhead is popular for day hikers to Adams Falls. Hike the East Inlet Trail for about 4.4 miles to the Gray Jay Group site sign. The campsite is off to the left of the trail over a log foot bridge. It takes about 4 hours to reach the site. The first half of the hike is easy with the rest being moderate to strenuous.

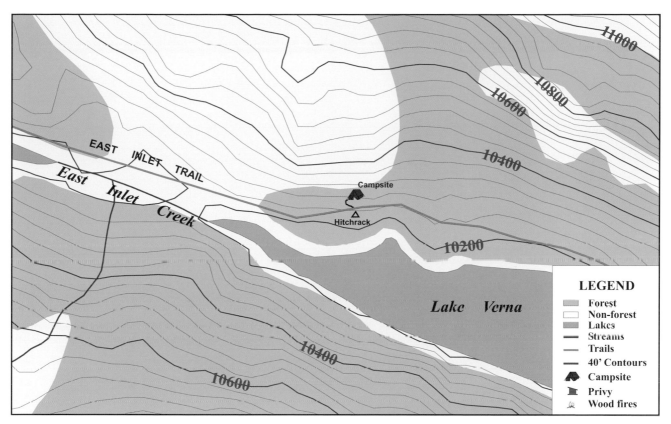

Lake Verna

Description:

The Lake Verna campsite is located near the west end of Lake Verna. It is situated at an elevation of 10,200 feet on a small bench above the north shore of the lake. This level site lies under a canopy of spruce trees and has room for 1 to 2 tents. There are no toilet facilities near this campsite. Water is available from East Inlet Creek or Lake Verna. Wood or charcoal fires are not permitted at this site. Use camp stoves only. This campsite is the most popular campsite in this area with a 72% occupancy rate.

Lake Verna campsite.

Activities:

Fishing: East Inlet Creek, Lake Verna, Spirit Lake, Fourth Lake

Hiking: East Inlet Trail

Peaks nearby: Andrews Peak, The Cleaver, Tanima Peak, Isolation Peak, Mahana Peak

Scenic Features: Adams Falls, East Meadow, Lone Pine Lake, Lake Verna, Spirit Lake, Fourth Lake

Directions:

Take Trail Ridge Road to the west entrance to the Park. Continue south to the road leading into Grand Lake. Turn left toward Grand Lake and then bear left at Tunnel Road across from the Mountain Food Market, just past the stables. Continue on Tunnel Road to the East Inlet Trailhead at its end. There is room for about 30 vehicles at the trailhead. There are restroom facilities at the trailhead. This trailhead is popular for day hikers to Adams Falls. Hike the East Inlet Trail for about 6.1 miles to the hitchrack at the west end of Lake Verna. The campsite is up the hill to the left of the trail. It takes about 4 to 5 hours to reach the site. The first 2.2 miles and the last half mile of the hike are easy to hike. The rest of the trail is moderate to strenuous.

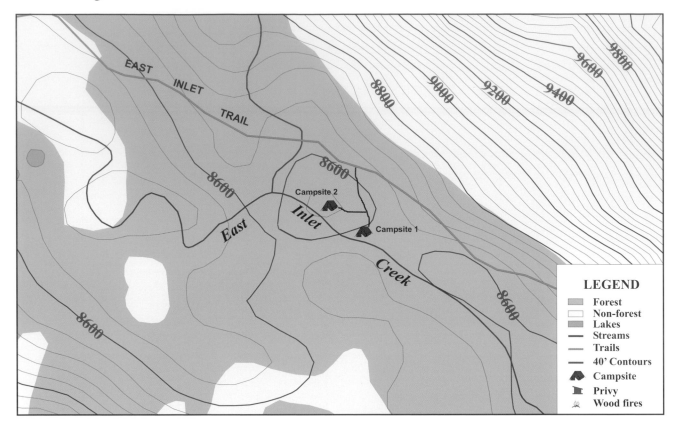

Lower East Inlet

Description:

The Lower East Inlet campsites are located south of the East Inlet Trail in an area of large rocks about 20 to 30 feet above East Inlet Creek. There are two individual sites situated at an elevation of 8,575 feet under a canopy of lodgepole pine. Campsite 1 is a level site about 200 feet below the trail. This site will accommodate 1 to 2 tents. Campsite 2 is about 200 feet downhill from campsite 1 next to the creek. It also will handle 1 to 2 tents. There are no toilet facilities near this campsite. Water is available from East Inlet Creek. Wood or charcoal fires are not permitted at this site. Use camp stoves only. Extra caution is advised when camping with children in this area. There are steep cliffs along the creek and the water in the stream is particularly fast moving. This campsite is the least utilized in the East Inlet area with an occupancy rate of 34%.

Activities:
Fishing: East Inlet Creek
Hiking: East Inlet Trail
Peaks nearby: Mount Westcott
Scenic features: Adams Falls, East Meadow

Lower East Inlet campsite 1.

Directions:

Take Trail Ridge Road to the west entrance to the Park. Continue south to the road leading into Grand Lake. Turn left toward Grand Lake and then bear left at Tunnel Road across from the Mountain Food Market, just past the stables. Continue on Tunnel Road to the East Inlet Trailhead at its end. There is room for about 30 vehicles at the trailhead. There are restroom facilities at the trailhead. This trailhead is popular for day hikers to Adams Falls. Hike the East Inlet Trail for about 2.2 miles to the Lower East Inlet sign. Follow the path to the right as it travels downhill to campsite 1. It takes about 1 - 1.5 hours of easy hiking to reach the site.

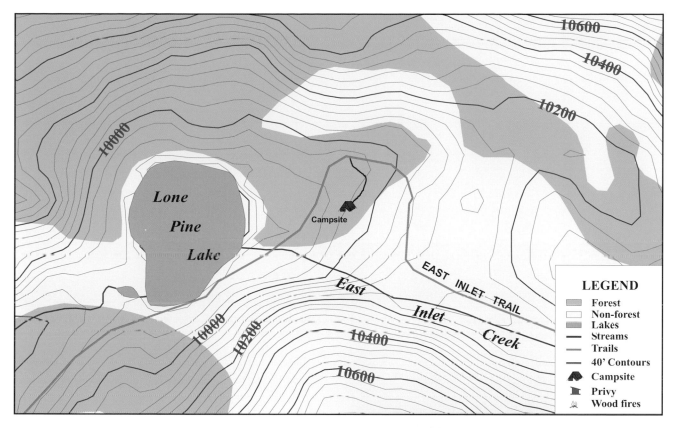

Slickrock

Description:

The Slickrock campsite is located amongst some rocks on a bench overlooking the East Inlet Creek drainage. The campsite is situated about 500 feet south of the East Inlet Trail at an elevation of 9,950 feet. The site has room for one tent and is fairly sunny with only a few spruce trees to provide shade. After crossing a small brook over a log foot bridge, the path to the  site winds its way to the right over some granite to the site. Some rock cairns will help to guide you. There are no toilet facilities near this campsite. Water is available from East Inlet Creek or the small brook crossed on the way to the site. Wood or charcoal fires are not permitted at this site. Use camp stoves only. The Slickrock campsite is occupied about 60% of the time

Activities:
Fishing: East Inlet Creek, Lone Pine Lake
Hiking: East Inlet Trail
Peaks nearby: Mount Craig, Andrews Peak
Scenic features: Adams Falls, East Meadow, Lone Pine Lake

Slickrock campsite.

Directions:

Take Trail Ridge Road to the west entrance to the Park. Continue south to the road leading into Grand Lake. Turn left toward Grand Lake and then bear left at Tunnel Road across from the Mountain Food Market, just past the stables. Continue on Tunnel Road to the East Inlet Trailhead at its end. There is room for about 30 vehicles at the trailhead. There are restroom facilities at the trailhead. This trailhead is popular for day hikers to Adams Falls. Hike the East Inlet Trail for about 5 miles to the Slickrock site sign. The campsite is off to the right of the trail over a log foot bridge. It takes about 3 to 4 hours to reach the site. The first half of the hike is easy with the rest being moderate to strenuous.

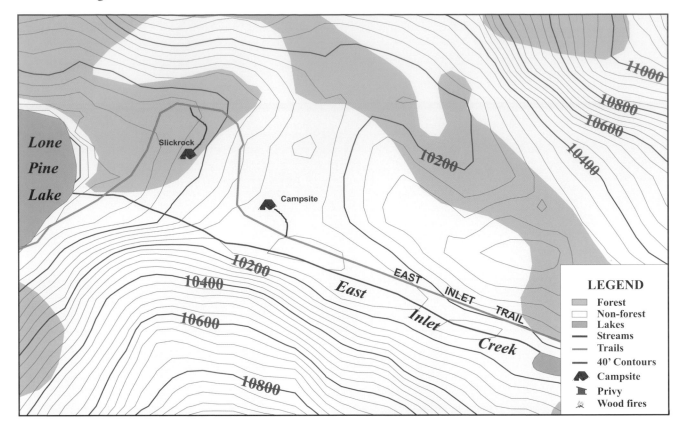

Solitaire

Description:

The Solitaire campsite is located on a small bench to the north of the East Inlet Trail. It is situated at an elevation of 10,120 feet in a clump of spruce trees. The site is level and well shaded with room for one tent. There are no toilet facilities near this campsite. Water is available from East Inlet Creek. Wood and

charcoal fires are not permitted here. Use camp stoves only. The Solitaire campsite has an occupancy rate of 47%.

Solitaire campsite.

Activities:

Fishing: East Inlet Creek, Lone Pine Lake, Lake Verna

Hiking: East Inlet Trail

Peaks nearby: Mount Craig, Andrews Peak

Scenic features: Adams Falls, East Meadow, Lone Pine Lake, Lake Verna

Directions:

Take Trail Ridge Road to the west entrance to the Park. Continue south to the road leading into Grand Lake. Turn left toward Grand Lake and then bear left at Tunnel Road across from the Mountain Food Market, just past the stables. Continue on Tunnel Road to the East Inlet Trailhead at its end. There is room for about 30 vehicles at the trailhead. There are restroom facilities at the trailhead. This trailhead is popular for day hikers to Adams Falls. Hike the East Inlet Trail for about 5.2 miles to the Solitaire site sign. The path to the site leaves the trail to the left and makes a sharp left after passing an uprooted tree stump. It takes about 3 to 4 hours to reach the site. The first 2.2 miles of the hike is easy with the rest being moderate to strenuous.

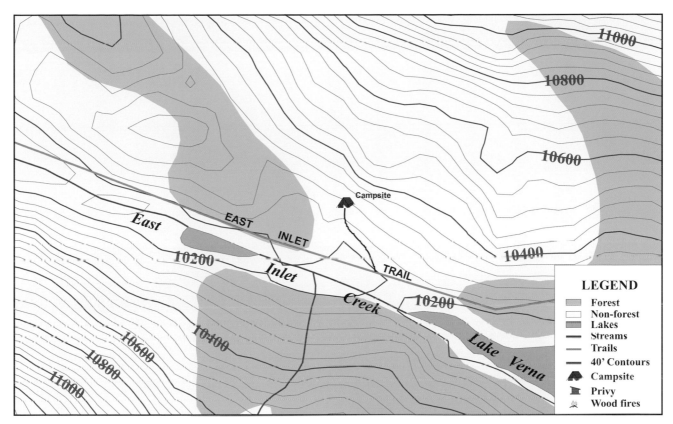

Upper East Inlet

Description:

The Upper East Inlet campsite is located on the north side of the East Inlet Trail about 600 feet before reaching Lake Verna. The path to the site follows a brook for a while before climbing a hill to the right. The campsite is situated at an elevation of 10,200 feet and well shaded by spruce trees. There is room for one tent. There are no toilet facilities near this campsite. Water can be obtained from East Inlet Creek. Wood and charcoal fires are not permitted here. Use camp stoves only. The Upper East Inlet campsite is one of the more popular sites in this area with an occupancy rate of 58%.

Activities:

Fishing: East Inlet Creek, Lake Verna, Spirit Lake, Fourth Lake

Hiking: East Inlet Trail

Peaks nearby: Andrews Peak, The Cleaver, Tanima Peak, Isolation Peak, Mahana Peak

Scenic Features: Adams Falls, East Meadow, Lone Pine Lake, Lake Verna, Spirit Lake, Fourth Lake

Upper East Inlet campsite.

Directions:

Take Trail Ridge Road to the west entrance to the Park. Continue south to the road leading into Grand Lake. Turn left toward Grand Lake and then bear left at Tunnel Road across from the Mountain Food Market, just past the stables. Continue on Tunnel Road to the East Inlet Trailhead at its end. There is room for about 30 vehicles at the trailhead. There are restroom facilities at the trailhead. This trailhead is popular for day hikers to Adams Falls. Hike the East Inlet Trail for about 5.9 miles to the Upper East Inlet site sign. The campsite is off to the left of the trail on a rise to the right of a small brook. It takes about 4 to 4.5 hours to reach the site.

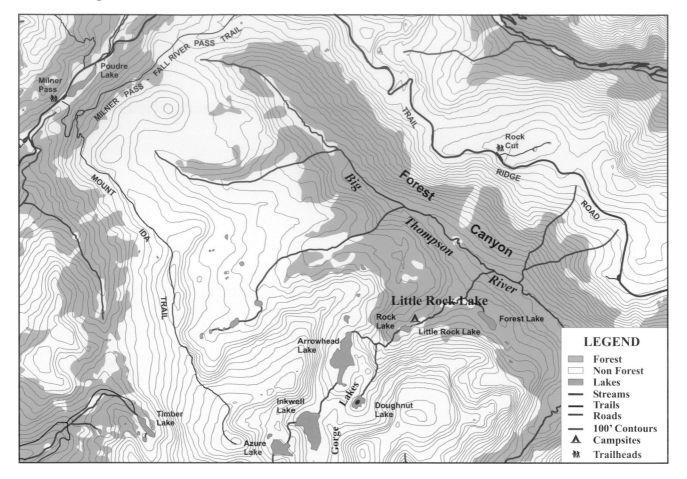

Gorge Lakes Area

The Gorge Lakes area, as its name implies, is a deep gorge containing a series of eight lakes. This gorge descends in a northeasterly direction from

The Gorge Lakes area as seen from Trail Ridge Road.

Mount Ida and Chief Cheley Peak at over 12,800 feet to the floor of Forest Canyon at less than 10,000 feet. The lakes include: Highest Lake, Azure Lake, Inkwell Lake, Doughnut Lake, Love Lake, Arrowhead Lake, Rock Lake, and Little Rock Lake. The Gorge Lakes area is readily visible from the Rock Cut area of Trail Ridge Road. Arrowhead Lake can be easily seen as a prominent landmark. This area is quite rugged and contains steep, unstable slopes. It is accessible by cross-country travel only.

There is only one campsite in the Gorge Lakes area. It is located at Little Rock Lake near the bottom of the gorge. Fishing is available in Rock Lake, Little Rock Lake, and Arrowhead Lake. Check with Park personnel for any restrictions. Peaks in the area include: Mount Ida (12,809'), Terra Tomah Mountain (12,718'), Mount Julian (12,928'), Chief Cheley Peak, and Cracktop.

There are several options for accessing this area. One is to descend into Forest Canyon from Rock Cut and follow the outlet stream to Little Rock Lake. Another is to take the Milner Pass - Fall River Pass Trail to Forest Canyon Pass and head southeast across gently sloping terrain toward the lake. Yet another is to take the Mount Ida Trail and to descend from the continental divide near Mount Ida. Topographic maps that cover the area include the Fall River, Trail Ridge, Grand Lake, and McHenrys Peak quads.

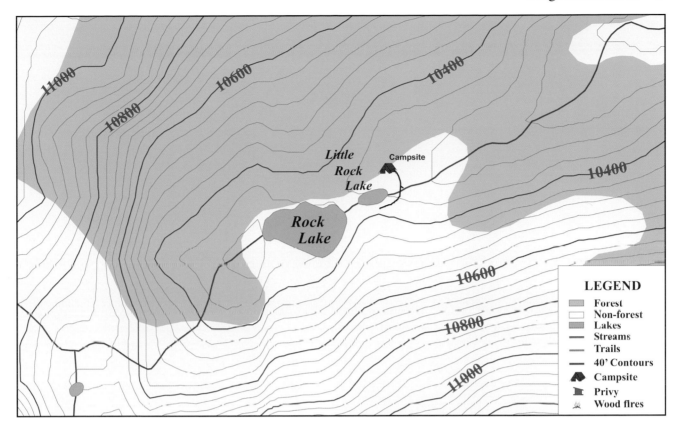

Little Rock Lake

Description:

The Little Rock Lake campsite is located at the north end of Little Rock Lake. The site is situated in a small meadow surrounded by trees at an elevation of 10,320 feet. There are no toilet facilities near this campsite. Water is available from the outlet of Little Rock Lake. Wood and charcoal fires are not permitted here. Use camp stoves only. This site is occupied 40% of the time.

Activities:

Fishing: Rock Lake, Arrowhead Lake

Hiking: Cross-country travel only

Peaks nearby: Mount Ida, Terra Tomah Mountain, Mount Julian, Chief Cheley Peak, Cracktop

Scenic features: Forest Canyon, Gorge Lakes

Directions:

This is the most difficult campsite in the Park to reach. Only those people experienced in cross-country travel using topographic maps should attempt this. There are two trailheads that can be used to access this campsite. They are the Rock Cut and Milner Pass parking areas. From Rock Cut you can descend into Forest Canyon and up the other side following the outlet of Little Rock Lake. Although shorter, this route is

The rugged terrain of the Gorge Lakes area is evident from this view below Mount Ida.

very difficult. The slopes of Forest Canyon are steep and covered with dense dead fall making it very difficult to navigate. From Milner Pass you can take the Milner Pass - Fall River Pass Trail to Forest Canyon Pass. From here head southeast across the gently sloping tundra and through a stretch of forest to the site. This route may cross several wet and boggy areas. You can also take the Mount Ida Trail from Milner Pass and descend from the continental divide near Mount Ida. All routes off of the divide may be covered by steep snowfields in spring or summer. Crampons and ice axes may be necessary under such conditions.

Hague Creek Area Campsites

Campsite	No. of sites	Wood Fires	Elevation	Privy	Nearest Trailhead	Distance	Elevation Change	Travel Time	Stock	Use
Cache	2	stoves only	10,320 ft	no	Milner Pass*	5.1 mi	910 ft	2 -3 hr	no	18%
Chapin Creek Group	1 grp	stoves only	10,340 ft	yes	Milner Pass*	5.7 mi	970 ft	3 - 3.5 hr	no	11%
Desolation	1	stoves only	9,860 ft	no	Corral Creek	2.5 mi	615 ft	1.5 hr	no	19%
Flatiron	1	yes	9,930 ft	no	Corral Creek	3.4 mi	770 ft	1.5 - 2 hr	no	31%
Hague Creek	2 + 1 grp	stoves only	9,720 ft	yes	Corral Creek	2.0 mi	460 ft	1 hr	yes	16%
Koenig	1	stoves only	10,680 ft	no	Corral Creek	5.6 mi	1,740 ft	3 -3.5 hr	yes	18%
Mirror Lake	3	stoves only	10,960 ft	no	Corral Creek	6.4 mi	2,040 ft	3.5 - 4 hr	no	34%
Mummy Pass Creek	2	yes	10,690 ft	no	Corral Creek	5.1 mi	1,650 ft	2.5 - 3 hr	no	28%

*The Chapin Pass Trailhead is the nearest trailhead but parking is very limited. The trail is more difficult and requires crosscountry travel through very wet areas.

The Poudre River Trail leads the way to some campsites in the Hague Creek area.

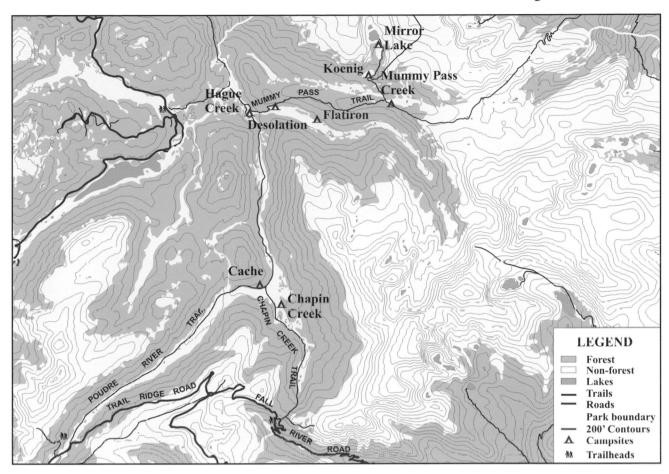

Hague Creek Area

The Hague Creek area is located in the northwest section of the Park . There are eight camping locations and 14 campsites in the Hague Creek area. Two of the

Hague Creek flows through a large meadow near the Flatiron campsite.

sites are suitable for camping with live stock. Twelve sites are individual campsites and two are designated for groups of 8 to 12 people. Elevations range from 9,720 feet at the Hague Creek campsite to 10,960 feet at the Mirror Lake campsite. All of the campsites are

located in forested areas or clumps of trees next to meadows. Some have more trees than others. Two of the sites permit the use of wood fires. The two group sites are the only sites that have privies.

Most of the campsites offer easy access to stream or lake fishing. Fishing is available in the Cache La Poudre River, Chapin Creek, Hague Creek, Cascade Creek, Mummy Pass Creek, and Mirror Lake. Check with Park personnel for any special restrictions. Peaks in the area include: Comanche Peak (12,702'), Fall Mountain (12,258'), and Flatiron Mountain (12,335').

Access to the campsites is available from the Corral Creek, Milner Pass, and Chapin Pass trailheads. Additional access is available from the Emmaline Lake Trailhead near Pingree Park. The distance from the trailhead to campsites ranges from 2 miles to 6.3 miles with hiking times ranging from 1 hour to 4 hours. Topographic maps that cover the area include the Chambers Lake, Comanche Peak, Fall River, and Trail Ridge quads.

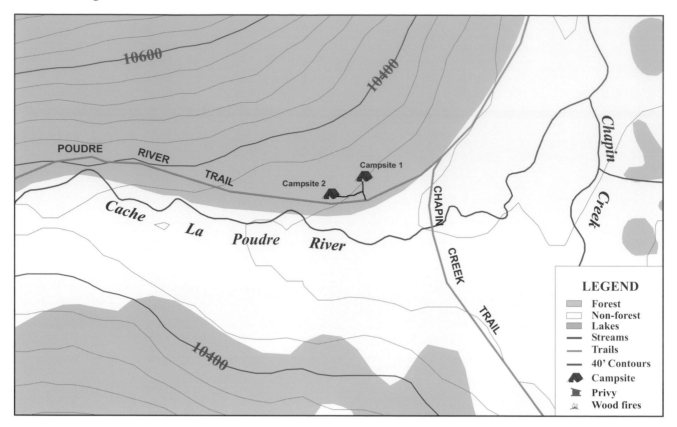

Cache

Description:

The Cache campsites are located in an area of lodgepole pines north of the Poudre River Trail at an elevation of 10,320 feet. It is a short distance to the confluence of Chapin Creek and the Cache La Poudre River. This campsite has two individual sites. Campsite 1 is about 50 yards to the right while campsite 2 is off to the left. Both campsites are level and have room for 1 to 2 tents. Campsite 2 is closer to the trail and the river. There are bears in this area and a bear box is located where the paths to the campsites spilt. You are required to use the bear box to store your food. Water is available from the Poudre River. There are no toilet facilities near this campsite. Wood or charcoal fires are not permitted at this site. Use camp stoves only. These campsites are only used about 18% of the time.

Activities:

Fishing: Cache La Poudre River, Chapin Creek
Hiking: Poudre River Trail, Chapin Creek Trail
Peaks nearby: Flatiron Mountain

Directions:

The shortest route to this campsite is via the Chapin Creek Trail. This route has limited parking (requires permission from Park Service for overnight), is more

Cache campsite 2.

strenuous, and requires cross-country travel through wet areas. The recommended route is via the Poudre River Trail. Take Trail Ridge Road to the Milner Pass Trailhead. The Poudre River Trail begins just north of the parking area near the north end of Poudre Lake. There is limited parking near the beginning of the trail. Follow the easy hiking trail for 5.1 miles to the campsite sign on the left. You will have to negotiate some wet areas on this trail and it becomes faint as you cross an open area before getting to the campsite. Just follow the river and you'll pick it up again. It take about 2 to 3 hours to hike to this campsite.

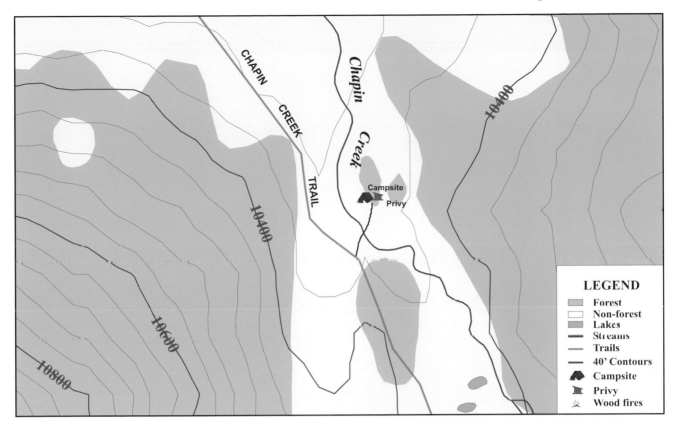

Chapin Creek Group

Description:

    The Chapin Creek Group campsite is located in a clump of lodgepole pines on the north side of Chapin Creek about .55 miles from the Poudre River. It is situated at an elevation of 10,340 feet. The Chapin Creek Trail is unimproved but is easy to follow on this end. The campsite is 300 to 400 feet across some willows and Chapin Creek from the trail. There are two areas to camp. The smaller one is well shaded under lodgepole pine trees. The other area is larger but has little shade. Bears are occasionally seen in this area so be sure to hang all food and scented items 10' from the ground and 4' horizontal from the trunk of a tree. Water is available from Chapin Creek. There is an pit toilet privy (3 walls) near the site. Wood or charcoal fires are not permitted at this site. Use camp stoves only.

Activities:
Fishing: Cache La Poudre River, Chapin Creek
Hiking: Poudre River Trail, Chapin Creek Trail
Peaks nearby: Flatiron Mountain

Directions:

    The shortest route to this campsite is via the Chapin Creek Trail. This route has limited parking (re-

Chapin Creek Group campsite.

quires permission from Park Service for overnight), is more strenuous, and requires cross-country travel through wet areas. The recommended route is via the Poudre River Trail. Take Trail Ridge Road to the Milner Pass Trailhead. The Poudre River Trail begins just north of the parking area near the north end of Poudre Lake. There is limited parking near the beginning of the trail. Follow the easy hiking trail for 5.1 miles to the Chapin Creek Trail. Take this trail over a log foot bridge across the Poudre River and follow it for about a half mile to the Chapin Creek campsite sign. The campsite is about 300 to 400 feet north of the trail through some willows and across Chapin Creek. Hiking time is 3 to 3.5 hours.

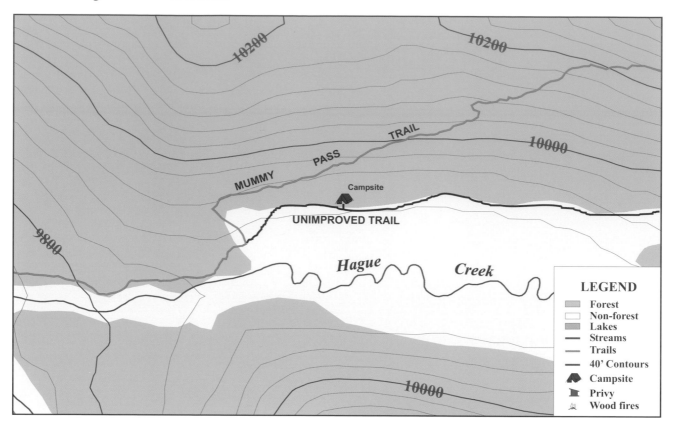

Desolation

Description:

The Desolation campsite is located in a stand of young lodgepole pines on the north edge of a large meadow containing Hague Creek. The campsite is situated at an elevation of 9,860 feet about 100 feet to the left of a foot path that travels along the north side of the meadow. This site is well shaded by the dense stand of trees. It is level and has room for 2 to 3 tents. Water is available from Hague Creek. There are no toilet facilities near this campsite. Wood or charcoal fires are not permitted at this site. Use camp stoves only. This area is a great spot to camp and provides good privacy from the Mummy Pass Trail. The Desolation campsite has an occupancy rate of about 19%.

Activities:

Fishing: Hague Creek
Hiking: Mummy Pass Trail, Poudre River Trail
Peaks nearby: Flatiron Mountain
Scenic features: Mirror Lake, Mummy Pass

Directions:

The nearest trailhead to this campsite is the Corral Creek Trailhead on the Long Draw Road. Take Highway 287 north from Fort Collins to La Porte.

Desolation campsite.

Continue on 287 north to Highway 14. Travel west on 14 for 52 miles to the Long Draw Road. Turn left and travel ten miles to the trailhead. The trailhead is on the left hand side of the road. Hike the Corral Creek Trail for 1.3 miles to the Poudre River Trail. Travel south on the Poudre River Trail into the Park. Continue this easy hike for about a half-mile to the Mummy Pass Trail. Cross the Poudre River over a wooden bridge and travel about .7 miles to the west end of a large meadow. Here a sign points the way on a foot path across the meadow to the campsite. It takes about 1.5 hours to hike to this campsite.

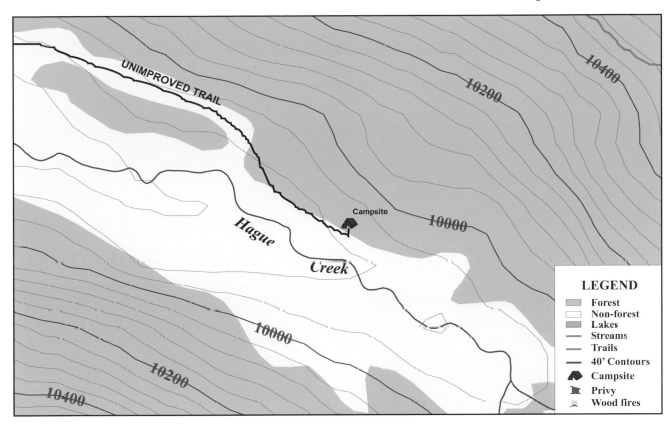

Flatiron

Description:

The Flatiron campsite is located in a stand of lodgepole pines on the north edge of a large meadow containing Hague Creek. The campsite is situated at an elevation of 9,930 feet about 1.4 miles along a foot path from the west end of the meadow. This site is well shaded by this dense stand of trees. It is level and has room for 2 to 3 tents. Water is available from Hague Creek. There are no toilet facilities near this campsite. Wood fires are permitted at this campsite. Metal fire grates are provided at each site. Fires can only be built within these grates. Do not place rocks in or around your fire. Use only dead and down wood.

Activities:

Fishing: Hague Creek
Hiking: Mummy Pass Trail, Poudre River Trail
Peaks nearby: Flatiron Mountain
Scenic features: Mirror Lake, Mummy Pass

Directions:

The nearest trailhead to this campsite is the Corral Creek Trailhead on the Long Draw Road. Take Highway 287 north from Fort Collins to La Porte. Continue on 287 north to Highway 14. Travel west on

Flatiron campsite.

14 for 52 miles to the Long Draw Road. Turn left and travel ten miles to the trailhead. The trailhead is on the left hand side of the road. Hike the Corral Creek Trail for 1.3 miles to the Poudre River Trail. Travel south on the Poudre River Trail into the Park. Continue this easy hike for about a half-mile to the Mummy Pass Trail. Cross the Poudre River over a wooden bridge and travel about .6 miles to the west end of a large meadow. Here a sign points the way on a foot path across the meadow to the trees on the north side. The path follows the north edge of the meadow for about a mile to the campsite. It takes about 1.5 to 2 hours to reach this site.

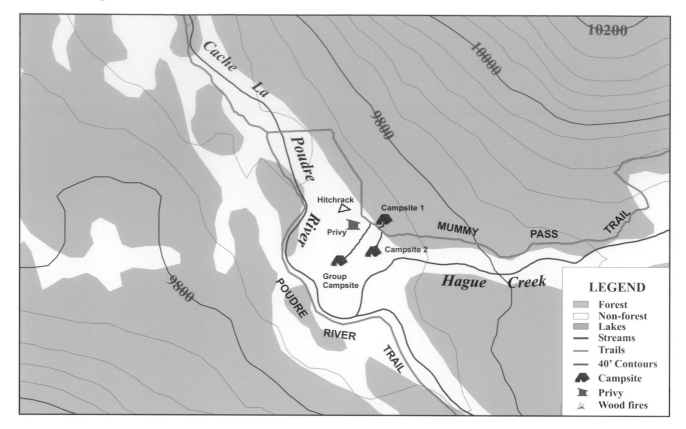

Hague Creek

Description:

The Hague Creek campsite is located at the bottom of the Hague Creek drainage just east of where the creek empties into the Poudre River. There are two individual campsites and one group/stock site. They are situated at an elevation of 9,720 feet. Campsite 1 is located in a rocky area to the left of the trail. Campsite 2 is to the right of the trail in the trees on the other side of an open area. Both sites are well shaded. The group/stock site is more sunny at the edge of a sagebrush meadow. A hitchrack is provided for horse parties. Water is available from Hague Creek or the Poudre River. A pit toilet privy (3 walls) is located to the right of the trail. Wood or charcoal fires are not permitted at this site. Use camp stoves only. The Hague Creek campsites are only used about 16% of the time.

Activities:
Fishing: Hague Creek, Poudre River
Hiking: Mummy Pass Trail, Poudre River Trail
Peaks nearby: Flatiron Mountain
Scenic features: Mirror Lake, Mummy Pass

Directions:

The nearest trailhead to this campsite is the Corral Creek Trailhead on the Long Draw Road. Take

Hague Creek Group / Stock campsite.

Highway 287 north from Fort Collins to La Porte. Continue on 287 north to Highway 14. Travel west on 14 for 52 miles to the Long Draw Road. Turn left and travel ten miles to the trailhead. The trailhead is on the left hand side of the road. Hike the Corral Creek Trail for 1.3 miles to the Poudre River Trail. Travel south on the Poudre River Trail into the Park. Continue this easy hike for about a half-mile to the Mummy Pass Trail. Cross the Poudre River over a wooden bridge and travel about .2 miles to the campsite. Campsite 1 is on the left side of the trail and Campsite 2 and the group site are on the right side of the trail. It takes about an hour to hike to this campsite.

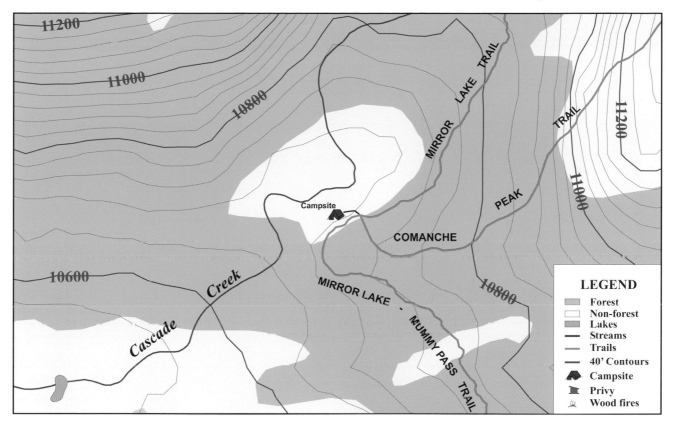

Koenig

Description:

The Koenig campsite is located in a clump of spruce trees on the edge of a meadow containing Cascade Creek. The campsite is situated at an elevation of 10,680 feet just south of a hitchrack near the intersection of the Mirror Lake and Comanche Peak trails. The trees are large and provide adequate shade. The campsite is level and has room for 2 tents. Livestock are permitted here and must be confined to the hitchrack area. Horses are not permitted on the Mirror Lake Trail. Water is available from Cascade Creek. There are no toilet facilities near this campsite. Wood or charcoal fires are not permitted at this site. Use camp stoves only.

Activities:

Fishing: Cascade Creek, Mirror Lake
Hiking: Mummy Pass Trail, Poudre River Trail, Mirror Lake Trail, Comanche Peak Trail
Peaks nearby: Comanche Peak, Fall Mountain
Scenic features: Mirror Lake, Mummy Pass

Directions:

The nearest trailhead to this campsite is the Corral Creek Trailhead on the Long Draw Road. Take Highway 287 north from Fort Collins to La Porte.

Koenig campsite.

Continue on 287 north to Highway 14. Travel west on 14 for 52 miles to the Long Draw Road. Turn left and travel ten miles to the trailhead. The trailhead is on the left hand side of the road. Hike the Corral Creek Trail for 1.3 miles to the Poudre River Trail. Travel south on the Poudre River Trail into the Park. Continue this easy hike for about a half-mile to the Mummy Pass Trail. Cross the Poudre River over a wooden bridge and travel about 3.2 miles to the intersection with the Mummy Pass - Mirror Lake Trail. Turn left on this trail and travel about .6 miles to the Mirror Lake Trail. The campsite is just south of the hitchrack to the left of the trail. It takes 3 to 3.5 hours to reach this campsite.

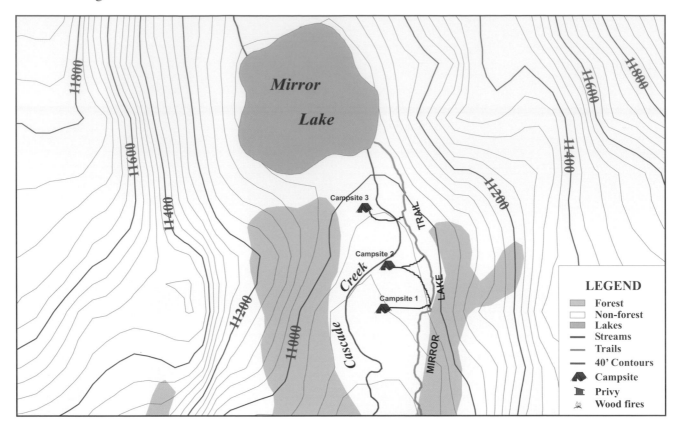

Mirror Lake

Description:

The Mirror Lake campsite has three individual campsites situated in clumps of spruce trees from 75 to 300 yards below the Mirror Lake at 10,960 feet. All of the sites are mostly open, being shaded only part of the day. Campsite 1 is located on a grassy knoll directly west of the foot path leading to the campsites. The grassy surface will accommodate 1 tent. Campsite 2 is about 100 yards to the north of campsite 1. It has room for 1 to 2 tents. Campsite 3 is located about 75 yards south of the lake on a small bench west of Cascade Creek. Water is available from Cascade Creek. There are no toilet facilities near this campsite. Use camp stoves only at these sites.

Activities:

Fishing: Cascade Creek, Mirror Lake

Hiking: Mummy Pass Trail, Mirror Lake Trail, Comanche Peak Trail

Peaks nearby: Comanche Peak, Fall Mountain

Scenic features: Mirror Lake, Mummy Pass

Directions:

The nearest trailhead to this campsite is the Corral Creek Trailhead on the Long Draw Road. Take Highway 287 north from Fort Collins to La Porte.

Mirror Lake campsite 2.

Continue on 287 north to Highway 14. Travel west on 14 for 52 miles to the Long Draw Road. Turn left and travel ten miles to the trailhead. The trailhead is on the left hand side of the road. Hike the Corral Creek Trail for 1.3 miles to the Poudre River Trail. Travel south on the Poudre River Trail into the Park. Continue this easy hike for about a half-mile to the Mummy Pass Trail. Cross the Poudre River over a wooden bridge and travel about 3.2 miles to the intersection with the Mummy Pass - Mirror Lake Trail. Turn left on this trail and travel about .6 miles to the Mirror Lake Trail. Follow the Mirror Lake Trail for about .8 miles to the campsites. Hiking time 3.5 to 4 hours.

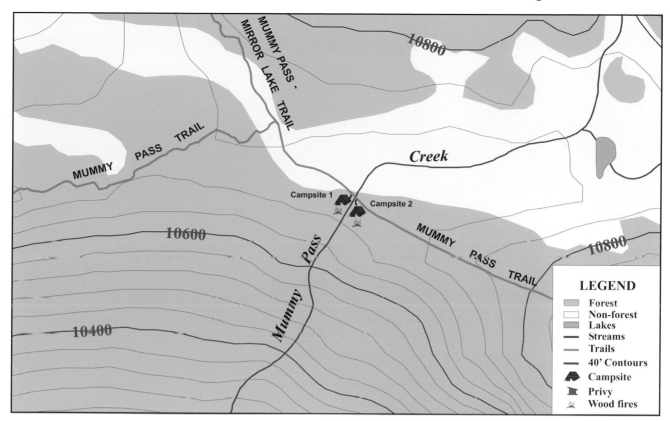

Mummy Pass Creek

Description:

The Mummy Pass Creek campsite is located near the southwest edge of a large meadow where Mummy Pass Creek flows down from Mummy Pass. There are two individual campsites, each located on either side of Mummy Pass Creek. They are situated at an elevation of 10,690 feet. Campsite 1 is located down hill from the trail on a bench above the west side of the creek. This is a large site having room for 4 to 5 tents. Campsite 2 is to the right of the trail just after crossing the creek. This site will accommodate 2 to 3 tents. There are no toilet facilities near this campsite. Wood fires are permitted at these campsites. Metal fire grates are provided at each site. Fires can only be built within these grates. Do not place rocks in or around your fire. Use only dead and down wood.

Activities:
Fishing: Mirror Lake, Mummy Pass Creek
Hiking: Mummy Pass Trail, Mirror Lake Trail
Peaks nearby: Comanche Peak, Fall Mountain
Scenic features: Mirror Lake, Mummy Pass

Directions:

The nearest trailhead to this campsite is the Corral Creek Trailhead on the Long Draw Road. Take

Mummy Pass Creek campsite 1.

Highway 287 north from Fort Collins to La Porte. Continue on 287 north to Highway 14. Travel west on 14 for 52 miles to the Long Draw Road. Turn left and travel ten miles to the trailhead. The trailhead is on the left hand side of the road. Hike the Corral Creek Trail for 1.3 miles to the Poudre River Trail. Travel south on the Poudre River Trail into the Park. Continue this easy hike for about a half-mile to the Mummy Pass Trail. Cross the Poudre River over a wooden bridge and travel about 3.2 miles to the Mummy Pass - Mirror Lake Trail. Turn right and travel about 250 yards to the campsites. It takes 2.5 to 3 hours to reach this campsite.

Longs Peak Area Campsites

Campsite	No. of sites	Wood Fires	Elevation	Privy	Nearest Trailhead	Distance	Elevation Change	Travel Time	Stock	Use
Battle Mountain Group	1 grp	stoves only	10,900 ft	yes	Longs Peak	2.7 mi	1,630 ft	1 - 2 hr	no	84%
Boulderfield	9	stoves only	12,760 ft	yes	Longs Peak	5.8 mi	3,360 ft	5 - 6 hr	no	63%
Goblins Forest	6	stoves only	10,120 ft	yes	Longs Peak	1.2 mi	720 ft	1 hr	no	54%
Moore Park	2	stoves only	9,725 ft	yes	Longs Peak	1.7 mi	640 ft	1.5 - 2 hr	no	46%

The Keyhole marks the way to the summit of Longs Peak.

The Jim's Grove Trail is a less crowded path down from the Granite Pass area.

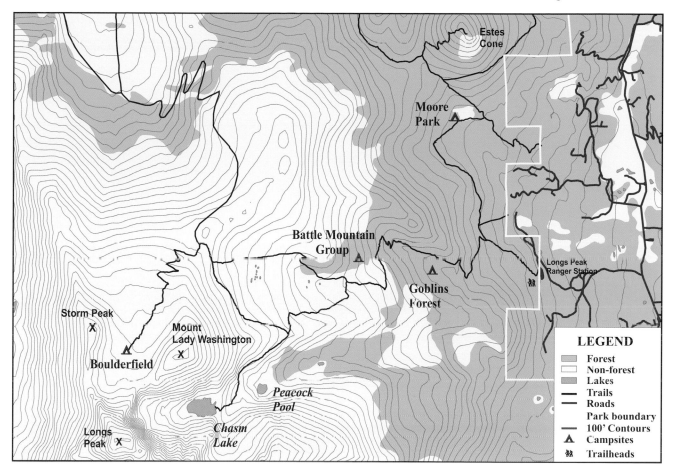

Longs Peak Area

The Longs Peak area is located in the southeast section of the Park. This area is very popular for day hikers traveling to Chasm Lake and Longs Peak. There

Longs Peak is a very popular destination for day hikers in the Longs Peak area.

are four camping locations and 18 campsites in the Longs Peak area. Seventeen sites are individual campsites and one is designated for groups of 8 to 12 people. Elevations range from 9,725 feet at the Moore Park campsite to 12,760 feet at the Boulderfield campsite.

All but the Boulderfield campsites are located in forested areas. Some have more trees than others. All of the campsites have toilet facilities. The Longs Peak area is the second most popular backcountry camping area in the Park.

This is not a very good area for fishing. Fishing is available in Peacock Pool and perhaps some of the small streams may hold some small brook trout. Check with Park personnel for any special restrictions. Peaks in the area include: Longs Peak (14,255'), Storm Peak (13,326'), Mt. Lady Washington (13,281'), Mt. Meeker (13,911'), and Estes Cone (11,006').

Access to the campsites is available from the trailhead at the Longs Peak Ranger Station. Because of the popularity of this area, it is advisable to arrive early to get a parking spot. The distance from the trailhead to campsites ranges from 1.2 miles to 5.8 miles with hiking times ranging from 1 hour to 6 hours. Topographic maps that cover the area include the Longs Peak quad.

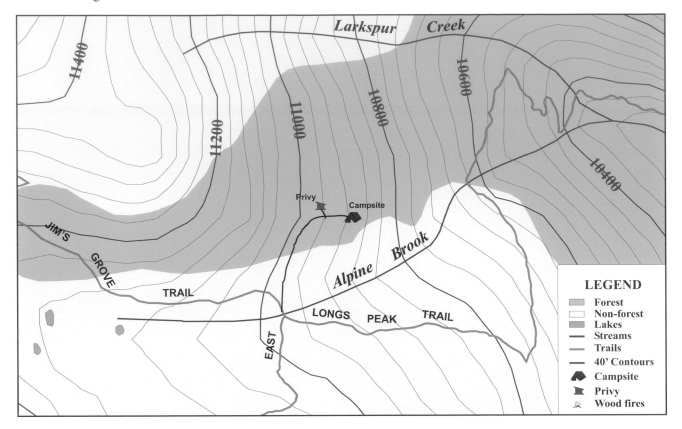

Battle Mountain Group

Description:

The Battle Mountain Group campsite is located in an area of subalpine fir and limber pines north of the junction of the East Longs Peak and Jim's Grove trails at an elevation of 10,900 feet. The campsite is about .25 miles on a path that travels northeast from the Jim's Grove Trail just after it crosses Alpine Brook. The trees here are not large and provide limited shade. The ground is fairly rocky. There is room for 6 to 8 tents scattered among the trees. Water is available from a creek fed by a snow field above Jim's Grove or from Alpine Brook. There is a pit toilet (privacy sides) near this campsite. Wood or charcoal fires are not permitted at this site. Use camp stoves only. This campsite is the most popular group campsite in the Park with an 84% occupancy rate.

Activities:

Hiking: East Longs Peak Trail, North Longs Peak Trail, Chasm Lake Trail

Peaks nearby: Longs Peak, Storm Peak, Mt. Lady Washington, Mt. Meeker

Scenic features: Longs Peak, Chasm Lake, Peacock Pool, Columbine Falls

Battle Mountain Group campsite.

Directions:

Take Highway 7 south from Estes Park about seven miles to the Longs Peak Area turnoff. Turn right and follow the road to the Longs Peak Ranger Station. There is parking for about 60 to 70 vehicles near the Ranger Station. Additional parking is available along the south side of the entrance road. The East Longs Peak Trail begins near the Ranger Station. Follow this trail for about 2.6 miles to the junction with the Jim's Grove Trail. You will make a moderate climb of about 1,600 feet on this trail. Cross Alpine Brook and turn right at the sign. Travel about .25 miles to the campsite. It takes about 1 to 2 hours to reach this campsite.

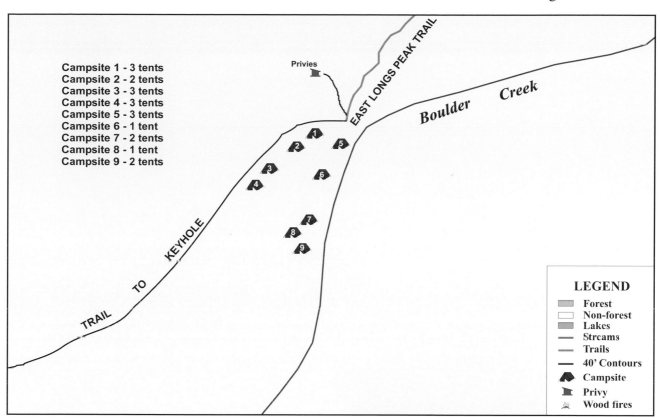

Campsite 1 - 3 tents
Campsite 2 - 2 tents
Campsite 3 - 3 tents
Campsite 4 - 3 tents
Campsite 5 - 3 tents
Campsite 6 - 1 tent
Campsite 7 - 2 tents
Campsite 8 - 1 tent
Campsite 9 - 2 tents

Privies

EAST LONGS PEAK TRAIL

Boulder Creek

TRAIL TO KEYHOLE

LEGEND
Forest
Non-forest
Lakes
Streams
Trails
40' Contours
Campsite
Privy
Wood fires

Boulderfield

Description:

The Boulderfield campsites are located in the boulderfield north of Longs Peak. The elevation here is 12,760 feet. There are nine campsites with room for about 20 tents. The campsites are level areas where the rocks have been removed and the ground smoothed out. They are bordered by three foot high rock walls for protection from the frequent high winds in this area. Food storage boxes are provided to protect your food from the numerous, brazen marmots that inhabit this area. Water is available from Boulder Brook that flows through the boulderfield. There are two solar outhouses about 50 yards northwest of the horse hitchrack. Wood or charcoal fires are not permitted at this site. Use camp stoves only. These campsites are occupied about 63% of the time.

Activities:

Hiking: East Longs Peak Trail, North Longs Peak Trail, Chasm Lake Trail

Peaks nearby: Longs Peak, Storm Peak, Mt. Lady Washington, Mt. Meeker

Scenic features: Longs Peak, Chasm Lake, Peacock Pool, Columbine Falls

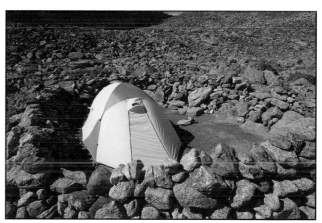

Boulderfield campsite 8.

Directions:

Take Highway 7 south from Estes Park about seven miles to the Longs Peak Area turnoff. Turn right and follow the road to the Longs Peak Ranger Station. There is parking for about 60 to 70 vehicles near the Ranger Station. Additional parking is available along the south side of the entrance road. The East Longs Peak Trail begins near the Ranger Station. Follow this trail for about 2.6 miles to the junction with the Jim's Grove Trail. Make a sharp turn to the left before getting to Alpine Brook. Continue to make a moderate climb for 1.8 miles to Granite Pass. From here it is about a 1.4 mile climb over several switchbacks to the Boulderfield. Hiking time is about 5 to 6 hours.

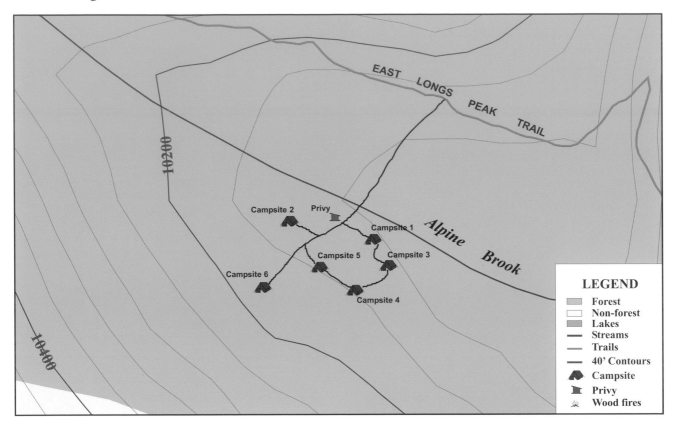

Goblins Forest

Description:

The Goblins Forest campsites are located in a stand of lodgepole pines and spruce below Alpine Brook. There are six individual sites located to either side of the main foot path. There is a pit toilet (3 walls) just right of the path after you cross the stream. Campsite 2 is off to the right of the main path and will accommodate 2 to 3 tents. Campsite 6 is at the end of the main path and has room for 3 to 4 tents. Campsites 1, 3, 4, and 5 are on a loop to the left of the main path. These sites will each accommodate 2 to 3 tents. Campsite 5 has three distinctly marked tent pads. All of the sites in this area are well shaded by dense forest. Water is available from Alpine Brook. Wood or charcoal fires are not permitted at this site. Use camp stoves only. The Goblins Forest sites are occupied about 54% of the season.

Activities:

Hiking: East Longs Peak Trail, North Longs Peak Trail, Chasm Lake Trail
Peaks nearby: Longs Peak, Storm Peak, Mt. Lady Washington, Mt. Meeker
Scenic features: Longs Peak, Chasm Lake, Peacock Pool, Columbine Falls

Goblins Forest campsite 4.

Directions:

Take Highway 7 south from Estes Park about seven miles to the Longs Peak Area turnoff. Turn right and follow the road to the Longs Peak Ranger Station. There is parking for about 60 to 70 vehicles near the Ranger Station. Additional parking is available along the south side of the entrance road. The East Longs Peak Trail begins near the Ranger Station. Follow this trail for about 1.2 miles to the Goblins Forest campsite sign. Turn left and follow the path down hill to a log foot bridge over Alpine Brook. The campsites are located on both sides of the foot path. It takes about an hour to hike to the Goblins Forest campsites.

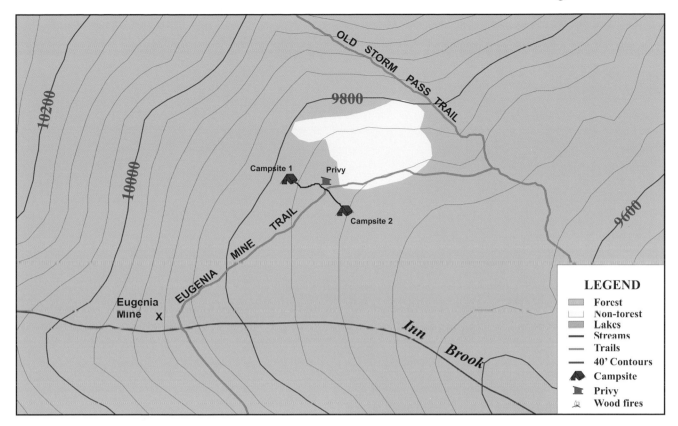

Moore Park

Description:

The Moore Park campsites are located in stands of spruce and lodgepole pines at an elevation of 9,725 feet. There are two campsites, each on either side of the Eugenia Mine Trail. Moore Park is a large meadow just a short distance beyond the campsites. Campsite 1 is to the left of the trail. The path passes a compost type toilet with three privacy walls and winds its way through the forest for about 300 to 400 yards to the campsite. This level site will accommodate 2 to 3 tents and is well shaded by lodgepole pines. Campsite 2 it a short distance to the right of the trail. This site is a large flat area bounded by lodgepole pine logs. Campsite 2 has room for 2 to 3 tents. Water is available from Inn Brook. Wood or charcoal fires are not permitted at this site. Use camp stoves only. These campsites are occupied about 46% of the time.

Activities:

Hiking: East Longs Peak Trail, Eugenia Mine Trail, Storm Pass Trail, Estes Cone Trail

Peaks nearby: Estes Cone

Scenic features: Longs Peak, Estes Cone, Eugenia Mine

Moore Park campsite 2.

Directions:

Take Highway 7 south from Estes Park about seven miles to the Longs Peak Area turnoff. Turn right and follow the road to the Longs Peak Ranger Station. There is parking for about 60 to 70 vehicles near the Ranger Station. Additional parking is available along the south side of the entrance road. The East Longs Peak Trail begins near the Ranger Station. Follow this trail for about .5 miles to the Eugenia Mine Trail. Turn right and follow this trail to the Eugenia Mine site. Continue on this trail for another .25 miles to the Moore Park campsite sign. The campsites are located on both sides of the trail. It takes about 1.5 to 2 hours to hike to these campsites.

Mummy Range Area Campsites

Campsite	No. of sites	Wood Fires	Elevation	Privy	Nearest Trailhead	Distance	Elevation Change	Travel Time	Stock	Use
Cutbank	1	stoves only	9,590 ft	yes	Lawn Lake	2.8 mi	1,030 ft	1.5 - 2 hr	no	54%
Golden Banner	1	stoves only	9,640 ft	yes	Lawn Lake	2.9 mi	1,090 ft	1.5 - 2 hr	no	70%
Lawn Lake	5	stoves only	11,130 ft	yes	Lawn Lake	6.1 mi	2,520 ft	4 - 5 hr	yes	64%
Lower Tileston Meadows	1	stoves only	10,730 ft	yes	Lawn Lake	6.3 mi	2,960 ft	5 - 6 hr	no	15%
Tileston Meadows	2	stoves only	10,830 ft	yes	Lawn Lake	6.0 mi	2,850 ft	5 - 6 hr	no	30%
Upper Chipmunk	2	stoves only	10,700 ft	yes	Lawn Lake	4.3 mi	2,230 ft	4 - 5 hr	no	57%
Ypsilon Creek	1	stoves only	9,510 ft	yes	Lawn Lake	3.0 mi	1,080 ft	1.5 - 2 hr	no	64%

You get a great view of Ypsilon Mountain from Chipmunk Lake on the way to the Upper Chipmunk campsites.

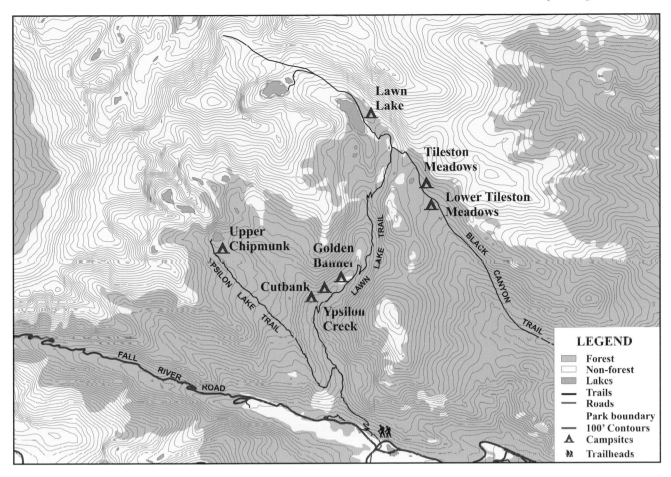

Mummy Range Area

The Mummy Range area is centered around the Roaring River as it flows from Lawn Lake. There are five trails in this area including: Lawn Lake Trail,

Mummy Mountain is a prominent point in the Mummy Range area.

Ypsilon Lake Trail, Black Canyon Trail, Crystal Lake Trail, and the Saddle Trail. This area has eight camping locations containing 13 campsites. All of the sites are individual campsites with one permitting the use of horses or llamas. All of the campsites have toilet facilities and are well shaded by forest. Elevations range from 9,510 feet at Ypsilon Creek to 11,130 feet at Lawn Lake.

The majority of the campsites offer easy access to stream or lake fishing. Look for signs indicating catch and release fishing only on Lawn Lake, Big Crystal Lake, and Roaring River. Check with Park personnel to be sure. Numerous peaks are found in this area. Some of these include: Mummy Mountain (13,425'), Hagues Peak (13,560'), Fairchild Mountain (13,502'), Bighorn Mountain (11,463'), Dark Mountain (10,859'), and Mt. Tileston (11,254'), Ypsilon Mountain (13,514'), Mt. Chiquita (13.069'), Mt. Chapin.

Two trailheads provide access to the campsites in this area. They are: the Lawn Lake Trailhead and the Twin Owls Trailhead. The Lawn Lake Trailhead is the closest one to all of the campsites. The distance from a trailhead to campsites ranges from 2.8 miles to 6.3 miles with hiking times ranging from 1.5 - 2 hours to 5 - 6 hours. Topographic maps that cover the area include the Trail Ridge and Estes Park quads.

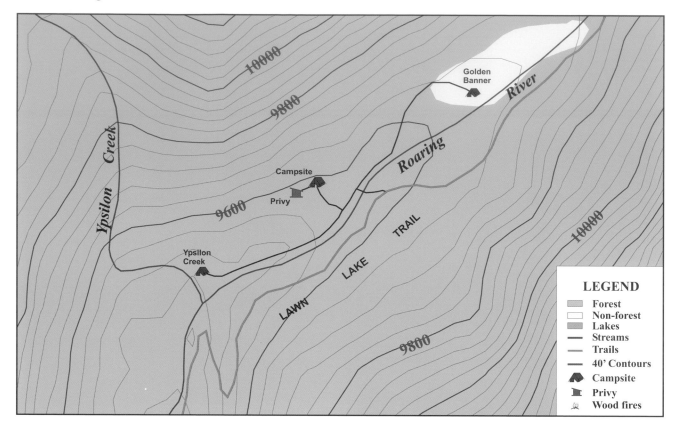

Cutbank

Description:

The Cutbank campsite is located west of Roaring River in an open forest of lodgepole pine at an elevation of 9,590 feet. Red arrowheads mark the path to the campsite. The campsite is slightly sloping but not

excessively so. There are two tent pads with room for 2 to 3 tents. A pit toilet (no walls) is located about 200 feet south of the site. Privacy is limited by the openness of the forest. The rushing waters of the river provide a soothing atmosphere for sleeping. Water is available from Roaring River. Wood or charcoal fires are not permitted here. Use camp stoves only. The Cutbank campsite is occupied about 54% of the season.

Activities:
Fishing: Roaring River, Lawn Lake, Ypsilon Lake
Hiking: Lawn Lake Trail, Ypsilon Lake Trail
Peaks nearby: Mummy Mountain, Fairchild Mountain, Hagues Peak
Scenic features: Alluvial Fan, Roaring River, Ypsilon Lake, Lawn Lake

Cutbank campsite.

Directions:

The Lawn Lake Trailhead is the nearest trailhead to the campsite. Take Highway 36 to its intersection with Highway 34. Turn right and travel to Horseshoe Park. Turn left onto the road to the Endovalley Picnic Area and then immediately right into the trailhead parking area. There is parking for horse trailers a little farther along the Endovalley Road. Take the Lawn Lake Trail for about 2.7 miles to a sign pointing the way across Roaring River over a foot bridge (about 1.3 miles past the Ypsilon Lake Trail). The path to the campsite is about 100 yards south of the sign on the west bank of the stream. It takes about 1.5 to 2 hours to hike to this campsite.

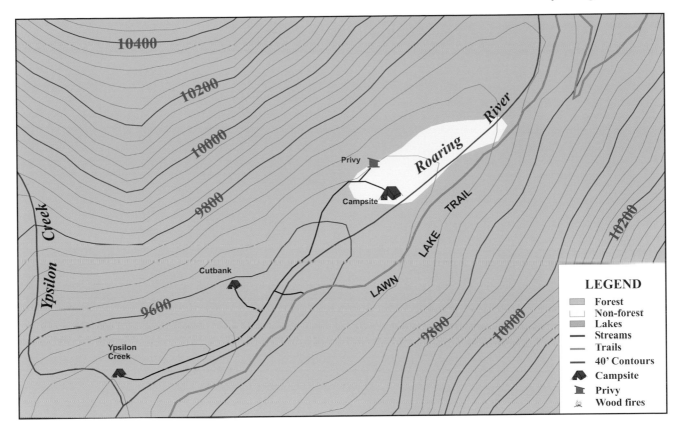

Golden Banner

Description:

The Golden Banner campsite is located west of Roaring River between the river and a lodgepole pine forest at an elevation of 9,640 feet. Red arrowheads mark the path to the campsite. The campsite is in a sandy area with limited shade. There is ample room to pitch 4 to 5 tents. A pit toilet (no walls) is located north of the site. Privacy is limited here as the site can be seen from the Lawn Lake Trail across the river. The rushing waters of the river provide a soothing atmosphere for sleeping. Water is available from Roaring River. Wood or charcoal fires are not permitted here. Use camp stoves only. At a 70% occupancy rate, this site is the most popular in this area.

Golden Banner campsite.

Activities:
Fishing: Roaring River, Lawn Lake, Ypsilon Lake
Hiking: Lawn Lake Trail, Ypsilon Lake Trail
Peaks nearby: Mummy Mountain, Fairchild Mountain, Hagues Peak
Scenic features: Alluvial Fan, Roaring River, Ypsilon Lake, Lawn Lake

Directions:

The Lawn Lake Trailhead is the nearest trailhead to the campsite. Take Highway 36 to its intersection with Highway 34. Turn right and travel to Horseshoe Park. Turn left onto the road to the Endovalley Picnic Area and then immediately right into the trailhead parking area. There is parking for horse trailers a little farther along the EndoValley Road. Take the Lawn Lake Trail for about 2.7 miles to a sign pointing the way across Roaring River over a foot bridge (about 1.3 miles past the Ypsilon Lake Trail). The path to the campsite heads north from the sign on the west bank of the stream. It travels away from the river up hill through the forest for about .15 miles before turning back to the campsite near the river. It takes about 1.5 to 2 hours to hike to this campsite.

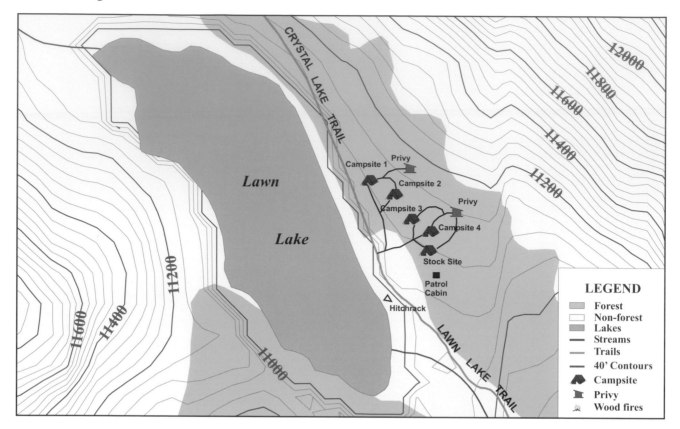

Lawn Lake

Description:

The Lawn Lake campsites are located in a spruce/ fir forest along the ridge to the east of Lawn Lake. They are situated at an elevation of 11,130 feet. There are four individual campsites and one individual/stock site. The stock site is the southern most site of the group. There are llama tethering posts near the site. Horses must be tied at the hitchrack near the lake. There are two tent pads at the stock site. Campsites 1-4 are located north to south along the ridge. Each site has well defined tent pads accommodating 1 to 3 tents. There are two pit toilets (no walls) to serve the campsites. Water is available from Lawn Lake but best from the lake inlet. Wood or charcoal fires are not permitted here. Use camp stoves only.

Activities:

Fishing: Roaring River, Lawn Lake, Big Crystal Lake

Hiking: Lawn Lake Trail, Crystal Lake Trail, Saddle Trail, Black Canyon Trail

Peaks nearby: Mummy Mountain, Fairchild Moun tain, Hagues Peak

Scenic features: Roaring River, Lawn Lake, Crystal Lakes

Lawn Lake campsite 4.

Directions:

The Lawn Lake Trailhead is the nearest trailhead to the campsite. Take Highway 36 to its intersection with Highway 34. Turn right and travel to Horseshoe Park. Turn left onto the road to the Endovalley Picnic Area and then immediately right into the trailhead parking area. There is parking for horse trailers a little farther along the EndoValley Road. Take the Lawn Lake Trail for about 6.1 miles to Lawn Lake. The horse hitchrack is to the left near the southeast end of the lake. The paths to the campsites are farther down the trail and to the right. It takes about 4 to 5 hours to hike to this campsite.

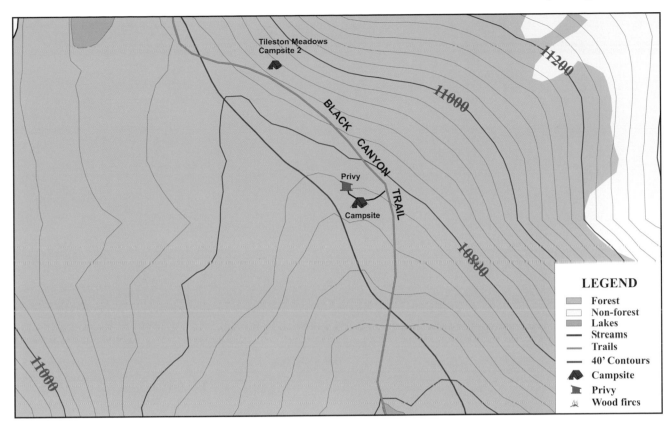

Lower Tileston Meadows

Description:

The Lower Tileston Meadows campsite is located about a quarter-mile below Tileston Meadows in a clump of young spruce trees south of the Black Canyon Trail. The campsite is situated at an elevation of 10,730 feet. Do not confuse this site with the Tileston Meadows campsite 2 at the lower end of Tileston Meadows. A permit for Lower Tileston Meadows does not permit you to camp at Tileston Meadows. This site is quite level in a clear area surrounded by trees. There is room for two tents. A pit toilet (no walls) is located northwest of the campsite. Water is available from Black Canyon Creek. Wood or charcoal fires are not permitted here. Use camp stoves only.

Activities:
Hiking: Lawn Lake Trail, Black Canyon Trail
Peaks nearby: Bighorn Mountain, Mount Tileston, Dark Mountain
Scenic features: Roaring River, Lawn Lake

Directions:

The Lawn Lake Trailhead is the nearest trailhead to the campsite. Take Highway 36 to its intersection with Highway 34. Turn right and travel to Horseshoe

Lower Tileston Meadows campsite.

Park. Turn left onto the road to the Endovalley Picnic Area and then immediately right into the trailhead parking area. There is parking for horse trailers a little farther along the EndoValley Road. Take the Lawn Lake Trail for about 5.4 miles to the Black Canyon Trail turnoff. The turnoff is located opposite a large rubble field below Lawn Lake. This trail makes a moderate to steep climb over a ridge and down into Black Canyon. Hike the Black Canyon Trail for about .9 miles through Tileston Meadows to the campsite on the right of the trail. The path to the campsite is about a quarter-mile below the last campsite at Tileston Meadows. It takes about 5 to 6 hours to hike to this campsite.

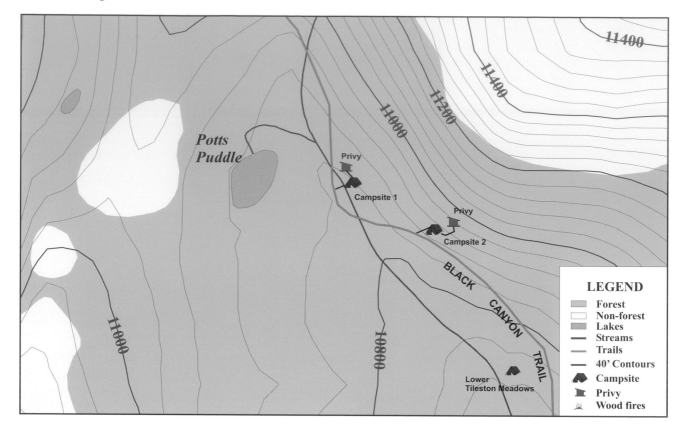

Tileston Meadows

Description:

The Tileston Meadows campsites are located in a forested area to the east of Tileston Meadows. This location has two campsites situated at an elevation of 10,830 feet. There are signs in the meadow pointing the way to the campsites. Both campsites are surrounded by dense spruce trees offering excellent privacy. Campsite 1 is located near the north end of the meadow and has room for 1 to 2 tents. There is a pit toilet (no walls) about 50 yards northwest of the site. Campsite 2 is at the south end of the meadow and will accommodate 2 to 3 tents. A pit toilet (no walls) is located about 100 feet north of the campsite. Water is available from Black Canyon Creek. Wood or charcoal fires are not permitted here. Use camp stoves only. The occupancy rate for the Tileston Meadows campsites is about 30%.

Activities:
Hiking: Lawn Lake Trail, Black Canyon Trail
Peaks nearby: Bighorn Mountain, Mount Tileston, Dark Mountain
Scenic features: Roaring River, Lawn Lake

Directions:

The Lawn Lake Trailhead is the nearest trailhead

Tileston Meadows campsite 1.

to the campsite. Take Highway 36 to its intersection with Highway 34. Turn right and travel to Horseshoe Park. Turn left onto the road to the Endovalley Picnic Area and then immediately right into the trailhead parking area. There is parking for horse trailers a little farther along the EndoValley Road. Take the Lawn Lake Trail for about 5.4 miles to the Black Canyon Trail turnoff. The turnoff is located opposite a large rubble field below Lawn Lake. This trail makes a moderate to steep climb over a ridge and down into Black Canyon. Hike the Black Canyon Trail for about .6 miles to Tileston Meadows. It takes about 5 to 6 hours to hike to this campsite.

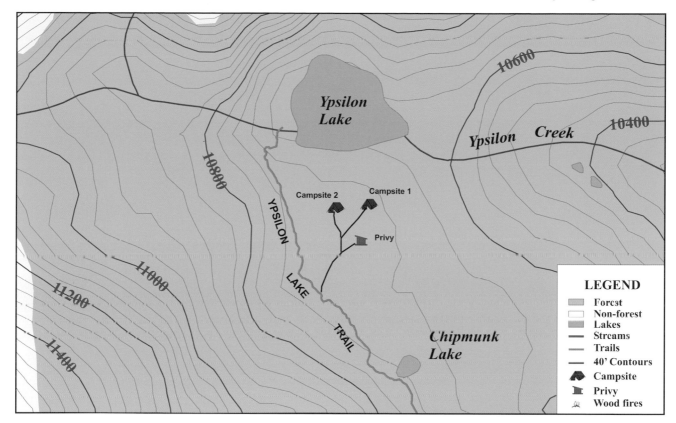

Upper Chipmunk

Description:

The Upper Chipmunk campsites are located south of Ypsilon Lake at an elevation of 10,700 feet (about 100 feet above the lake). There are two campsites with the path to their location marked with red arrowheads on the trees. The campsites are situated in a dense spruce forest. Both sites are well shaded. Campsite 1 has one tent pad with room for two tents. Campsite 2 has three tent pads accommodating one tent each. A pit toilet (no walls) is located to the right of the path just before reaching the campsites. Water is available from the outlet of a nearby pond or from Ypsilon Lake. Wood or charcoal fires are not permitted here. Use camp stoves only. The Upper Chipmunk campsites are occupied about 57% of the time.

Activities:

Fishing: Ypsilon Lake

Hiking: Lawn Lake Trail, Ypsilon Lake Trail

Peaks nearby: Ypsilon Mountain, Mt. Chiquita, Mt. Chapin

Scenic features: Alluvial Fan, Roaring River, Ypsilon Lake

Directions:

The Lawn Lake Trailhead is the nearest trailhead

Upper Chipmunk campsite 1.

to the campsite. Take Highway 36 to its intersection with Highway 34. Turn right and travel to Horseshoe Park. Turn left onto the road to the Endovalley Picnic Area and then immediately right into the trailhead parking area. There is parking for horse trailers a little farther along the EndoValley Road. Take the Lawn Lake Trail for about 1.4 miles to the Ypsilon Lake Trail that crosses Roaring River. Continue a moderate climb for about 2.7 miles to Chipmunk Lake. From here it is an easy hike for .2 miles to the path leading to the campsites. The path leaves the trail to the right just past a boulder field. It takes about 4 to 5 hours to hike to this campsite.

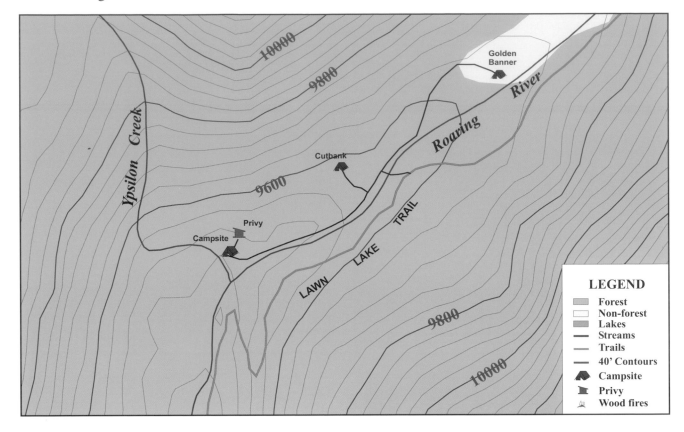

Ypsilon Creek

Description:

The Ypsilon Creek campsite is located west of Roaring River in an open forest of lodgepole pine and spruce at an elevation of 9,510 feet. The path follows the river to the campsite just above Ypsilon Creek where

it flows into Roaring River. Red arrowheads mark the path to the campsite. There is room for 2 to 3 tents. A pit toilet (no walls) is located northwest of the site. Privacy is limited by the openness of the forest. The rushing waters of the creek provide a soothing atmosphere for sleeping. Water is available from Roaring River or Ypsilon Creek. Wood or charcoal fires are not permitted here. Use camp stoves only. The occupancy rate for this campsite is about 64%.

Activities:

Fishing: Roaring River, Lawn Lake, Ypsilon Lake
Hiking: Lawn Lake Trail, Ypsilon Lake Trail
Peaks nearby: Mummy Mountain, Fairchild Mountain, Hagues Peak
Scenic features: Alluvial Fan, Roaring River, Ypsilon Lake, Lawn Lake

Ypsilon Creek campsite.

Directions:

The Lawn Lake Trailhead is the nearest trailhead to the campsite. Take Highway 36 to its intersection with Highway 34. Turn right and travel to Horseshoe Park. Turn left onto the road to the Endovalley Picnic Area and then immediately right into the trailhead parking area. There is parking for horse trailers a little farther along the EndoValley Road. Take the Lawn Lake Trail for about 2.7 miles to a sign pointing the way across Roaring River over a foot bridge (about 1.3 miles past the Ypsilon Lake Trail). The path to the campsite follows Roaring River south for about .3 miles. It takes about 1.5 to 2 hours to hike to this campsite.

Lawn Lake has four individual sites and one stock campsite.

Ypsilon Lake has good fishing for cutthroat trout.

Never Summer Range

Campsite	No. of sites	Wood Fires	Elevation	Privy	Nearest Trailhead	Distance	Elevation Change	Travel Time	Stock	Use
Box Canyon	2	stoves only	10,480 ft	no	Never Summer	3.8 mi	900 ft	2 - 3 hr	no	43%
Ditch Camp	2 + 1grp	stoves only	10,160 ft	yes	Never Summer	3.3 mi	670 ft	2 - 3 hr	yes	22%
Dutch Town	1	stoves only	10,760 ft	no	Colorado River	6.0 mi	2,170 ft	3 - 4 hr	no	32%
Hitchens Gulch	2	stoves only	10,480 ft	no	Colorado River	5.6 mi	1,930 ft	3 - 4 hr	no	19%
La Poudre Pass	3	stoves only	10,230 ft	no	Never Summer	.4 mi	30 ft	30 min	no	7%
Opposition Creek	1	stoves only	10,460 ft	no	Colorado River	4.9 mi	1,760 ft	2 - 3 hr	no	21%
Red Gulch Group	1grp	stoves only	10,320 ft	yes	Colorado River	6.4 mi	2,010 ft	3 - 4 hr	no	18%
Skeleton Gulch	1	stoves only	10,600 ft	no	Never Summer	4.4 mi	1,140 ft	2 - 3 hr	no	33%
Stage Road	1	stoves only	9,530 ft	no	Never Summer	2.5 mi	870 ft	1 - 2 hr	no	49%
Valley View	2	stoves only	10,260 ft	no	Colorado River	3.8 mi	1,410 ft	2 - 3 hr	no	19%

Mount Richthofen surveys the landscape in the Never Summer Range.

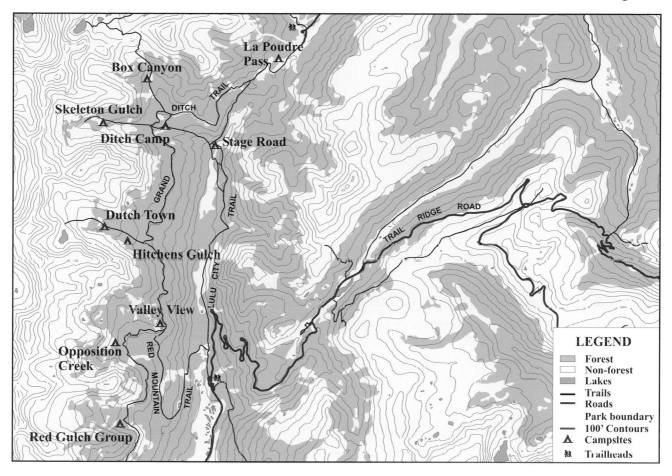

Never Summer Range

The Never Summer Range is located in the north-west section of the Park. Most of the campsites are situated above the Grand Ditch Trail. This trail pro-

The Grand Ditch Trail (ditch maintenance road) provides access to the campsites in the Never Summer Range.

vides great views and easy hiking to most of the camp-sites. There are 10 camping locations within this area containing 17 campsites. Two of these sites are group sites and one permits the use of livestock. Only the group sites have toilet facilities. All of the sites are located in forested areas. Some are more shaded than

others. Elevations range from 9,530 feet at the Stage Road campsite to 10,600 feet at the Skeleton Gulch campsite.

The only fishing here might be found in the small streams near the campsites (Lulu Creek, Sawmill Creek, Big Dutch Creek, Opposition Creek) or in the Colorado River. Numerous peaks are found in this area. Some of these include: Mt. Richthofen (12,940'), Teepee Mtn., Static Peak, Thunder Mtn., Lulu Mtn. (12,228'), Baker Mtn. (12,387'), Mt. Nimbus (12,706'), Mt. Stratus, Mt. Cumulus (12,726'), Howard Mtn. (12,810'), Mt. Cirrus (12,797'), Lead Mtn. (12,357'), and Red Mtn. (11,805').

Access to this area is via the Colorado River and Never Summer trailheads. The distance from a trailhead to campsites ranges from .4 miles to 6.2 miles with hiking times ranging from 30 minutes to 4 hours. Topographic maps that cover the area include the Mount Richthofen and Fall River Pass quads.

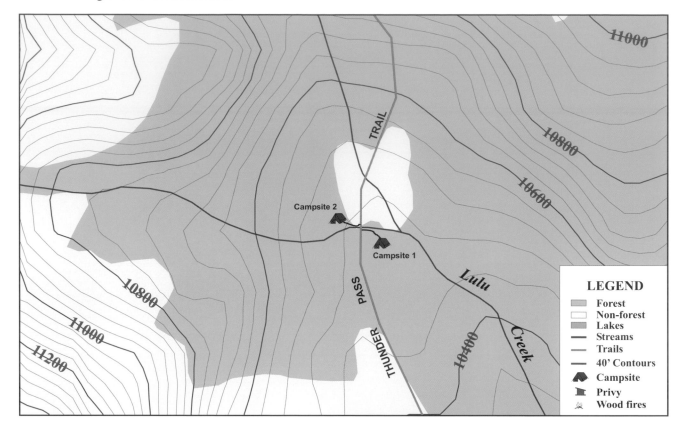

LEGEND
Forest
Non-forest
Lakes
Streams
Trails
40' Contours
Campsite
Privy
Wood fires

Box Canyon

Description:

The Box Canyon campsites are located in a forested area near a large meadow below Thunder Pass. There are two sites situated underneath a canopy of spruce trees at an elevation of 10,480 feet. Campsite 1

is east of the Thunder Pass Trail just south of Lulu Creek. It is a small cleared area with room for one tent. Campsite 2 is west of the trail after crossing Lulu Creek. This site is larger and more open with room for 1 to 2 tents. Water is available from Lulu Creek. There are no toilet facilities at this campsite. Wood and charcoal fires are not permitted here. Use camp stoves only.

Activities:

Fishing: Lulu Creek, Michigan Lakes
Hiking: Thunder Pass Trail, Grand Ditch Trail
Peaks nearby: Thunder Mountain, Lulu Mountain,
   Mount Richthofen, Static Peak
Scenic Features: Thunder Pass, Michigan Lakes

Box Canyon campsite 1.

Directions:

The nearest trailhead to this campsite is the Never Summer Trailhead on the Long Draw Road. Take Highway 287 north from Fort Collins to La Porte. Continue on 287 north to Highway 14. Travel west on 14 for 52 miles to the Long Draw Road. Turn left and travel 12.5 miles to the trailhead at the end of the road. Take the Grand Ditch Trail for 3.2 miles to the Thunder Pass Trail. Cross the ditch over a wooden bridge and hike about .6 miles to the campsites. Most of the hike is easy along the Grand Ditch Trail. The Thunder Pass Trail is of moderate difficulty. It takes 2 to 3 hours to hike to this campsite.

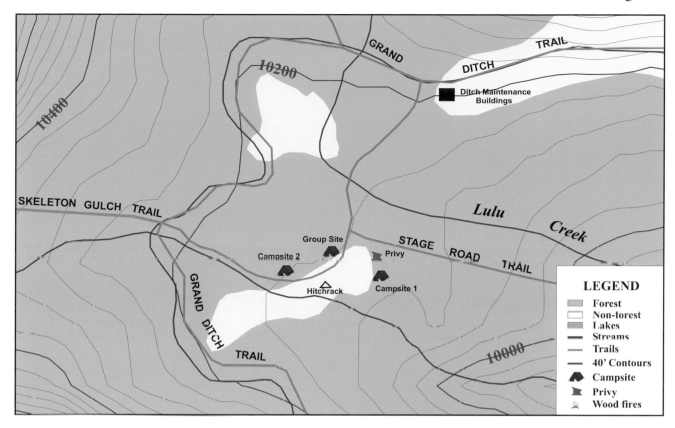

Ditch Camp

Description:

The Ditch Camp campsites are located in a spruce forest surrounding an open area. They are situated at an elevation of 10,160 feet. There are three sites, a group/stock site and two individual sites. The group site and campsite 1 are near the northeast edge of the meadow while campsite 2 is farther back in the trees. The group/stock site has room for 5 to 6 tents. There is a hitchrack about 50 yards down in the meadow. Campsite 1 is directly across from the group site and will accommodate 1 to 2 tents. Campsite 2 is just to the right of the loop trail back toward the Skeleton Gulch Trail. There is a sign in the meadow. A pit toilet (3 walls) is located north of campsite 1. Water is available from Sawmill Creek that runs through the open area. There are some old buildings here that are remnants of the turn of the century ditch construction camp. Wood and charcoal fires are not permitted here. Use camp stoves only.

Activities:

Fishing: Sawmill Creek, Lulu Creek

Hiking: Grand Ditch Trail, Thunder Pass Trail, Stage Road Trail, Lulu City Trail, Little Yellowstone Trail, Skeleton Gulch Trail

Peaks nearby: Thunder Mountain, Lulu Mountain,

Ditch Camp Group/Stock campsite.

Mount Richthofen, Static Peak

Scenic Features: Thunder Pass, Michigan Lakes

Directions:

The nearest trailhead to this campsite is the Never Summer Trailhead on the Long Draw Road. Take Highway 287 north from Fort Collins to La Porte. Continue on 287 north to Highway 14. Travel west on 14 for 52 miles to the Long Draw Road. Turn left and travel 12.5 miles to the trailhead at the end of the road. Take the Grand Ditch Trail for 3.1 miles to the ditch maintenance buildings. Turn left on the road just past the buildings for about .2 miles to the campsites. Hiking time is 2 to 3 hours.

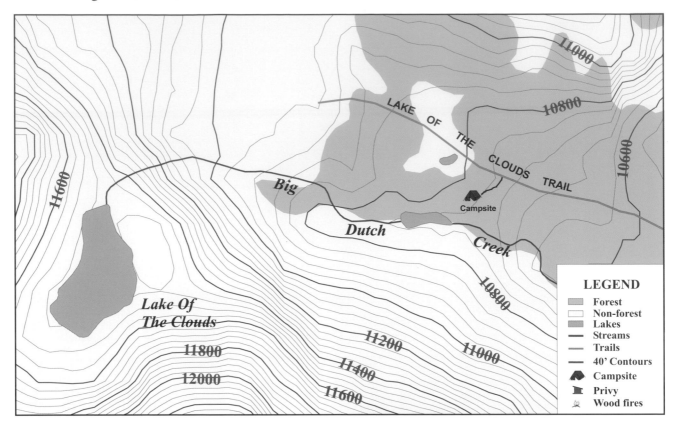

Dutch Town

Description:

The Dutch Town campsite is located in a forested area toward the end of the Lake of the Clouds Trail. The path to the site climbs over a rise and down to the site at an elevation of 10,760 feet. This campsite is level and has room for one tent. Water is available from Big Dutch Creek below the site. There are no toilet facilities at this campsite. Wood and charcoal fires are not permitted here. Use camp stoves only. It is a short distance to timberline and the boulder field that surrounds the Lake of the Clouds. This lake, however, is not easy to find and requires a fair amount of rock scrambling to get to it. Dutch Town has a 32% occupancy rate.

Activities:

Fishing: Big Dutch Creek

Hiking: Lake of the Clouds Trail, Grand Ditch Trail

Peaks nearby: Lead Mountain, Mount Cirrus, Howard Mountain

Scenic Features: Lake of the Clouds

Directions:

The nearest trailhead to this campsite is the Colorado River Trailhead on the west side of the Park. The

Dutch Town campsite.

trailhead is just west of Trail Ridge Road about 10.2 miles north of the Grand Lake Entrance and about 31 miles from the Beaver Meadows Entrance. Take the Lulu City Trail for about .44 miles to its intersection with the Red Mountain Trail. Turn left and cross the Colorado River over a wooden bridge. The Red Mountain Trail makes a moderate climb for 3.2 miles to the Grand Ditch Trail. Turn right here and travel 1.75 miles to the Lake of the Clouds Trail near Big Dutch Creek. Cross the ditch over a log foot bridge and make a moderate climb for .6 miles to the Dutch Town sign. Turn left and travel about 200 feet over a rise to the campsite. It takes 3 to 4 hours to reach the campsite.

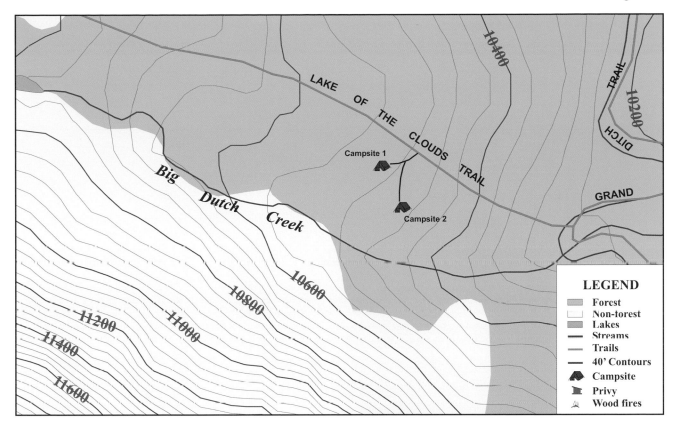

Hitchens Gulch

Description:

The Hitchens Gulch campsites are located in a forested area about .3 miles west of Grand Ditch to the left of the Lake of the Clouds Trail. There are two campsites about 50 to 100 yards apart, both situated at an elevation of 10,480 feet. They are near some ruins of old cabins built in the late 1800's by prospectors seeking gold. Campsite 1 is a level, bare area under some spruce trees. Campsite 2 is off to the left and downhill from campsite 1 and is slightly smaller. Both sites will accommodate one tent. Water is available from Big Dutch Creek below the site. There are no toilet facilities at this campsite. Wood and charcoal fires are not permitted here. Use camp stoves only. Hitchens Gulch is occupied only 19% of the time.

Activities:
Fishing: Big Dutch Creek
Hiking: Lake of the Clouds Trail, Grand Ditch Trail
Peaks nearby: Lead Mountain, Mount Cirrus, Howard Mountain
Scenic Features: Lake of the Clouds

Directions:

The nearest trailhead to this campsite is the

Hitchens Gulch campsite 1.

Colorado River Trailhead on the west side of the Park. The trailhead is just west of Trail Ridge Road about 10.2 miles north of the Grand Lake Entrance and about 31 miles from the Beaver Meadows Entrance. Take the Lulu City Trail for about .44 miles to its intersection with the Red Mountain Trail. Turn left and cross the Colorado River over a wooden bridge. The Red Mountain Trail makes a moderate climb for 3.2 miles to the Grand Ditch Trail. Turn right and travel 1.75 miles to the Lake of the Clouds Trail near Big Dutch Creek. Cross the ditch over a log foot bridge and make a moderate climb for .2 miles to the cabin ruins. The sites are off to the left. It takes about 3 to 4 hours to reach this campsite.

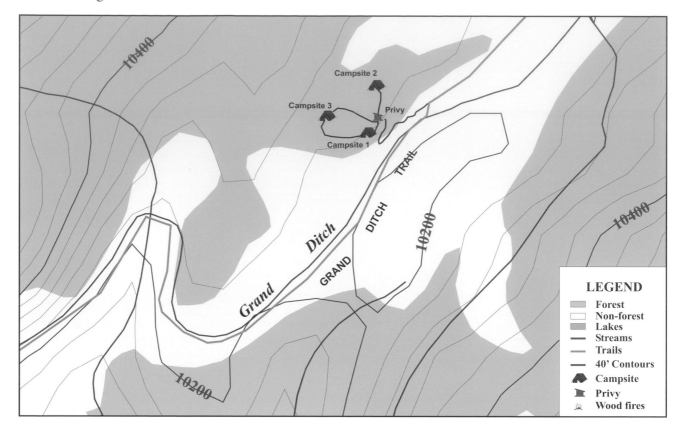

La Poudre Pass

Description:

The La Poudre Pass campsites are located on the ridge above and south of the Park Service patrol cabin. This area is situated at an elevation of 10,230 feet. There are three campsites here with an outhouse centrally located. Campsite 1 is nearest the outhouse. A path traveling behind the outhouse leads to campsite 2. This campsite is about 250 to 300 yards from the outhouse and to the left of the path. Campsite 3 is northwest of the outhouse in some trees above the meadow. Some small rock cairns mark the way. The silver post stands in front of some trees with the tent area behind them. All of these campsites will accommodate one tent. Water is available from Grand Ditch below. Wood and charcoal fires are not permitted here. Use camp stoves only. These campsites are the least utilized in the Park with only a 7% occupancy rate.

Activities:

Fishing: Bennett Creek, Neota Creek

Hiking: Grand Ditch Trail, Thunder Pass Trail, Stage Road Trail, Lulu City Trail, Little Yellowstone Trail

Peaks nearby: Thunder Mountain, Lulu Mountain, Mount Richthofen, Static Peak

La Poudre Pass campsite 2.

Scenic Features: Thunder Pass, Michigan Lakes

Directions:

The nearest trailhead to this campsite is the Never Summer Trailhead on the Long Draw Road. Take Highway 287 north from Fort Collins to La Porte. Continue on 287 north to Highway 14. Travel west on 14 for 52 miles to the Long Draw Road. Turn left and travel 12.5 miles to the trailhead at the end of the road. Take the Grand Ditch Trail for about .4 miles to the Park Service patrol cabin. There is a road veering off to the right just before the ditch road crosses the ditch. Follow this road a short distance to the campsites. It take about 30 minutes to hike to this campsite.

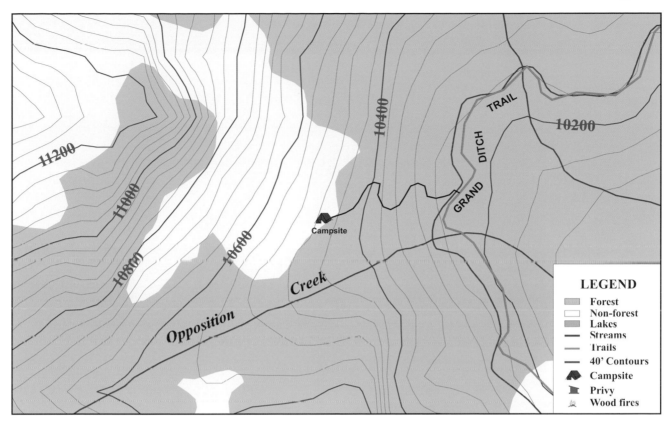

Opposition Creek

Description:

The Opposition Creek campsite is located in a grassy area next to some spruce trees just east of a rock talus slope. The site is situated at an elevation of 10,460 feet. Much of the area is in the open and is only shaded for part of the day. This campsite is level and will accommodate 2 to 3 tents. Water is available from Opposition Creek below the site. There are no toilet facilities at this campsite. Wood and charcoal fires are not permitted here. Use camp stoves only. This campsite provides good privacy from the Grand Ditch Trail below. The Opposition Creek campsite is occupied 21% of the time.

Activities:

Fishing: Opposition Creek

Hiking: Lake of the Clouds Trail, Grand Ditch Trail

Peaks nearby: Mount Nimbus, Mount Cumulus, Howard Mountain

Scenic Features: Lake of the Clouds

Directions:

The nearest trailhead to this campsite is the Colorado River Trailhead on the west side of the Park. The trailhead is just west of Trail Ridge Road about 10.2

Opposition Creek campsite.

miles north of the Grand Lake Entrance and about 31 miles from the Beaver Meadows Entrance. Take the Lulu City Trail for about .44 miles to its intersection with the Red Mountain Trail. Turn left and cross the Colorado River over a wooden bridge. The Red Mountain Trail makes a moderate climb for 3.2 miles to the Grand Ditch Trail. Turn left and travel a mile to the sign for Opposition Creek. Cross the ditch over a log foot bridge and make a moderate climb for about .25 miles to the campsite. It takes about 2 to 3 hours to reach this campsite.

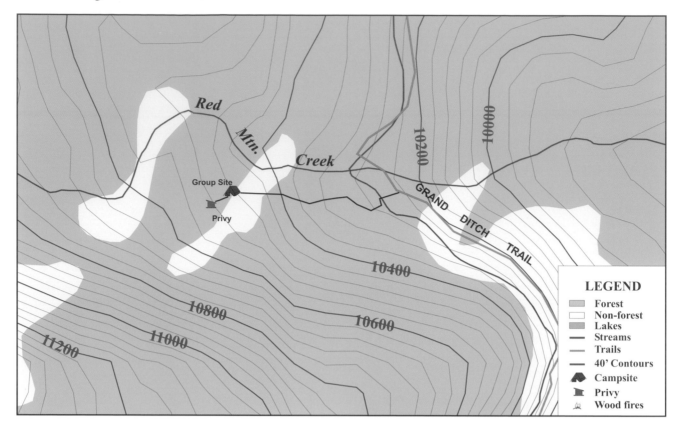

Red Gulch Group

Description:

The Red Gulch Group campsite is located on the edge of an open area about .2 miles above the Grand Ditch Trail. It is situated at an elevation of 10,320 feet in Red Gulch, above and to the south of Red Mountain Creek. A large bare area next to some spruce trees will accommodate 3 to 4 tents. Water is available from Grand Ditch. There is a pit toilet (4 walls) about 200 feet to the left of the campsite. Wood and charcoal fires are not permitted here. Use camp stoves only. This group campsite is utilized about 18% of the time.

Red Gulch Group campsite.

Activities:

Fishing: Red Mountain Creek

Hiking: Grand Ditch Trail

Peaks nearby: Mount Nimbus, Mount Stratus, Baker Mountain

Scenic Features: Views of Kawuneeche Valley and Lakes to the south

Directions:

The nearest trailhead to this campsite is the Colorado River Trailhead on the west side of the Park. The trailhead is just west of Trail Ridge Road about 10.2 miles north of the Grand Lake Entrance and about 31 miles from the Beaver Meadows Entrance. Take the Lulu City Trail for about .44 miles to its intersection with the Red Mountain Trail. Turn left and cross the Colorado River over a wooden bridge. The Red Mountain Trail makes a moderate climb for 3.2 miles to the Grand Ditch Trail. Turn left and travel 2.6 miles to the sign for Red Mountain Creek. The path to the campsite is a few hundred yards south of this sign. Cross the ditch over a shaky log foot bridge and make a moderate climb for about .2 miles to the campsite. The campsite is just ahead after the path levels off. It takes about 3 to 4 hours to reach this campsite.

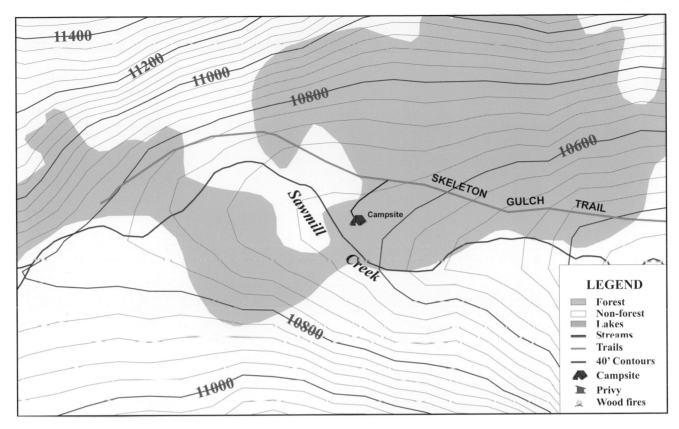

Skeleton Gulch

Description:

The Skeleton Gulch campsite is located in a hollow surrounded by rocks and spruce trees at an elevation of 10,600 feet. The path leaves the Skeleton Gulch Trail just before it reaches a meadow and travels to the  left for about 150 yards and then drops down to the site. This campsite has a small bare area surrounded by grass. There is room for 1 to 2 tents. There are no toilet facilities at this campsite. Water is available from Sawmill Creek that runs below the campsite. Wood and charcoal fires are not permitted here. Use camp stoves only. The Skeleton Gulch campsite has an occupancy rate of about 33%.

Activities:

Fishing: Sawmill Creek

Hiking: Grand Ditch Trail, Thunder Pass Trail, Stage Road Trail, Skeleton Gulch Trail

Peaks nearby: Thunder Mountain, Lulu Mountain, Mount Richthofen, Static Peak, Teepee Mountain, Lead Mountain

Scenic Features: Thunder Pass, Michigan Lakes

Skeleton Gulch campsite.

Directions:

The nearest trailhead to this campsite is the Never Summer Trailhead on the Long Draw Road. Take Highway 287 north from Fort Collins to La Porte. Continue on 287 north to Highway 14. Travel west on 14 for 52 miles to the Long Draw Road. Turn left and travel 12.5 miles to the trailhead at the end of the road. Take the Grand Ditch Trail for 3.7 miles to the Skeleton Gulch Trail. This is about a half-mile past the Thunder Pass Trail. Cross the ditch over a log bridge and hike .7 miles to the campsite. It takes about 2 to 3 hours to reach this campsite.

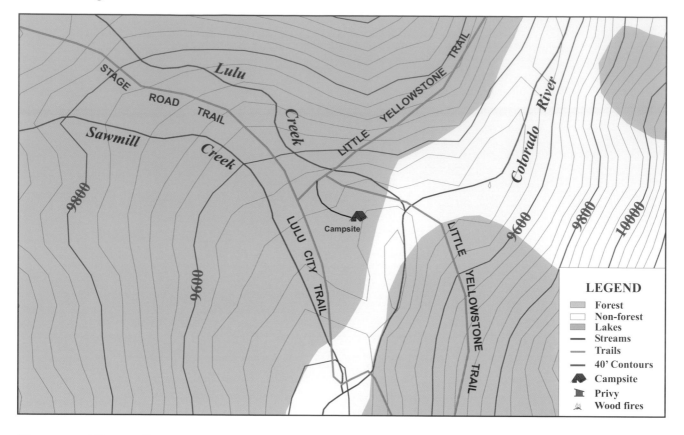

Stage Road

Description:

    The Stage Road campsite is located on a bench above Lulu Creek under a canopy of spruce trees. It is situated at an elevation of 9,530 feet. The campsite is well shaded and has room for 1 to 2 tents. This centrally located site offers opportunities for exploring the Lulu City town site and Little Yellowstone Canyon. The Stage Road Trail follows the old wagon road used to deliver supplies to Lulu City and Teller City in the late 1800's. There are no toilet facilities at this campsite. Water is available from Lulu Creek that runs below the campsite. Wood and charcoal fires are not permitted here. Use camp stoves only. The occupancy rate for this site is about 49%.

Activities:
Fishing: Lulu Creek, Colorado River
Hiking: Grand Ditch Trail, Little Yellowstone Trail, Stage Road Trail, Lulu City Trail, Thunder Pass Trail, Skeleton Gulch Trail
Peaks nearby: Thunder Mountain, Lulu Mountain, Mount Richthofen, Static Peak, Teepee Mountain, Lead Mountain
Scenic Features: Thunder Pass, Michigan Lakes, Little Yellowstone Canyon

Stage Road campsite.

Directions:

    The nearest trailhead to this campsite is the Never Summer Trailhead on the Long Draw Road. Take Highway 287 north from Fort Collins to La Porte. Continue on 287 north to Highway 14. Travel west on 14 for 52 miles to the Long Draw Road. Turn left and travel 12.5 miles to the trailhead at the end of the road. Take the Grand Ditch Trail for 1.3 miles to the Little Yellowstone Trail. Turn left and follow the trail down through Little Yellowstone Canyon to its junction with the Lulu City Trail (just after crossing Lulu Creek). Turn right and make a short climb to the campsite sign. The campsite is about 100 yards to the left in the trees. It takes 1 to 2 hours to hike to this campsite.

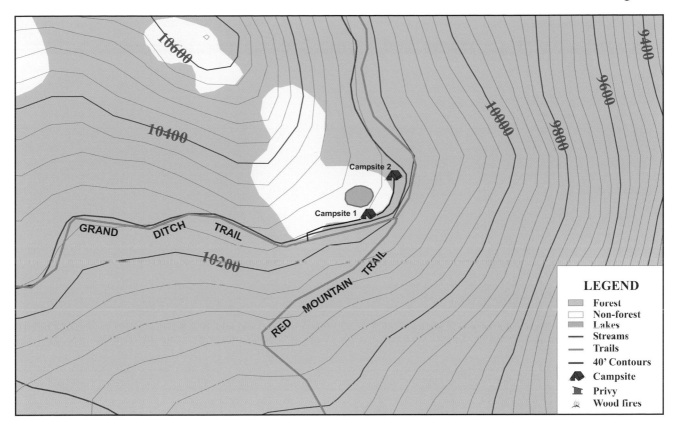

Valley View

Description:

The Valley View campsites are located on the ridge to the west of the Grand Ditch Trail near a pond that dries up in the summer. There are two campsites situated at an elevation of 10,260 feet. Campsite 1 offers a view of the Kawuneeche Valley below and is about 300 to 400 yards from the Grand Ditch Trail. Campsite 2 is 100 to 200 yards farther along the ridge to the north. Both sites are located under a spruce canopy and have room for 1 to 2 tents. Water is available from Grand Ditch below the sites. There are no toilet facilities at this campsite. Wood and charcoal fires are not permitted here. Use camp stoves only.

Activities:

Fishing: Opposition Creek

Hiking: Lake of the Clouds Trail, Grand Ditch Trail

Peaks nearby: Mount Nimbus, Mount Cumulus, Howard Mountain

Scenic Features: Lake of the Clouds

Directions:

The nearest trailhead to this campsite is the Colo-

Valley View campsite 2.

rado River Trailhead on the west side of the Park.   The trailhead is just west of Trail Ridge Road about 10.2 miles north of the Grand Lake Entrance and about 31 miles from the Beaver Meadows Entrance. Take the Lulu City Trail for about .44 miles to its intersection with the Red Mountain Trail. Turn left and cross the Colorado River over a wooden bridge. The Red Mountain Trail makes a moderate climb for 3.2 miles to the Grand Ditch Trail. Turn left and travel a short distance to the sign for the Valley View campsites. Cross the ditch over a log foot bridge and make a moderate climb to the campsites. It takes about 2 to 3 hours to reach this campsite.

North Fork Area Campsites

Campsite	No. of sites	Wood Fires	Elevation	Privy	Nearest Trailhead	Distance	Elevation Change	Travel Time	Stock	Use
Aspen Meadow Group	1grp	yes	9,390 ft	yes	Dunraven	6.0 mi	2,160 ft	4 - 5 hr	no	32%
Bighorn Mountain Group	1 grp	yes	10,600 ft	yes	Twin Owls	6.4 mi	3,700 ft	4 - 5 hr	yes	17%
Boundary Creek	2	yes	9,000 ft	yes	Dunraven	4.6 mi	1,650 ft	3 - 4 hr	no	44%
Halfway	2	yes	9,360 ft	yes	Dunraven	5.6 mi	2,040 ft	4 - 5 hr	no	27%
Happily Lost	1	yes	9,560 ft	yes	Dunraven	6.5 mi	2,290 ft	4 - 5 hr	no	41%
Kettle Tarn	2	stoves only	9,200 ft	yes	Dunraven	5.2 mi	2,000 ft	3 - 4 hr	no	57%
Lost Falls	2	yes	9,560 ft	yes	Dunraven	6.8 mi	2,370 ft	5 - 6 hr	no	41%
Lost Lake	4	stoves only	10,714 ft	yes	Dunraven	9.2 mi	3,490 ft	8 - 10 hr	no	36%
Lost Meadow	1 + 1grp	stoves only	10,390 ft	yes	Dunraven	8.2 mi	3,170 ft	8 - 9 hr	yes	25%
McGregor Mountain	2	yes	9,070 ft	yes	Twin Owls	3.9 mi	1,980 ft	3 - 4 hr	no	40%
Peregrine	1	stoves only	8,290 ft	yes	Cow Creek	2.1 mi	490 ft	1 - 2 hr	no	58%
Rabbit Ears	1	stoves only	8,100 ft	yes	Cow Creek	1.4 mi	310 ft	1 hr	no	77%
Silvanmere	2	yes	9,340 ft	yes	Dunraven	5.8 mi	2,080 ft	4 - 5 hr	no	12%
Stormy Peaks	2 + 1grp	stoves only	10,890 ft	yes	Stormy Peaks	4.1 mi	1,850 ft	4 - 5 hr	no	11%
Stormy Peaks South	1	stoves only	10,800 ft	yes	Stormy Peaks	6.4 mi	3,520 ft	6 - 7 hr	no	20%
Sugarloaf	1	stoves only	10,290 ft	yes	Dunraven	8.0 mi	3,090 ft	6 - 8 hr	no	20%

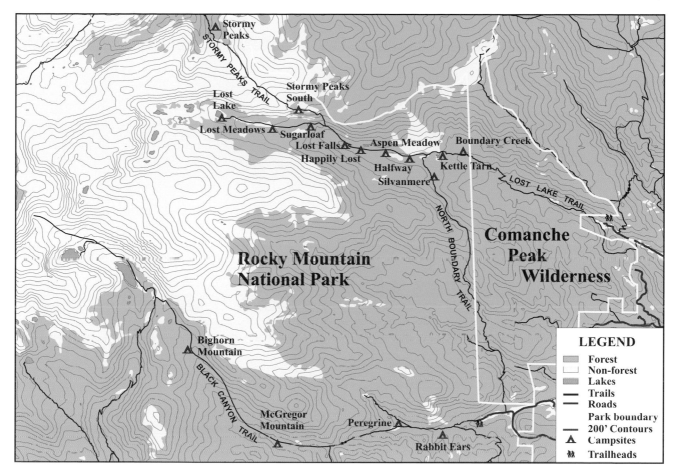

North Fork Area

The North Fork area is located in the northeast section of the Park. There are eight trails in this area

Lost Lake is a popular destination in the North Fork Area.

including: Lost Lake, Stormy Peaks, North Boundary, West Creek, Black Canyon, Cow Creek, Dark Mountain, and Lawn Lake.   Sixteen camping locations are found within this area with a total of 28 campsites. Four of these sites are group sites and two permit the use of livestock. All of the sites have toilet facilities. Eight of the sites permit the use of wood fires. All of

the sites are located in forested areas. Some are more shaded than others. Elevations range from 8,100 feet at Rabbit Ears to 10,890 feet at the Stormy Peaks campsite.

Most of the campsites offer easy access to stream or lake fishing. Look for signs indicating catch and release fishing only on many of the waters in the Park. Lost Lake , Lake Husted, Lake Louise and the North Fork Big Thompson River above Lost Falls are catch and release. Check with Park personnel to be sure. Numerous peaks are found in this area. Some of these include: Stormy Peaks (12,148'), Sugarloaf Mtn., Ramsey Peak (11,582'), Mt. Dunraven (12,571'), Mt. Dickinson (11,831'), Dark Mtn. (10,859'), and Sheep Mtn.

Trailheads providing access to campsites in this area include: Dunraven, Stormy Peaks, Cow Creek, Twin Owls, and Lawn Lake.   The distance from a trailhead to campsites ranges from 1.4 miles to 9.2 miles with hiking times ranging from 1 to 10 hours. Topographic maps that cover the area include the Comanche Peak, Pingree Park, Crystal Mountain, Trail Ridge, Estes Park, and Glen Haven quads.

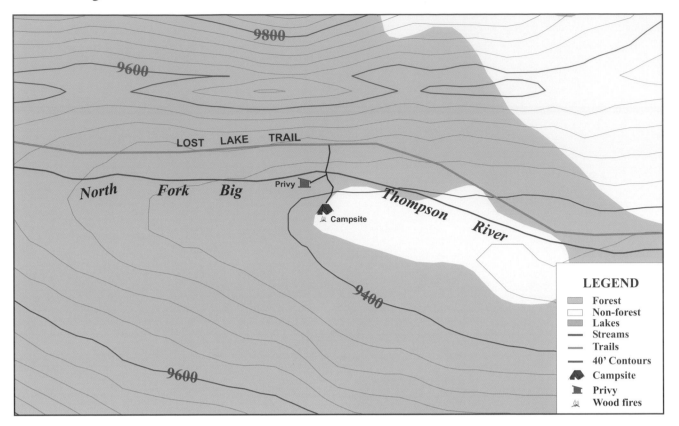

Aspen Meadow Group campsite.

Aspen Meadow Group

Description:

The Aspen Meadow Group campsite is located south of the Lost Lake Trail near a small dry meadow surrounded by aspen and spruce trees. The path to the site is marked with red arrowheads on the trees. It crosses the North Fork Big Thompson River over a log foot bridge and travels a short distance to the site. The meadow is situated at an elevation of 9,390 feet. There is a pit toilet (no walls) to the right just after crossing the stream. Wood fires are permitted at this campsite. Metal fire grates are provided at the site. Fires can only be built within these grates. Do not place rocks in or around your fire. Use only dead and down wood. Water may be obtained from the river. The site has room for 4 to 5 tents and offers a pleasant atmosphere for group camping. This group campsite is occupied 32% of the time.

Activities:
Fishing: North Fork Big Thompson River
Hiking: Lost Lake Trail, Stormy PeaksTrail
Peaks nearby: Stormy Peaks, Sugarloaf Mountain, Ramsey Peak
Scenic Features: Lost Lake, Lost Falls

Directions:

The nearest access to this campsite is via the Forest Service Dunraven Trailhead. Take Highway 34 from Loveland to Drake. Turn right on County Road 43 and travel about 6 miles to County Road 518. There is a sign marking the way to the trailhead. Turn right and go about 2 miles to the Dunraven Trailhead and the south end of the trail. Follow the Forest Service North Fork Trail for 4.4 miles through the Comanche Peak Wilderness to the Park boundary. The trail becomes the Lost Lake Trail in the Park. It is another 1.6 miles (about .75 miles beyond the North Boundary Trail) to the sign for the Aspen Meadow Group campsite. Turn left and cross the river over a log foot bridge to reach the site. Travel time is 4 to 5 hours.

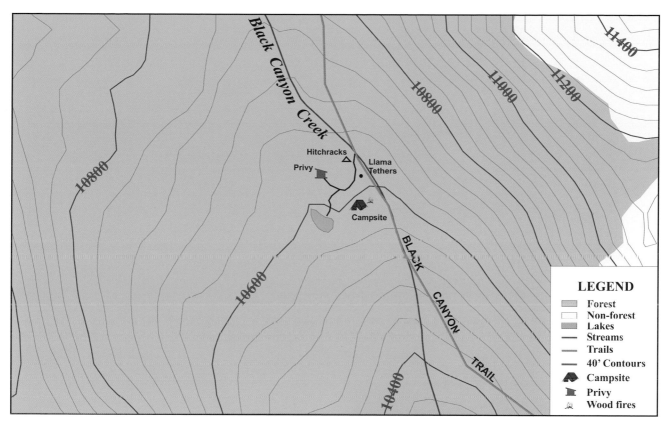

LEGEND
- Forest
- Non-forest
- Lakes
- Streams
- Trails
- 40' Contours
- Campsite
- Privy
- Wood fires

Bighorn Mountain Group

Description:

The Bighorn Mountain Group campsite is located about 6.4 miles from the Twin Owls parking area just south of the Black Canyon Trail. The site is situated at an elevation of 10,600 feet. This is a great stock site. There are two hitchracks and several llama tethering posts. There also is a large pond to the south of the site for watering stock. This campsite has five tent pads that will accommodate 8 to 10 tents. There is a pit toilet (no walls) 50 to 100 yards to the right of the tent pads. A separate fire pit area is great for group gatherings. Wood fires are permitted at this campsite. Metal fire grates are provided at the site. Fires can only be built within these grates. Do not place rocks in or around your fire. Use only dead and down wood. Water is available from Black Canyon Creek. The site offers a pleasant atmosphere for group camping. Occupancy rate is about 17%.

Activities:
Fishing: Black Canyon Creek
Hiking: Black Canyon Trail, Lawn Lake Trail
Peaks nearby: Bighorn Mountain, Mount Tileston, Dark Mountain
Scenic features: Roaring River, Lawn Lake

Bighorn Mountain tent area.

Directions:

The nearest access to this campsite is via the Twin Owls Trailhead. Travel west on Highway 34 toward the Fall River Entrance. Turn right on Devils Gulch Road and go about .75 miles to the MacGregor Ranch. Follow the ranch road for about .7 miles to the parking area. Take the Black Canyon Trail from the west end of the parking area for three miles to its intersection with the Dark Mountain Trail. Continue along Black Canyon Creek into Black Canyon. It is about 3.4 miles to the Bighorn Mountain campsite sign. The campsite is off to the left in the spruce forest. Plan on 4 to 5 hours to reach this campsite. Horse campers are better off using the Lawn Lake Trail to Black Canyon (trailer parking).

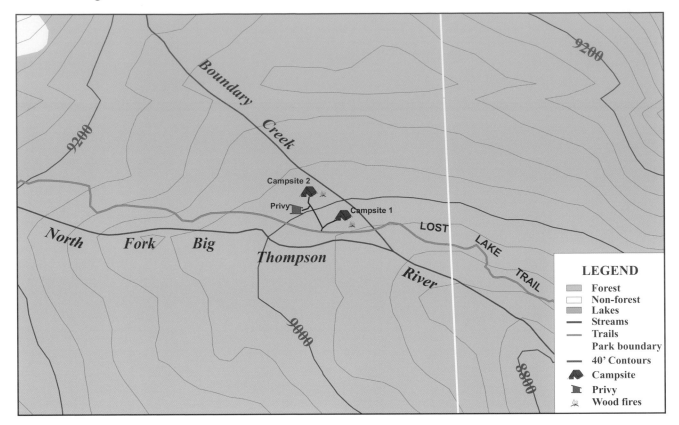

Boundary Creek

Description:

The Boundary Creek campsites are located north of the Lost Lake Trail near an open area just west of Boundary Creek. There are two campsites situated at an elevation of 9,000 feet about 100 yards apart. Camp-

site 1 is closer to the trail and is located in a fairly open area. The trees are small and provide little shade. This site has two gravel filled tent pads. Campsite 2 is farther up the hill and has two tent pads also. There is a pit toilet (no walls) southwest of campsite 2. Wood fires are permitted at this campsite. Metal fire grates are provided at the site. Fires can only be built within these grates. Do not place rocks in or around your fire. Use only dead and down wood. Water may be obtained from Boundary Creek. These campsites have a 44% occupancy rate.

Activities:

Fishing: Boundary Creek, North Fork Big
   Thompson River
Hiking: Lost Lake Trail, Stormy PeaksTrail
Peaks nearby: Stormy Peaks, Mt. Dickinson, South
   Signal Mtn.

Boundary Creek campsite 2.

Directions:

The nearest access to this campsite is via the Forest Service Dunraven Trailhead. Take Highway 34 from Loveland to Drake. Turn right on County Road 43 and travel about 6 miles to County Road 518. There is a sign marking the way to the trailhead. Turn right and go about 2 miles to the Dunraven Trailhead and the south end of the trail. Follow the Forest Service North Fork Trail for 4.4 miles through the Comanche Peak Wilderness to the Park boundary. The trail becomes the Lost Lake Trail in the Park. It is another .2 miles to the sign for the Boundary Creek campsite. The campsites are on the right above the trail. It takes about 3 to 4 hours to hike to this campsite.

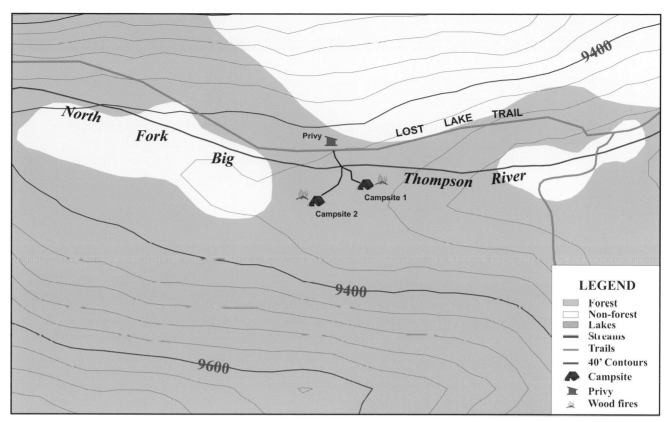

Halfway

Description:

The Halfway campsites are located south of the Lost Lake Trail across the river from a small meadow. The path to the sites is marked with red arrowheads on the trees. There are two campsites situated at an elevation of 9,360 feet. The path to campsite 1 winds down through the forest to the left. This site has two tent pads under a spruce canopy. Campsite 2 is to the right after crossing the stream. An outhouse is located north of the Lost Lake Trail opposite the path to the campsites. Wood fires are permitted at this campsite. Metal fire grates are provided at the site. Fires can only be built within these grates. Do not place rocks in or around your fire. Use only dead and down wood. Water may be obtained from the river.

Activities:

Fishing: North Fork Big Thompson River

Hiking: Lost Lake Trail, Stormy PeaksTrail

Peaks nearby: Stormy Peaks, Sugarloaf Mountain, Ramsey Peak, Mount Dickinson, Mount Dunraven

Scenic Features: Lost Lake, Lost Falls

Halfway campsite 1.

Directions:

The nearest access to this campsite is via the Forest Service Dunraven Trailhead. Take Highway 34 from Loveland to Drake. Turn right on County Road 43 and travel about 6 miles to County Road 518. There is a sign marking the way to the trailhead. Turn right and go about 2 miles to the Dunraven Trailhead and the south end of the trail. Follow the Forest Service North Fork Trail for 4.4 miles through the Comanche Peak Wilderness to the Park boundary. The trail becomes the Lost Lake Trail in the Park. It is another 1.2 miles (about .3 miles beyond the North Boundary Trail) to the sign for the Halfway campsite. Turn left and cross the river over a log foot bridge to reach the site.

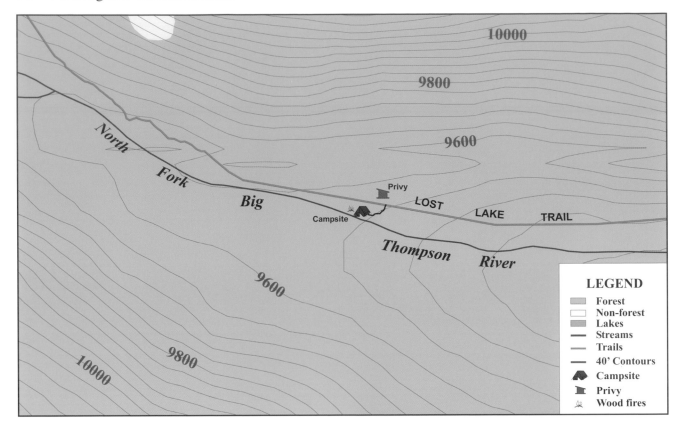

Happily Lost

Description:

The Happily Lost campsite is located south of the Lost Lake Trail in a heavily forested area between the trail and the North Fork Big Thompson River. The path to the site is marked with red arrowheads on the trees. The campsite is located in a sunny area of an otherwise dense spruce forest. It is situated at an elevation of 9,560 feet. There are two tent pads about 60 to 70 feet above the river. A pit toilet (no walls) is located near the trail. Wood fires are permitted at this campsite. Metal fire grates are provided at the site. Fires can only be built within these grates. Do not place rocks in or around your fire. Use only dead and down wood. Water may be obtained from the river. This campsite is occupied 41% of the time.

Activities:
Fishing: North Fork Big Thompson River
Hiking: Lost Lake Trail, Stormy Peaks Trail
Peaks nearby: Stormy Peaks, Sugarloaf Mountain, Ramsey Peak, Mount Dickinson, Mount Dunraven
Scenic Features: Lost Lake, Lost Falls

Directions:

The nearest access to this campsite is via the For-

Happily Lost campsite.

est Service Dunraven Trailhead. Take Highway 34 from Loveland to Drake. Turn right on County Road 43 and travel about 6 miles to County Road 518. There is a sign marking the way to the trailhead. Turn right and go about 2 miles to the Dunraven Trailhead and the south end of the trail. Follow the Forest Service North Fork Trail for 4.4 miles through the Comanche Peak Wilderness to the Park boundary. The trail becomes the Lost Lake Trail in the Park. It is another 2.1 miles (about 1.2 miles beyond the North Boundary Trail) to the sign for the Happily Lost campsite. Turn left and follow the red arrowheads to reach the site. Hiking time is about 4 to 5 hours from the trailhead.

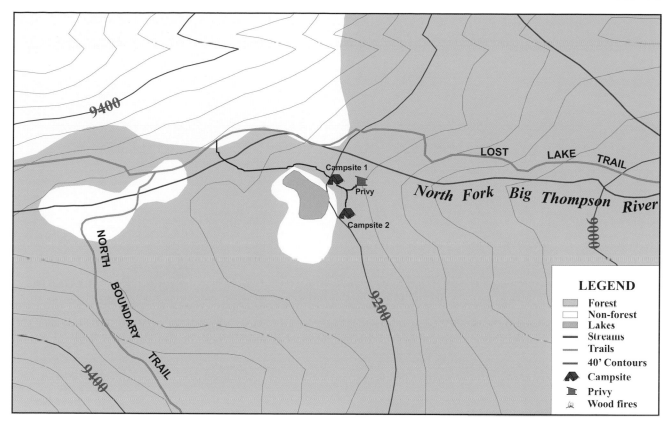

Kettle Tarn

Description:

The Kettle Tarn campsites are located south of the Lost Lake Trail above a small pond or glacial kettle (Kettle Tarn). There are two campsites situated at an elevation of 9,200 feet about 100 yards apart. Campsite 1 is on the ridge to the north of the pond under a canopy of lodgepole pines. This site has room for one tent. A pit toilet (no walls) is located east of campsite 1 and down the north side of the ridge. Campsite 2 is on the ridge above the east edge of the pond and has room for 1 to 2 tents. Water may be obtained from the North Fork of Big Thompson River or Kettle Tarn. Wood and charcoal fires are not permitted here. Use camp stoves only. The occupancy rate for Kettle Tarn is about 57%.

Activities:

Fishing: Boundary Creek, North Fork Big
    Thompson River
Hiking: Lost Lake Trail, Stormy Peaks Trail
Peaks nearby: Stormy Peaks, Mt. Dickinson, South
    Signal Mtn.

Directions:

The nearest access to this campsite is via the Forest Service Dunraven Trailhead. Take Highway 34 from

Kettle Tarn campsite 2.

Loveland to Drake. Turn right on County Road 43 and travel about 6 miles to County Road 518. There is a sign marking the way to the trailhead. Turn right and go about 2 miles to the Dunraven Trailhead and the south end of the trail. Follow the Forest Service North Fork Trail for 4.4 miles through the Comanche Peak Wilderness to the Park boundary. The trail becomes the Lost Lake Trail in the Park. It is another .8 miles to the sign for the Kettle Tarn campsite. Turn left and follow the path over a log foot bridge across the river. The path then turns east and climbs a ridge above a pond. The campsites area located on the ridge above the pond to the north and east. It takes 3 to 4 hours to reach this campsite.

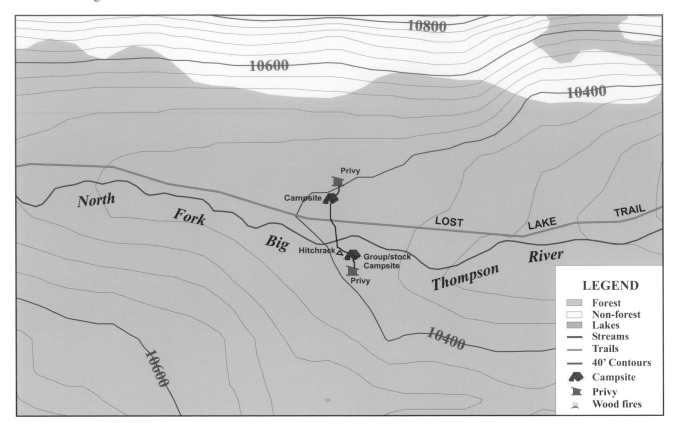

Lost Meadow

Description:

The Lost Meadow campsites are located on the north and south sides of a small meadow. A sign in the middle of the meadow marks the path to the sites. The elevation here is 10,390 feet. This camping area has two sites: a group/stock campsite and an individual campsite. The group site is south of the Lost Lake Trail across the river. There are two hitchracks for horses and two marked tent pads accommodating a total of 3 to 4 tents. A pit toilet (no walls) is located in the spruce trees southeast of the tent sites. The individual campsite is to the north of the Lost Lake Trail just inside the trees. There are two tent pads at this well shaded campsite with a toilet to the north. Water may be obtained from the river. Wood and charcoal fires are not permitted here. Use camp stoves only.

Activities:
Fishing: Lost Lake, Lake Husted, Lake Louise, North Fork Big Thompson River
Hiking: Lost Lake Trail
Peaks nearby: Mount Dunraven, Sugarloaf Mountain

Directions:

The nearest access to this campsite is via the For-

Lost Meadow group/stock hitchracks.

est Service Dunraven Trailhead. Take Highway 34 from Loveland to Drake. Turn right on County Road 43 and travel about 6 miles to County Road 518. There is a sign marking the way to the trailhead. Turn right and go about 2 miles to the Dunraven Trailhead and the south end of the trail. Follow the Forest Service North Fork Trail for 4.4 miles through the Comanche Peak Wilderness to the Park boundary. The trail becomes the Lost Lake Trail in the Park. It is another 3.8 miles to Lost Meadow, about a mile below Lost Lake. There is a sign in the middle of the meadow. The group/stock site is to the left and the individual site is to the right. Travel time to this campsite is 8 to 9 hours.

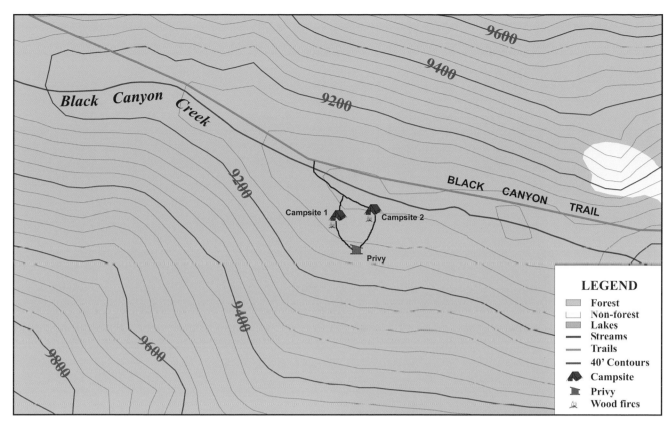

McGregor Mountain

Description:

The McGregor Mountain campsites are located about 3.9 miles from the Twin Owls parking area in a lodgepole pine forest just south of the Black Canyon Trail. The site is situated at an elevation of 9,070 feet. There are two individual campsites here. The path to the sites crosses Black Canyon Creek over a log foot bridge and turns east back along the creek. Campsite 1 is off to the right and campsite 2 is straight ahead. Both campsites have two well marked tent pads. A pit toilet (3 walls) is located on a path between the sites. Wood fires are permitted at this campsite. Metal fire grates are provided at the site. Fires can only be built within these grates. Do not place rocks in or around your fire. Use only dead and down wood. Water may be obtained from Black Canyon Creek. The occupancy rate for these campsites is about 40%.

Activities:

Fishing: Black Canyon Creek
Hiking: Black Canyon Trail, Dark Mountain Trail
Peaks nearby: Bighorn Mountain, Mount Tileston, Dark Mountain
Scenic features: Roaring River, Lawn Lake

McGregor Mountain campsite 1.

Directions:

The nearest access to this campsite is via the Twin Owls Trailhead. Travel west on Highway 34 toward the Fall River Entrance. Turn right on Devils Gulch Road and go about .75 miles to the MacGregor Ranch. Follow the ranch road for about .7 miles to the parking area. Take the Black Canyon Trail from the west end of the parking area for three miles to its intersection with the Dark Mountain Trail. Continue along Black Canyon Creek into Black Canyon. It is about .9 miles to the McGregor Mountain campsite sign. The campsites are off to the left across Black Canyon Creek in the lodgepole pine and spruce forest. It takes about 3 to 4 hours to hike to this campsite.

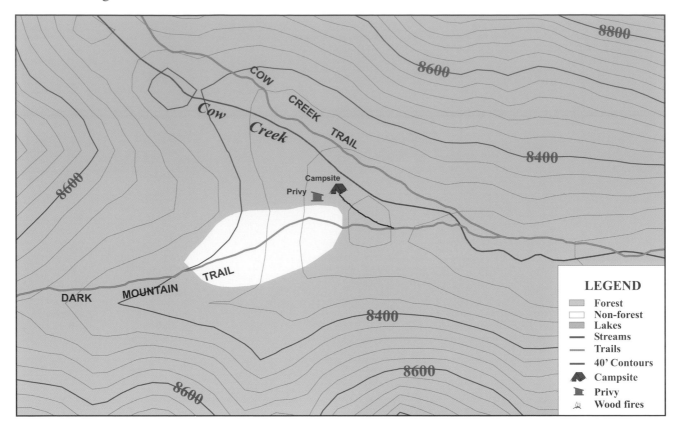

Peregrine

Description:

The Peregrine campsite is located north of the Dark Mountain Trail just past its intersection with the trail to Bridal Veil Falls. This well shaded campsite is situated at an elevation of 8,290 feet under a canopy of ponderosa pines. The site is next to a small stream and will accommodate 1 to 2 tents. A pit toilet (no walls) is located a short distance southwest of the site. There is a meadow south of the campsite containing numer-

ous aspens. Its low elevation and gold coloration make this campsite a great spot in the fall. Water can be obtained from the nearby stream. Wood or charcoal fires are not permitted here. Use camp stoves only. The Peregrine campsite is the most popular site in this area with an occupancy rate of about 77%.

Activities:
Fishing: Cow Creek
Hiking: Cow Creek Trail, Dark Mountain Trail
Peaks nearby: Sheep Mountain , Dark Mountain
Scenic features: Bridal Veil Falls, Balanced Rock, Gem Lake

Peregrine campsite.

Directions:

The Cow Creek Trailhead is the nearest trailhead to this site. Travel west on Highway 34 toward the Fall River Entrance. Turn right on Devils Gulch Road and go about four miles to a dirt road signed "McGraw Ranch". Turn left and travel about two miles to the end of the road and the McGraw Ranch at the bottom of hill. Parking is permitted on the west side of the road only. There is a turnaround at the end of the road. Take the Cow Creek Trail past the buildings to the west. Continue west for about two miles to the Dark Mountain Trail. Proceed west for a short distance to the sign for the Peregrine campsite. It takes 1 to 2 hours to hike to this campsite.

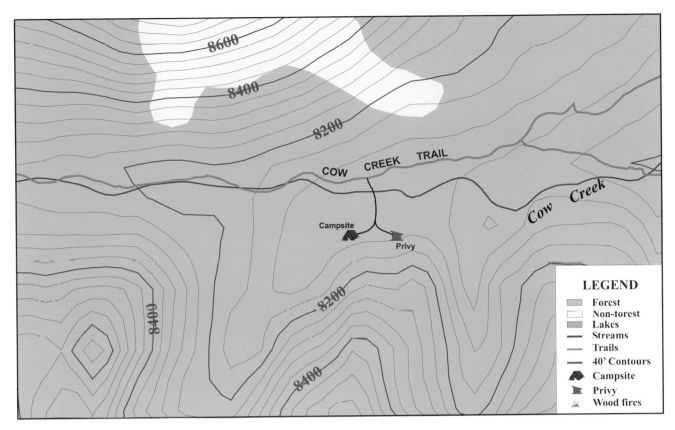

Rabbit Ears

Description:

The Rabbit Ears campsite is located in an open grassy area south of Cow Creek. The site is situated at an elevation of 8,100 feet, making the lowest back-country campsite in the Park. This sunny campsite is surrounded by a mix of aspen, ponderosa pine, and spruce trees. The tent area is level and will accommodate 1 to 2 tents. A pit toilet (no walls) is located in the trees to the east of the site. The low elevation of this campsite makes it ideal for early spring or late fall camping. Water can be obtained from Cow Creek. Wood or charcoal fires are not permitted here. Use camp stoves only. This campsite is occupied about 58% of the time.

Activities:

Fishing: Cow Creek, West Creek
Hiking: Cow Creek Trail, Dark Mountain Trail, North Boundary Trail
Peaks nearby: Sheep Mountain , Dark Mountain
Scenic features: Bridal Veil Falls, Balanced Rock, Gem Lake, West Creek Falls

Directions:

The Cow Creek Trailhead is the nearest trailhead to this site. Travel west on Highway 34 toward the

Rabbit Ears campsite.

Fall River Entrance. Turn right on Devils Gulch Road and go about four miles to a dirt road signed "McGraw Ranch". Turn left and travel about two miles to the end of the road and the McGraw Ranch at the bottom of hill. Parking is permitted on the west side of the road only. There is a turnaround at the end of the road. Take the Cow Creek Trail past the buildings to the west. Continue west for about 1.2 miles to the Gem Lake Trail intersection. The path to the campsite is located about .2 miles beyond the intersection. Red arrow-heads on the trees mark the path to the site south of Cow Creek. It takes about an hour to reach this campsite.

Silvanmere

Description:

The Silvanmere campsites are located east of the North Boundary Trail about a half-mile south of the Lost Lake Trail. There are two campsites situated at an elevation of 9,340 feet about 100 yards apart. Campsite 1 is about 50 yards east and downhill from the North Boundary Trail. It is a bare area under some lodgepole pines that will accommodate 1 to 2 tents. Campsite 2 is farther downhill and is a bit more open. There is a pit toilet (no walls) north of the sites. Wood fires are permitted at this campsite. Metal fire grates are provided at the site. Fires can only be built within these grates. Do not place rocks in or around your fire. Use only dead and down wood. Water may be obtained from a small stream east of the site but may be dry after June 30. The Silvanmere campsites are occupied only 12% of the time.

Activities:

Fishing: Boundary Creek, North Fork Big Thompson River, West Creek

Hiking: Lost Lake Trail, Stormy PeaksTrail, North Boundary Trail

Peaks nearby: Stormy Peaks, Mt. Dickinson

Scenic features: West Creek Falls

Silvanmere campsite1.

Directions:

The nearest access to this campsite is via the Forest Service Dunraven Trailhead. Take Highway 34 from Loveland to Drake. Turn right on County Road 43 and travel about 6 miles to County Road 518. There is a sign marking the way to the trailhead. Turn right and go about 2 miles to the Dunraven Trailhead and the south end of the trail. Follow the Forest Service North Fork Trail for 4.4 miles through the Comanche Peak Wilderness to the Park boundary. The trail becomes the Lost Lake Trail in the Park. Follow the trail for another .85 miles to the North Boundary Trail. Travel the North Boundary Trail south for about a half-mile to the Silvanmere sign. The campsites are off to the left. Travel time is 4 to 5 hours.

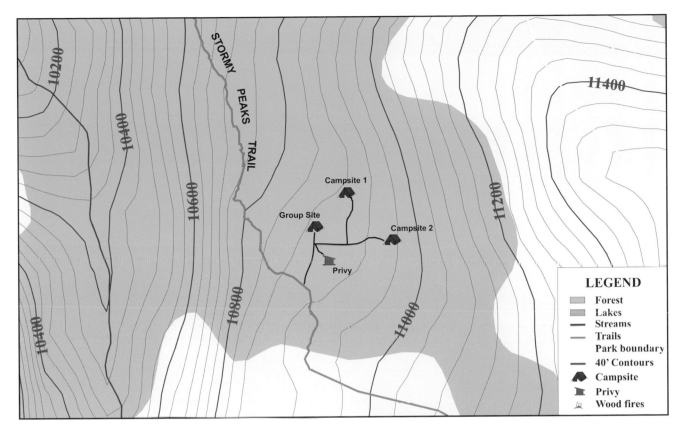

Stormy Peaks

Description:

    The Stormy Peaks campsites are located in a spruce forest north of the Stormy Peaks Trail. There are two individual sites and one group site situated at an elevation of 10,890 feet. It is a short distance from the Stormy Peaks Trail to a sign directing you to the various campsites. The group site, to the left, is a large area under some spruce trees. This site will accommodate 6 to 7 tents. There is a pit toilet (no walls) off to the right. Red arrowheads on the trees mark the path to the individual sites. Follow them up the hill and across the meadow. The path to Campsite 1 goes to the left on the other side of the meadow. This campsite is level and well defined with room for 1 to 2 tents. The path to campsite 2 continues uphill. This campsite is in a grassy area to the right of where the red arrowheads stop. Water is available from the spring near the trail to the individual sites. Wood and charcoal fires are not permitted here. Use camp stoves only. The occupancy rate for these campsites is about 11%.

Activities:

Hiking: Stormy Peaks Trail

Peaks nearby: Stormy Peaks, Sugarloaf Mountain, Ramsey Peak

Scenic features: Pingree Park, Stormy Peaks Pass

Stormy Peaks group campsite.

Directions:

    The nearest trailhead is the Stormy Peaks Trailhead near Pingree Park. Take Highway 287 north from Fort Collins to La Porte. Continue on 287 north to Highway 14. Travel west on 14 for 24 miles to the Pingree Park Road. Turn left and travel about 14.5 miles to the trailhead. The trailhead is on the left side of the road. The Stormy Peaks Trail heads north before curving around to the south. You will make a moderate climb for a little over four miles before reaching the Stormy Peaks campsite sign. Turn left and follow the path to the sites. It takes 4 to 5 hours to reach these campsites.

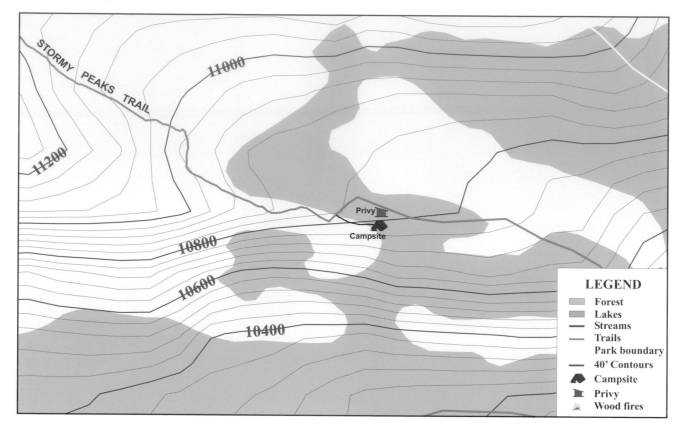

Stormy Peaks South

Description:

The Stormy Peaks South campsite is located in a clump of subalpine fir near treeline. The area around the campsite is fairly open with good views of Stormy Peaks. This campsite is located on the edge of a deep valley at an elevation of 10,800 feet. The site is a bare area under the trees with room for 2 to 3 tents. Large logs provide places to sit. There is a pit toilet (no walls) about 50 yards to the east of the campsite. Water is available from a small stream near the campsite. Wood and charcoal fires are not permitted here. Use camp stoves only. The Stormy Peaks South campsite is occupied about 20% of the time.

Activities:

Fishing: North Fork Big Thompson River
Hiking: Stormy Peaks Trail, Lost Lake Trail
Peaks nearby: Stormy Peaks, Sugarloaf Mountain, Ramsey Peak
Scenic features: Pingree Park, Stormy Peaks Pass

Directions:

The nearest trailhead is the Stormy Peaks Trailhead near Pingree Park. Take Highway 287 north from Fort Collins to La Porte. Continue on 287 north to Highway 14. Travel west on 14 for 24 miles to the Pingree

Stormy Peaks South campsite.

Park Road. Turn left and travel about 14.5 miles to the trailhead. The trailhead is on the left side of the road. The Stormy Peaks Trail heads north before curving around to the south. You will make a moderate climb for a little over four miles before reaching the Stormy Peaks campsite sign. Continue south through Stormy Peaks Pass for another 2.3 miles to the Stormy Peaks South sign. Turn right and follow the path to the campsite. It takes 6 to 7 hours to reach this campsite. An alternative route is to hike the Lost Lake Trail from the Dunraven Trailhead about 7.25 miles to the south end of the Stormy Peaks Trail. It is a very steep one mile hike from here to the campsite.

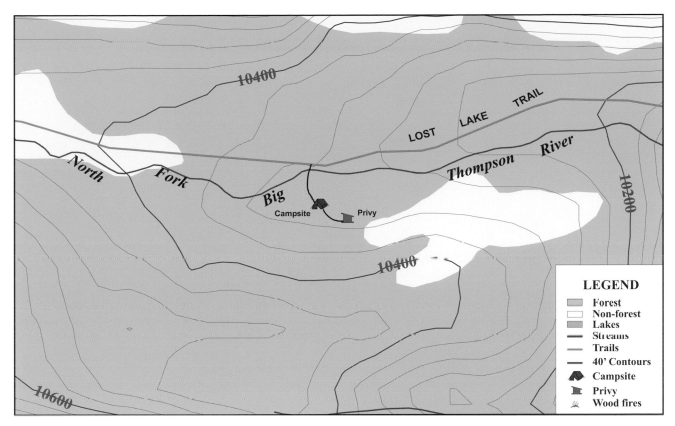

Sugarloaf

Description:

The Sugarloaf campsite is located to the south of the Lost Lake Trail on the other side of the North Fork Big Thompson River. The path crosses the river via a log foot bridge and is marked by red arrowheads. The campsite is situated at an elevation of 10,290 feet under a canopy of dense spruce trees. There is room for one tent here. A pit toilet (no walls) is off to the left of the site about 200 yards. Water may be obtained from the river. Wood and charcoal fires are not permitted here. Use camp stoves only. The Sugarloaf campsite has a low occupancy rate of about 20%.

Sugarloaf campsite.

Activities:

Fishing: Lost Lake, Lake Husted, Lake Louise, North Fork Big Thompson River

Hiking: Lost Lake Trail, Stormy Peaks Trail

Peaks nearby: Mount Dunraven, Sugarloaf Mountain, Stormy Peaks, Ramsey Peak

Directions:

The nearest access to this campsite is via the Forest Service Dunraven Trailhead. Take Highway 34 from Loveland to Drake. Turn right on County Road 43 and travel about 6 miles to County Road 518. There is a sign marking the way to the trailhead. Turn right and go about 2 miles to the Dunraven Trailhead and the south end of the trail. Follow the Forest Service North Fork Trail for 4.4 miles through the Comanche Peak Wilderness to the Park boundary. The trail becomes the Lost Lake Trail in the Park. It is another 2.8 miles to the intersection with the Stormy Peaks Trail. From here continue west for about .75 miles to the sign for Surgarloaf campsite. Turn left and cross the river over a log foot bridge. Follow the red arrowheads to the campsite. It takes about 6 to 8 hours to reach this campsite.

North Inlet Area Campsites

Campsite	No. of sites	Wood Fires	Elevation	Privy	Nearest Trailhead	Distance	Elevation Change	Travel Time	Stock	Use
Big Pool	2	stoves only	9,160 ft	no	North Inlet	4.3 mi	1,080 ft	2 - 3 hr	no	39%
Cascade Falls	1	stoves only	8,930 ft	yes	North Inlet	3.2 mi	790 ft	2 hr	no	69%
Footbridge	1	yes	9,290 ft	yes	North Inlet	5.9 mi	1,410 ft	3 - 4 hr	no	44%
Grouseberry	2	stoves only	9,300 ft	no	North Inlet	5.6 mi	1,360 ft	3 - 4 hr	no	22%
July	3+1grp	stoves only	10,800 ft	yes	North Inlet *	8.3 mi	2,860 ft	5 - 6 hr	no	54%
North Inlet Falls	1	stoves only	9,540 ft	no	North Inlet	6.9 mi	1,850 ft	4 - 5 hr	no	65%
North Inlet Horse Camp	1 grp	yes	9,290 ft	yes	North Inlet	5.7 mi	1,360 ft	3 - 4 hr	yes	43%
North Inlet Junction	3	stoves only	9,600 ft	yes	North Inlet	6.7 mi	1,760 ft	4 - 5 hr	no	49%
Pine Marten	2	stoves only	9,570 ft	no	North Inlet	7.0 mi	1,870 ft	4 - 5 hr	no	57%
Porcupine	2	yes	9,360 ft	no	North Inlet	6.2 mi	1,480 ft	4 - 5 hr	no	51%
Ptarmigan	1	stoves only	9,310 ft	no	North Inlet	5.8 mi	1,400 ft	3 - 4 hr	no	37%
Summerland Park	1+1grp	yes	8,535 ft	yes	North Inlet	0.9 mi	220 ft	45 min	no	48%
Twinberry	2	stoves only	8,700 ft	no	North Inlet	2.8 mi	600 ft	1.5 - 2 hr	no	36%

* It is a little shorter (7.5 miles) to hike from the Bear Lake Trailhead to the July campsite. However, the change in elevation is 50% more and the hike is much more strenuous.

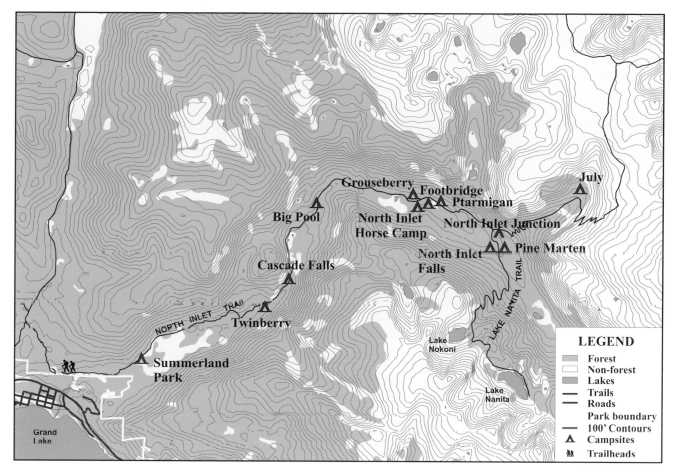

North Inlet Area

The North Inlet area is located in the southwest portion of the Park just north of the Grand Lake area.

The Bear Lake area encompases over 60 square miles of the Park.

There are just two trails in this area, the North Inlet Trail and the Nanita Lake Trail. Most of the campsites are located along the North Inlet Trail. There are 13 camping locations within this area containing 24 campsites. Three of these sites are group sites and one permits the use of horses. Six of the sites have toilet fa-

cilities. Four campsites permit the use of wood fires. All of the sites are located in heavily forested areas. Most are well shaded. Elevations range from 8,535 feet at Summerland Park to 10,800 feet at the July campsite. Campsites in this area average a 47% occupancy rate.

Most of the campsites offer easy access to stream or lake fishing. Look for signs indicating catch and release fishing only or closed areas on many of the waters in the Park. Check with Park personnel to be sure. Ptarmigan Creek above War Dance Falls and Bench Lake are currently closed for Colorado River Cutthroat restoration. Some of peaks in this area include: Hallett Peak (12,713'), Taylor Peak (13,153'), Ptarmigan Mountain (12,334'), Andrews Peak (12,565'), and Otis Peak.

Trailheads providing access to campsites in this area include: North Inlet and Bear Lake. The distance from a trailhead to campsites ranges from .9 miles to 8.3 miles with hiking times ranging from 45 minutes to 6 hours. Topographic maps that cover the area include the McHenrys Peak and Grand Lake quads.

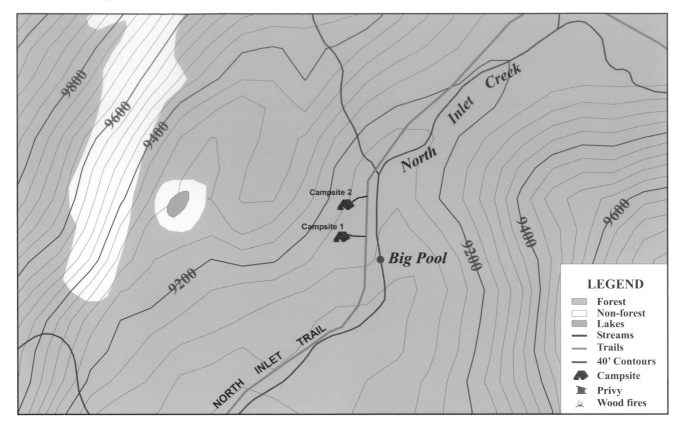

Big Pool

Description:

The Big Pool campsites are located just above the Big Pool in North Inlet Creek to the north of the North Inlet Trail. They are situated at an elevation of 9,160 feet on a rocky, wooded ridge. There are two camp-

sites. The path to campsite 1 leaves the trail just beyond the sign and travels about 60 to 70 yards up the ridge to the site. The campsite is a level spot with the ridge dropping off on two sides. This partially sunny site has room for 1 to 2 tents. Campsite 2 is located about 75 yards east along the ridge. There is a separate path leading from the trail. This campsite is located under a spruce and lodgepole pine canopy. It is a little more rocky than campsite 1. There are no toilet facilities near these campsites. Water is available from North Inlet Creek. Wood and charcoal fires are not permitted here. Use camp stoves only. These campsites are occupied about 39% of the time.

Activities:
Fishing: North Inlet Creek
Hiking: North Inlet Trail, Lake Nanita Trail
Scenic Features: Cascade Falls, Big Pool

Big Pool campsite 1.

Directions:

Take Trail Ridge Road to the west entrance to the Park. Continue south to the road leading into Grand Lake. Turn left toward Grand Lake and then bear left at Tunnel Road across from the Mountain Food Market, just past the stables. Continue on Tunnel Road a short distance to a dirt road going to the left that leads to the water works building (about .25 miles). Turn right at the water works building and follow the narrow road to the trailhead. The North Inlet Trail begins behind a locked gate on a dirt road. Follow this trail for about 4.3 miles to the Big Pool. The campsites are at the top of the hill beyond the pool. It takes 2 to 3 hours to reach the campsites.

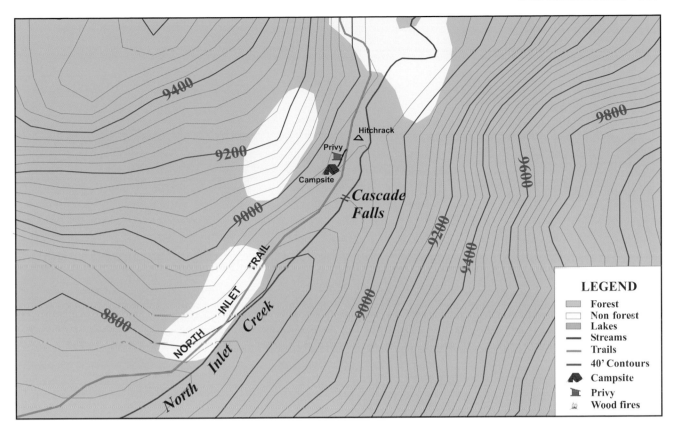

Cascade Falls

Description:

The Cascade Falls campsite is located west of the North Inlet Trail where it tops a rocky climb above Cascade Falls. It is situated at an elevation of 8,930 feet just inside a dense spruce forest. A pit toilet (3 walls) is located just off the trail from the campsite sign. The path to the campsite continues to the left of the privy for about 25 yards to the campsite. The tent site is level and smooth with room for one tent. Water is available from North Inlet Creek. Wood and charcoal fires are not permitted here. Use camp stoves only. Extreme caution is advised when camping at this site with children. There are steep cliffs and fast-moving water in this area. Cascade Falls is the most popular campsite in the North Inlet area. It has an occupancy rate of about 69%.

Activities:

Fishing: North Inlet Creek
Hiking: North Inlet Trail, Lake Nanita Trail
Scenic Features: Cascade Falls, Big Pool

Directions:

Take Trail Ridge Road to the west entrance to the Park. Continue south to the road leading into Grand Lake. Turn left toward Grand Lake and then bear left

Cascade Falls campsite.

at Tunnel Road across from the Mountain Food Market, just past the stables. Continue on Tunnel Road a short distance to a dirt road going to the left that leads to the water works building (about .25 miles). Turn right at the water works building and follow the narrow road to the trailhead. The North Inlet Trail begins behind a locked gate on a dirt road. Follow this trail for about 3.2 miles to Cascade Falls. The campsites are at the top of the hill beyond the falls. It takes about 2 hours of relatively easy hiking to reach the campsite.

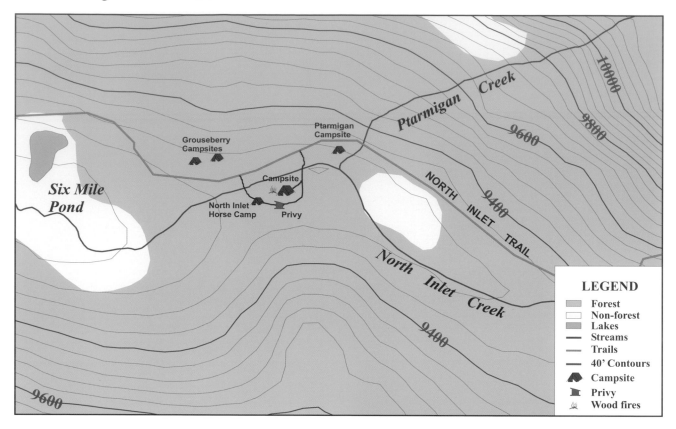

Footbridge

Description:

The Footbridge campsite is located south of the North Inlet Trail and North Inlet Creek at an elevation of 9,290 feet. It is located under a canopy of spruce and lodgepole pine trees in a rocky area on a ridge above the creek. The path to the campsite travels downstream a short distance before crossing the creek over a long foot bridge. Caution should be taken when crossing the bridge in wet conditions as it can be slippery. There is a sign just above the south bank pointing the way to the campsite (to the right). Follow the red arrowheads. A pit toilet (3 walls) is located on the path to the North Inlet Horse Camp. Wood fires are permitted at this campsite. Metal fire grates are provided at each site. Fires can only be built within these grates. Do not place rocks in or around your fire. Use only dead and down wood. Water is available from North Inlet Creek. Occupancy rate is 44%.

Activities:

Fishing: North Inlet Creek, Lake Nanita, Pettingell Lake

Hiking: North Inlet Trail, Lake Nanita Trail

Scenic Features: Cascade Falls, Big Pool, North Inlet Falls, Lake Nokoni, Lake Nanita

Footbridge campsite.

Directions:

Take Trail Ridge Road to the west entrance to the Park. Continue south to the road leading into Grand Lake. Turn left toward Grand Lake and then bear left at Tunnel Road across from the Mountain Food Market, just past the stables. Continue on Tunnel Road a short distance to a dirt road going to the left that leads to the water works building (about .25 miles). Turn right at the water works building and follow the narrow road to the trailhead. The North Inlet Trail begins behind a locked gate on a dirt road. Follow this trail for about 5.9 miles to the Footbridge sign. Turn right and follow the path over the long log foot bridge to the campsite. It takes 3 to 4 hours of relatively easy hiking to reach this campsite.

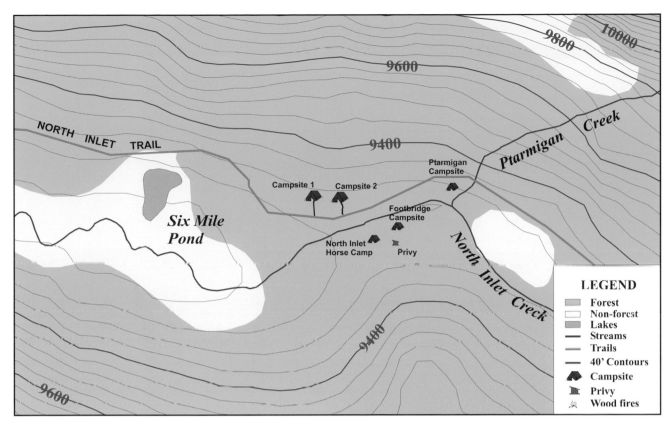

Grouseberry

Description:

The Grouseberry campsites are located north of the North Inlet Trail about 350 yards east of Six Mile Pond. They are situated at an elevation of 9,300 feet in a spruce and lodgepole pine forest. There are two campsites here. The path to campsite 1 travels about 50 to 60 yards uphill to the site. This campsite is level but a little rocky. It will accommodate 1 to 2 tents. The path to campsite 2 is about 100 yards farther east on the trail. This campsite is about 25 yards north of the trail in some spruce trees. It is not as level as campsite 1. There are no toilet facilities at these campsites. Water is available from North Inlet Creek. Wood or charcoal fires are not permitted at this site. Use camp stoves only. These campsites are occupied about 22% of the time.

Activities:

Fishing: North Inlet Creek, Lake Nanita, Pettingell Lake

Hiking: North Inlet Trail, Lake Nanita Trail

Scenic Features: Cascade Falls, Big Pool, North Inlet Falls, Lake Nokoni, Lake Nanita

Grouseberry campsite 1.

Directions:

Take Trail Ridge Road to the west entrance to the Park. Continue south to the road leading into Grand Lake. Turn left toward Grand Lake and then bear left at Tunnel Road across from the Mountain Food Market, just past the stables. Continue on Tunnel Road a short distance to a dirt road going to the left that leads to the water works building (about .25 miles). Turn right at the water works building and follow the narrow road to the trailhead. The North Inlet Trail begins behind a locked gate on a dirt road. Follow this trail for about 5.6 miles to the first Grouseberry sign. Turn left and follow the path up the hill to campsite 1. It takes 3 to 4 hours of relatively easy hiking to reach this campsite.

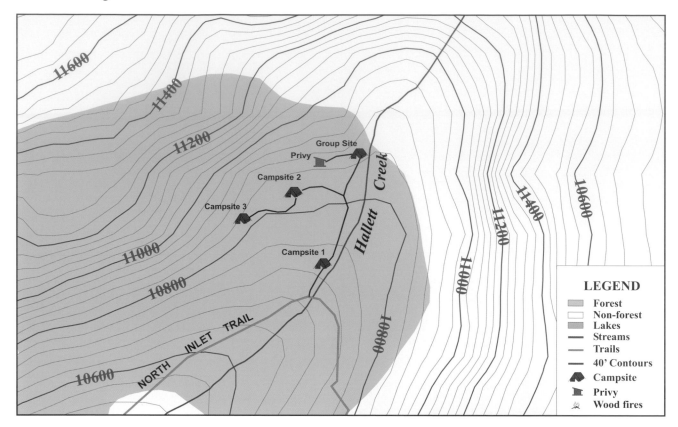

July

Description:

The July campsites are located just below treeline at an elevation of 10,800 feet. There are three individual campsites and one group site. The path to the sites travels north. Campsite 1 is just to the right of the path about 200 feet north of the trail. This site has two level tent pads. The path continues uphill to a sign pointing the way to the group site and other individual sites. Campsite 2 is to the left under a group of large spruce trees. Campsite 3 is southwest of campsite 2 on the other side of a small stream at the base of a rock slide. The group site is to the right of the sign about 200 feet. It is a large, level site with room for 6 to 8 tents. A pit toilet is located just west of the group site. Wood or charcoal fires are not permitted at this site (stoves only). Water is available from Hallett Creek. Occupancy rate is 54%.

Activities:

Fishing: North Inlet Creek, Lake Nanita, Pettingell Lake, Hallett Creek

Hiking: North Inlet Trail, Lake Nanita Trail

Peaks nearby: Hallett Peak, Otis Peak, Taylor Peak

Scenic Features: Cascade Falls, Big Pool, North Inlet Falls, Lake Nokoni, Lake Nanita

July campsite 2.

Directions:

Take Trail Ridge Road to the west entrance to the Park. Continue south to the road leading into Grand Lake. Turn left toward Grand Lake and then bear left at Tunnel Road across from the Mountain Food Market, just past the stables. Continue on Tunnel Road a short distance to a dirt road going to the left that leads to the water works building (about .25 miles). Turn right at the water works and follow the narrow road to the trailhead. The North Inlet Trail begins behind a locked gate on a dirt road. Follow this trail for about 8.3 miles to the sign before the foot bridge across Hallett Creek. Turn left at the sign. It takes about 5 to 6 hours to reach this campsite. A more strenuous route can be taken from the Bear Lake Trailhead (7.5 miles).

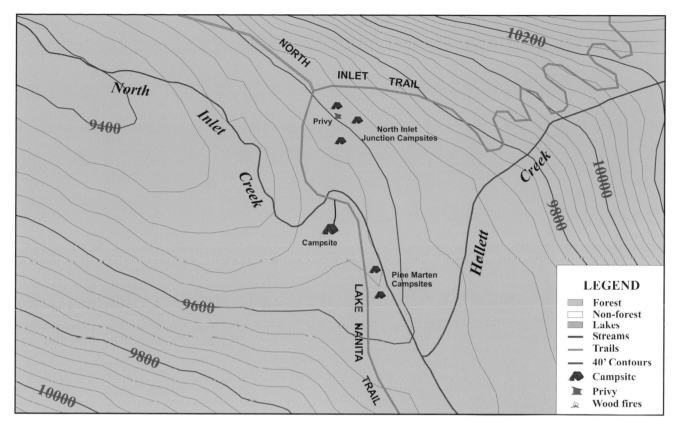

North Inlet Falls

Description:

The North Inlet Falls campsite is located just past the bridge below North Inlet Falls to the south of the Lake Nanita Trail. The campsite is situated at an elevation of 9,540 feet about 30 yards above the trail. This campsite is amongst some rocks under some smaller spruce trees. It will accommodate one tent. The roar from North Inlet Falls is sure to lull you to sleep at night here. There are no toilet facitlities at this campsite. Water is available from North Inlet Creek. Wood or charcoal fires are not permitted at this site. Use camp stoves only. This campsite is occupied about 65% of the time.

Activities:

Fishing: North Inlet Creek, Lake Nanita, Pettingell Lake, Hallett Creek

Hiking: North Inlet Trail, Lake Nanita Trail

Peaks nearby: Ptarmigan Mountain, Andrews Peak

Scenic Features: Cascade Falls, Big Pool, North Inlet Falls, Lake Nokoni, Lake Nanita

Directions:

Take Trail Ridge Road to the west entrance to the Park. Continue south to the road leading into Grand Lake. Turn left toward Grand Lake and then bear left

North Inlet Falls campsite.

at Tunnel Road across from the Mountain Food Market, just past the stables. Continue on Tunnel Road a short distance to a dirt road going to the left that leads to the water works building (about .25 miles). Turn right at the water works building and follow the narrow road to the trailhead. The North Inlet Trail begins behind a locked gate on a dirt road. Follow this trail for about 6.7 miles to its junction with the Lake Nanita Trail. Turn right and follow this trail for about .2 miles to North Inlet Falls. Cross the large wooden bridge. The path to the campsite is to the right just after crossing the bridge. It take about 4 to 5 hours to hike to this campsite.

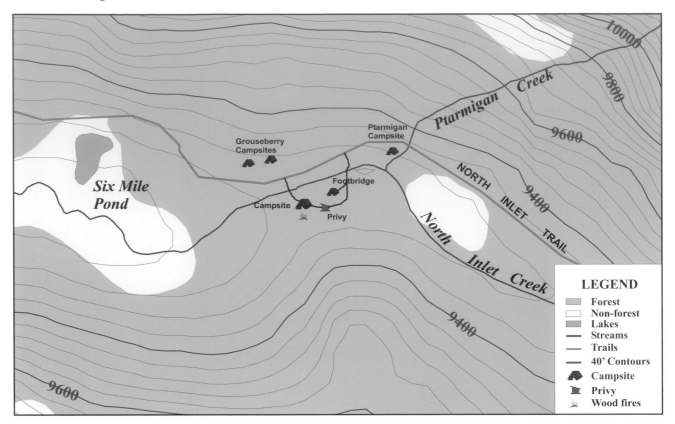

LEGEND

- ▨ Forest
- ▢ Non-forest
- ▨ Lakes
- — Streams
- — Trails
- — 40' Contours
- ▲ Campsite
- ▮ Privy
- ☗ Wood fires

North Inlet Horse Camp

Description:

The North Inlet Horse Camp (also group site) is located south of the North Inlet Trail and creek in a lodgepole pine forest. It is situated at an elevation of 9,290 feet. This campsite is in a relatively open forest and will accommodate 4 to 5 tents. There is a large horse corral (about 75 feet square) about 50 feet east of the tent area. A pit toilet (3 walls) is located just east of the corral. Water is available from North Inlet Creek. Wood fires are permitted at this campsite. Metal fire grates are provided at each site. Fires can only be built within these grates. Do not place rocks in or around your fire. Use only dead and down wood. The occupancy rate for this campsite is 43%.

Activities:

Fishing: North Inlet Creek, Lake Nanita, Pettingell Lake

Hiking: North Inlet Trail, Lake Nanita Trail

Scenic Features: Cascade Falls, Big Pool, North Inlet Falls, Lake Nokoni, Lake Nanita

Directions:

Take Trail Ridge Road to the west entrance to the Park. Continue south to the road leading into Grand Lake. Turn left toward Grand Lake and then bear left

Large horse corral at North Inlet Horse Camp.

at Tunnel Road across from the Mountain Food Market, just past the stables. Continue on Tunnel Road a short distance to a dirt road going to the left that leads to the water works building (about .25 miles). Turn right at the water works building and follow the narrow road to the trailhead. The North Inlet Trail begins behind a locked gate on a dirt road. Follow this trail for about 5.7 miles to the Horse Camp sign. Horses can cross the creek here and travel about 100 yards to the campsite. Hikers should continue on to the path to the Footbridge campsite and cross the creek over the log foot bridge. The path to the group campsite is marked by a sign and red arrowheads. Hiking time is about 3 to 4 hours.

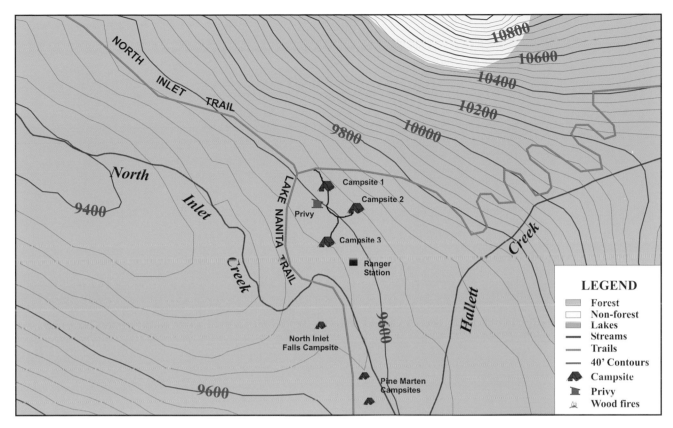

North Inlet Junction

Description:

The North Inlet Junction campsites are located in an open forested area about 50 yards beyond the intersection of the North Inlet and Lake Nanita Trails. The campsites are situated at an elevation of 9,600 feet. There are 3 campsites at this location. Campsite 1 is about 40 yards south of the North Inlet Trail. It has room for 1 to 2 tents. The path to the other sites continues downhill past an outhouse and splits off to sites 2 and 3. Campsite 2 is to the east near a small stream and will accommodate 2 tents. Campsite 3 is farther downhill just above a ranger station. This site is larger, having room for 2 to 3 tents. Wood or charcoal fires are not permitted at this site. Use camp stoves only. Water is available from North Inlet Creek or a small stream near campsite 2. There is a bear box above campsite 3. Occupancy rate is 49%.

Activities:

Fishing: North Inlet Creek, Lake Nanita, Pettingell Lake, Hallett Creek

Hiking: North Inlet Trail, Lake Nanita Trail

Peaks nearby: Ptarmigan Mountain, Andrews Peak

Scenic Features: Cascade Falls, Big Pool, North Inlet Falls, Lake Nokoni, Lake Nanita

North Inlet Junction campsite 1.

Directions:

Take Trail Ridge Road to the west entrance to the Park. Continue south to the road leading into Grand Lake. Turn left toward Grand Lake and then bear left at Tunnel Road across from the Mountain Food Market, just past the stables. Continue on Tunnel Road a short distance to a dirt road going to the left that leads to the water works building (about .25 miles). Turn right at the water works building and follow the narrow road to the trailhead. The North Inlet Trail begins behind a locked gate on a dirt road. Follow this trail for about 6.7 miles to the campsite sign. The campsites are downhill from the sign. It takes about 4 to 5 hours to reach these campsites.

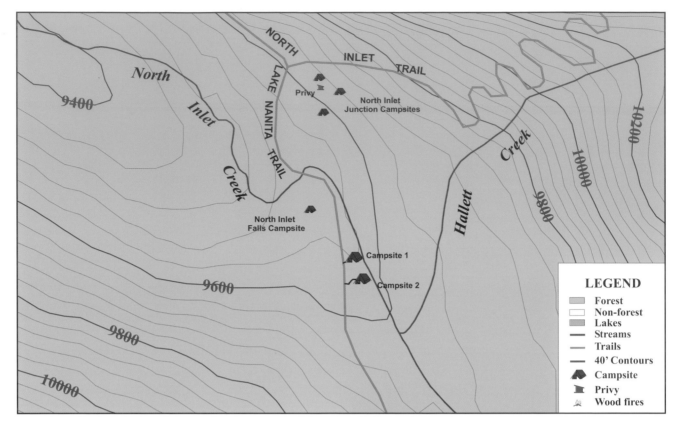

Pine Marten

Description:

The Pine Marten campsites are located above North Inlet Creek just east of the Lake Nanita Trail. They are situated in a spruce forest at an elevation of 9,570 feet. There are two campsites about 100 yards apart. The path to campsite 1 travels about 50 yards downhill to a level campsite that will accommodate 1 to 2 tents. The path to campsite 2 is about 60 yards farther up the Lake Nanita Trail. This campsite sits on a bluff above the creek with room for one tent. There are no toilet facitlities at these campsites. Water is available from North Inlet Creek. Wood or charcoal fires are not permitted at this site. Use camp stoves only. This area has steep cliffs and swift water. Caution is advised when camping with children. These campsites are occupied 57% of the time.

Activities:

Fishing: North Inlet Creek, Lake Nanita, Pettingell
    Lake, Hallett Creek
Hiking: North Inlet Trail, Lake Nanita Trail
Peaks nearby: Ptarmigan Mountain, Andrews Peak
Scenic Features: Cascade Falls, Big Pool, North
    Inlet Falls, Lake Nokoni, Lake Nanita

Pine Marten campsite 2.

Directions:

Take Trail Ridge Road to the west entrance to the Park. Continue south to the road leading into Grand Lake. Turn left toward Grand Lake and then bear left at Tunnel Road across from the Mountain Food Market, just past the stables. Continue on Tunnel Road a short distance to a dirt road going to the left that leads to the water works building (about .25 miles). Turn right at the water works building and follow the narrow road to the trailhead. The North Inlet Trail begins behind a locked gate on a dirt road. Follow this trail for about 6.7 miles to its junction with the Lake Nanita Trail. Turn right and follow this trail for about .3 miles to the path to campsite 1. It takes about 4 to 5 hours to hike to this campsite.

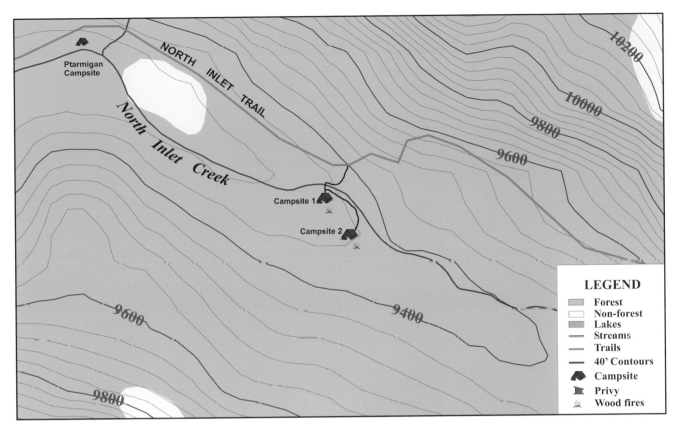

Porcupine

Description:

The Porcupine campsites are located in a spruce/fir and lodgepole pine forest just south of North Inlet Creek above its confluence with Ptarmigan Creek. It is situated at an elevation of 9,360 feet. There are two campsites here. The path to the sites leaves the North Inlet Trail just above Ptarmigan Creek and heads southeast down to the creek. There is a foot bridge a short distance downstream. Campsite 1 is directly up the bank after crossing the creek. This site has room for 2 to 3 tents. Campsite 2 is about 100 yards upstream and back to the right. There are no toilet facitlities at these campsites. Wood fires are permitted at this campsite. Metal fire grates are provided at each site. Fires can only be built within these grates. Use only dead and down wood. Water is available from North Inlet Creek. The occupancy rate for these campsites is 51%.

Activities:

Fishing: North Inlet Creek, Lake Nanita, Pettingell Lake

Hiking: North Inlet Trail, Lake Nanita Trail

Scenic Features: Cascade Falls, Big Pool, North Inlet Falls, Lake Nokoni, Lake Nanita

Porcupine campsite 2.

Directions:

Take Trail Ridge Road to the west entrance to the Park. Continue south to the road leading into Grand Lake. Turn left toward Grand Lake and then bear left at Tunnel Road across from the Mountain Food Market, just past the stables. Continue on Tunnel Road a short distance to a dirt road going to the left that leads to the water works building (about .25 miles). Turn right at the water works building and follow the narrow road to the trailhead. The North Inlet Trail begins behind a locked gate on a dirt road. Follow this trail for about 6.2 miles to the Porcupine sign. Turn right and follow the path over the log foot bridge to the campsite. It takes 4 to 5 hours to reach this campsite.

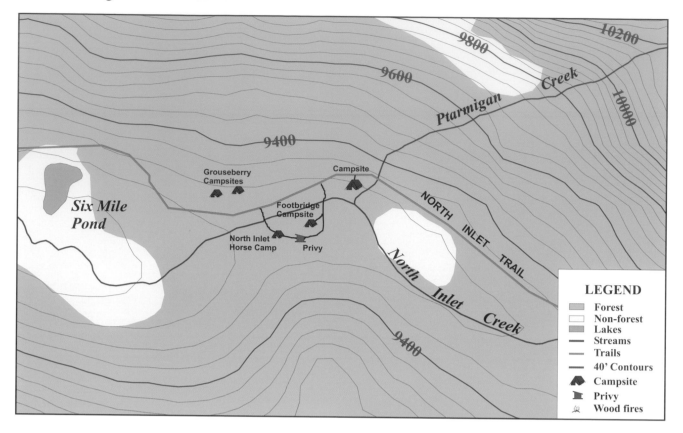

Ptarmigan

Description:

The Ptarmigan campsite is located in a dense stand of spruce trees between the North Inlet Trail and North Inlet Creek. The campsite is situated at an elevation of 9,310 feet. The path to the site is just west of

Ptarmigan Creek. There is one marked tent pad to the right of the path about 20 yards from the trail. Another area is located just beyond the silver arrow marking the site. This campsite has room for 2 to 3 tents. A nice meadow lies below the campsite. There are no toilet facitlities at these campsites. Wood or charcoal fires are not permitted at this site. Use camp stoves only. Water is available from North Inlet Creek. This campsite has a 37% occupancy rate.

Activities:

Fishing: North Inlet Creek, Lake Nanita, Pettingell Lake

Hiking: North Inlet Trail, Lake Nanita Trail

Scenic Features: Cascade Falls, Big Pool, North Inlet Falls, Lake Nokoni, Lake Nanita

Ptarmigan campsite.

Directions:

Take Trail Ridge Road to the west entrance to the Park. Continue south to the road leading into Grand Lake. Turn left toward Grand Lake and then bear left at Tunnel Road across from the Mountain Food Market, just past the stables. Continue on Tunnel Road a short distance to a dirt road going to the left that leads to the water works building (about .25 miles). Turn right at the water works building and follow the narrow road to the trailhead. The North Inlet Trail begins behind a locked gate on a dirt road. Follow this trail for about 5.8 miles to the Ptarmigan sign. Turn right and travel the short distance to the campsite. It takes 3 to 4 hours of hiking to reach this campsite.

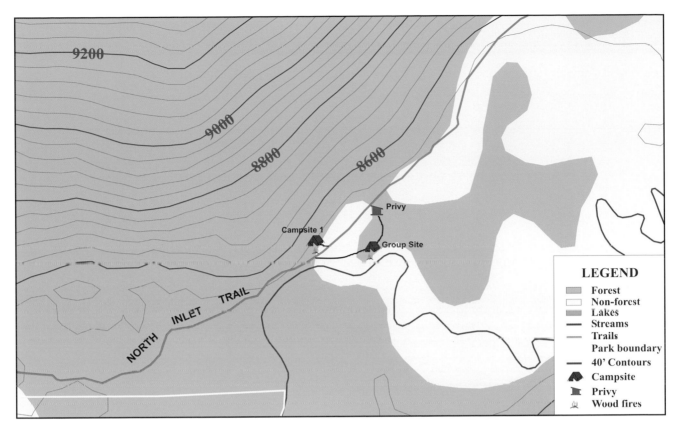

Summerland Park

Description:

The Summerland Park campsites are located about a mile from the North Inlet Trailhead. There are two campsites here. One individual campsite and a group campsite. The group campsite is located about 75 yards south of the trail in an open stand of lodgepole pines. This large campsite has room for 4 to 5 tents. It is situated at an elevation of 8,535 feet above a large meadow. The individual site is located at the edge of some sagebrush among some lodgepole pines. This is a sunny site and will accommodate one tent. Toilet facilities are located to the right of the trail just before it reenters the forest. This pit toilet has a wooden floor and a ramp. Water is available from North Inlet Creek. Wood fires are permitted at this campsite. Metal fire grates are provided at each site. Fires can only be built within these grates. Use only dead and down wood. Summerland Park has an occupancy rate of 48%.

Activities:

Fishing: North Inlet Creek
Hiking: North Inlet Trail
Scenic Features: Cascade Falls, Big Pool

Directions:

Take Trail Ridge Road to the west entrance to the

Summerland Park group campsite.

Park. Continue south to the road leading into Grand Lake. Turn left toward Grand Lake and then bear left at Tunnel Road across from the Mountain Food Market, just past the stables. Continue on Tunnel Road a short distance to a dirt road going to the left that leads to the water works building (about .25 miles). Turn right at the water works building and follow the narrow road to the trailhead. The North Inlet Trail begins behind a locked gate on a dirt road. Follow this trail for about .9 miles to the east end of Summerland Park. The path to the group site leads off to the right. The individual campsite is on the left side of the North Inlet Trail a short distance ahead. It is a short 45 minute hike to this campsite.

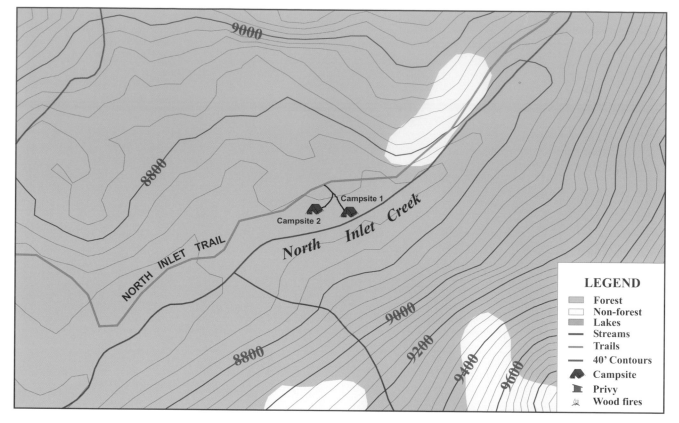

Twinberry

Description:

The Twinberry campsites are located on a rocky bench above North Inlet Creek just south of the North Inlet Trail. There are two campsites situated at an elevation of 8,700 feet. The path to the sites travels downhill where it splits. Campsite 1 is straight ahead while campsite 2 is off to the right. Campsite 1 lies below some granite slabs right above the creek. It has room for 1 to 2 tents. Campsite 2 is farther away from the creek. This larger site is more level and will accommodate 3 to 4 tents. Water is available from North Inlet Creek. Wood and charcoal fires are not permitted here. Use camp stoves only. Extreme caution is advised when camping at this site with children. There are steep cliffs and fast-moving water in this area. The occupancy rate for Twinberry is about 36%.

Activities:

Fishing: North Inlet Creek
Hiking: North Inlet Trail
Scenic Features: Cascade Falls, Big Pool

Directions:

Take Trail Ridge Road to the west entrance to the Park. Continue south to the road leading into Grand Lake. Turn left toward Grand Lake and then bear left

Twinberry campsite 1.

at Tunnel Road across from the Mountain Food Market, just past the stables. Continue on Tunnel Road a short distance to a dirt road going to the left that leads to the water works building (about .25 miles). Turn right at the water works building and follow the narrow road to the trailhead. The North Inlet Trail begins behind a locked gate on a dirt road. Follow this trail for about 2.8 miles to the Twinberry sign. Turn right and follow the path to campsite 1. Campsite 2 is off to the right. It takes about 2 hours of relatively easy hiking to reach the campsite.

Beautiful Cascade Falls is a great spot for a rest along the North Inlet Trail.

Timber Lake Area

Campsite	No. of sites	Wood Fires	Elevation	Privy	Nearest Trailhead	Distance	Elevation Change	Travel Time	Stock	Use
Jackstraw	2	stoves only	10,800 ft	yes	Timber Lake	3.8 mi	2,150 ft	2 -3 hr	no	22%
Rockslide	1	stoves only	10,930 ft	no	Timber Lake	4.2 mi	2,290 ft	2 -3 hr	no	37%
Snowbird	2	stoves only	11,010 ft	no	Timber Lake	4.3 mi	2,360 ft	2 -3 hr	no	37%
Timber Creek	2	stoves only	10,160 ft	no	Timber Lake	2.9 mi	1,670 ft	1.5 - 2 hr	no	21%

A family of marmots greets campers to the Timber Lake area.

One of my partners, Ginger, takes a well deserved rest near Jackstraw Meadow in the Timber Lake area.

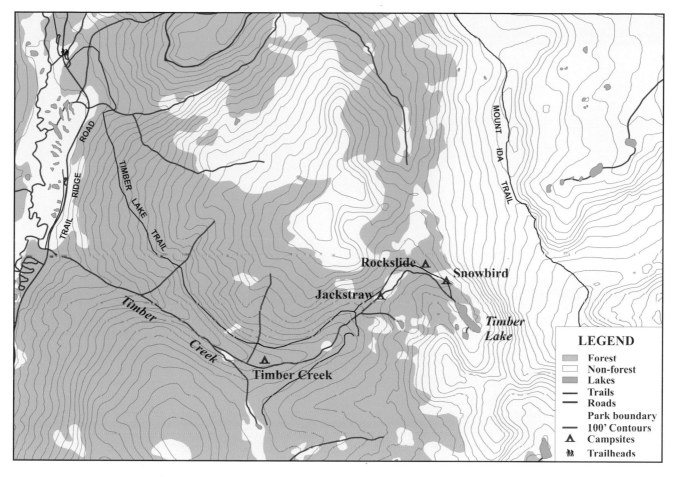

Timber Lake Area

The Timber Lake area is located in the western section of the Park and receives less use than areas on

Timber Lake is the reward at the end of a moderate to strenuous hike.

the east side.   There are four camping locations concentrated along the Timber Lake Trail. A total of 7 individual campsites are available. Only one campsite has toilet facilities. Wood fires are not permitted at any of these campsites. All of the campsites are situated above 10,000 feet and therefore open up later in the summer. Elevations range from 10,160 feet at Tim-

ber Creek to 11,010 feet at the Snowbird campsite. All of the campsites are located in forested areas. Some have more trees than others. This area does not receive heavy use as campsites have an average occupancy rate of 28%.

Fishing in this area is available in Timber Creek and Timber Lake. Catch and release policies apply to both of these waters. Check with Park personnel for any special restrictions.   Peaks in the area include: Mount Ida (12,809'), Jackstraw Mountain (11,704'), and Chief Cheley Peak.

Access to the campsites is available from the Timber Lake Trailhead. This is a large paved parking area with ample room for about 50 vehicles. Nine of the spaces are long pull-through type for RVs and horse trailers. The distance from the trailhead to campsites ranges from 2.9 miles to 4.3 miles with hiking times ranging from 1.5 to 3 hours. The Timber Lake Trail is moderate to strenuous to hike. Topographic maps that cover the area include the Fall River Pass and Grand Lake quads.

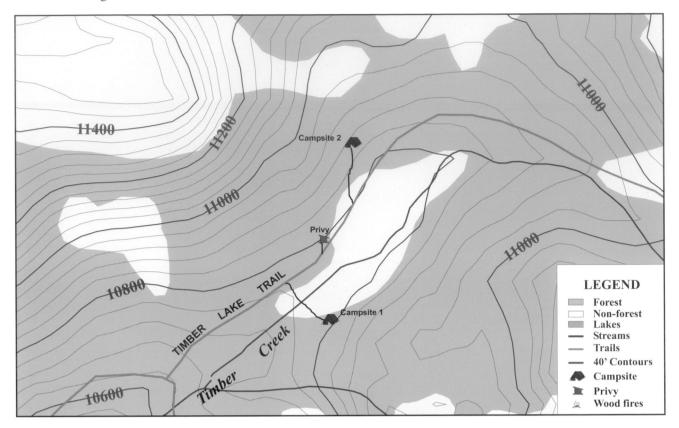

Jackstraw

Description:

The Jackstraw campsites are located near Jackstraw Meadow on both sides of the meadow. There are two campsites situated at an elevation of 10,800 feet. Campsite 1 is just off the south east edge of the meadow on a level bench. You must cross Timber Creek to get to this site. This campsite is level under some large spruce trees. It will accommodate 2 to 3 tents. Campsite 2 is located about 200 yards north of the trail about two thirds of the way up the meadow. It is a moderate climb through the trees to the site. The campsite is on a level spot about 50 feet above the meadow. There is a pit toilet (privacy sides) about 100 yards up the trail from the path to campsite 1. Water is available from Timber Creek. Wood or charcoal fires are not permitted at this site. Use camp stoves only. This campsite is occupied about 22% of the time.

Activities:

Fishing: Timber Creek, Timber Lake
Hiking: Timber Lake Trail, Mount Ida Trail
Peaks nearby: Jackstraw Mountain, Mount Ida, Chief Cheley Peak
Scenic features: Timber Lake

Jackstraw campsite 1.

Directions:

The nearest trailhead to this campsite is the Timber Lake Trailhead on the west side of the Park. The trailhead is just east of Trail Ridge Road about 10.2 miles north of the Grand Lake Entrance and about 31 miles from the Beaver Meadows Entrance. Take the Timber Lake Trail for about 3.8 miles to Jackstraw Meadow. Turn right and cross Timber Creek and follow the path to a bench above the meadow. This is campsite 1. Campsite 2 is farther up the meadow to the north up in the trees. It takes about 2 to 3 hours to reach this campsite.

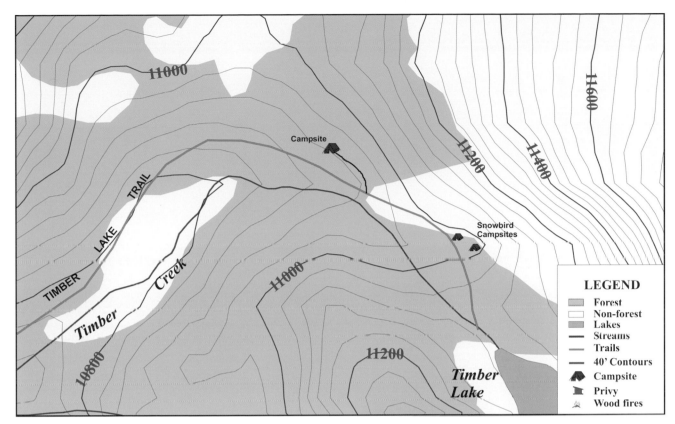

Rockslide

Description:

The Rockslide campsite is located near the base of a rocky slope about a quarter mile below Timber Lake. This campsite is situated at an elevation of 10,930 feet. The site is surrounded by spruce trees and is well shaded. There is a level, bare area that will accommo-

date 2 to 3 tents. There are no toilet facilities at this campsite. Water is available from Timber Creek. Wood or charcoal fires are not permitted at this site. Use camp stoves only. The Rockslide campsite has an occupancy rate of about 37%.

Activities:

Fishing: Timber Creek, Timber Lake
Hiking: Timber Lake Trail, Mount Ida Trail
Peaks nearby: Jackstraw Mountain, Mount Ida, Chief Cheley Peak
Scenic features: Timber Lake

Rockslide campsite.

Directions:

The nearest trailhead to this campsite is the Timber Lake Trailhead on the west side of the Park. The trailhead is just east of Trail Ridge Road about 10.2 miles north of the Grand Lake Entrance and about 31 miles from the Beaver Meadows Entrance. Take the Timber Lake Trail for about 4.2 miles to the campsite sign (about .2 miles beyond Jackstraw Meadow). Turn left and follow the path that heads back northwest for about 200 to 300 yards to the campsite. It takes about 2 to 3 hours to reach this campsite.

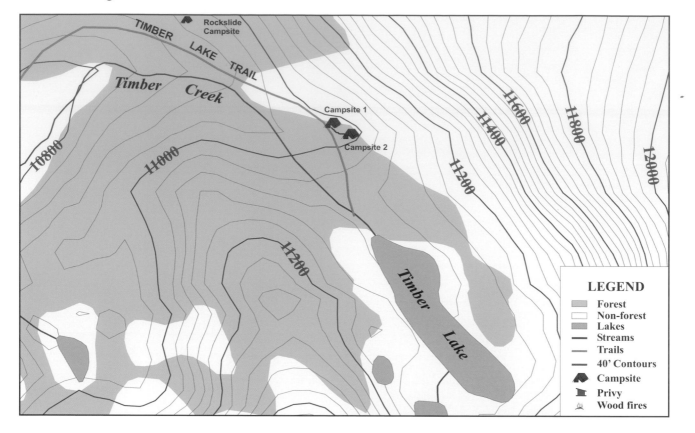

Snowbird

Description:

The Snowbird campsites are located on the other side of a small ridge a few hundred yards below Timber Lake. These campsites are situated at an elevation of 11,010 feet. The campsites are hidden from the trail by a small ridge. Campsite 1 is surrounded on three sides by dense spruce trees but is generally sunny when the sun is high. Space at this site is limited to one tent. Campsite 2 is 50 to 70 yards to the right of campsite 1. This campsite is larger than campsite 1 and has room for 1 to 2 tents. There are plenty of rocks and logs to sit on here. There are no toilet facilities at this campsite. Water is available from Timber Creek. Wood or charcoal fires are not permitted at this site. Use camp stoves only. The Snowbird campsites are occupied about 37% of the time.

Activities:
Fishing: Timber Creek, Timber Lake
Hiking: Timber Lake Trail, Mount Ida Trail
Peaks nearby: Jackstraw Mountain, Mount Ida, Chief Cheley Peak

Snowbird campsite 1.

Scenic features: Timber Lake

Directions:

The nearest trailhead to this campsite is the Timber Lake Trailhead on the west side of the Park. The trailhead is just east of Trail Ridge Road about 10.2 miles north of the Grand Lake Entrance and about 31 miles from the Beaver Meadows Entrance. Take the Timber Lake Trail for about 4.3 miles to the campsite sign (about .3 miles beyond Jackstraw Meadow). The path leaves the trail in a small meadow. Campsite 1 is to the left and campsite 2 is to the right. It takes 2 to 3 hours to reach these campsites.

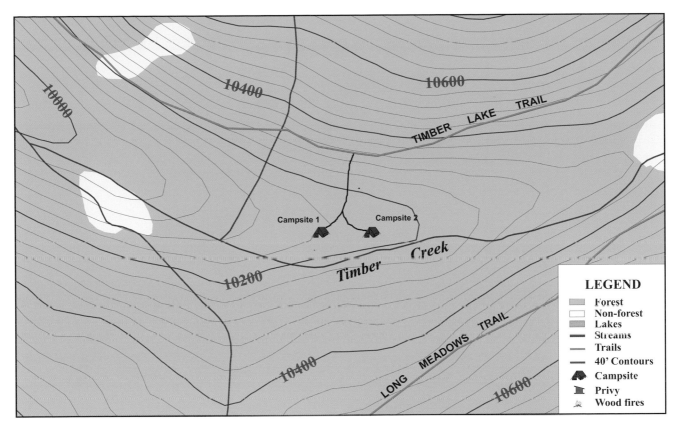

Timber Creek

Description:

The Timber Lake campsites are located in a heavily forested area about .6 miles west of the intersection of the Long Meadows and Timber Lake trails. These campsites are situated at an elevation of 10,160 feet. The path leaves the trail to the south and travels down-hill through a spruce forest. It splits as it nears the creek with campsite 1 to the right. This campsite is

level and well shaded. It has room for 2 to 3 tents. Campsite 2 is to the left next to Timber Creek. There is a small meadow across the creek. This campsite is also well shaded and will accom-modate two tents. There are no toilet facilities at this campsite. Water is available from Timber Creek. Wood or charcoal fires are not permitted at this site. Use camp stoves only. These campsites nave an occu-pancy rate of about 21%.

Activities:
Fishing: Timber Creek, Timber Lake
Hiking: Timber Lake Trail, Mount Ida Trail
Peaks nearby: Jackstraw Mountain, Mount Ida,

Timber Creek campsite 1.

Chief Cheley Peak
Scenic features: Timber Lake

Directions:

The nearest trailhead to this campsite is the Timber Lake Trailhead on the west side of the Park. The trailhead is just east of Trail Ridge Road about 10.2 miles north of the Grand Lake Entrance and about 31 miles from the Beaver Meadows Entrance. Take the Timber Lake Trail for about 2.9 miles to the camp-site sign. The path leaves the trail to the right and trav-els downhill toward Timber Creek. Campsite 1 is to the right and campsite 2 is to the left. Travel time to these campsites is about 1.5 to 2 hours.

Tonahutu Area

Campsite	No. of sites	Wood Fires	Elevation	Privy	Nearest Trailhead	Distance	Elevation Change	Travel Time	Stock	Use
Big Meadows Group	1grp	stoves only	9,400 ft	yes	Green Mountain	1.8 mi	710 ft	1 hr	no	67%
Granite Falls	2	stoves only	9,920 ft	no	Green Mountain	4.9 mi	1,280 ft	3 hr	no	51%
Haynach	2	stoves only	10,720 ft	no	Green Mountain	6.8 mi	2,170 ft	4 - 5 hr	llama	54%
Lodgepole	2	stoves only	9,150 ft	no	Kawuneeche VC	2.1 mi	630 ft	1 - 1.5 hr	no	22%
Lower Granite Falls	2	stoves only	9,770 ft	no	Green Mountain	4.6 mi	1,150 ft	2 - 3 hr	no	41%
Onahu Bridge	2	stoves only	9,710 ft	no	Onahu Creek	2.8 mi	950 ft	1.5 - 2 hr	no	13%
Onahu Creek	2	stoves only	9,570 ft	no	Onahu Creek	1.9 mi	720 ft	1 - 1.5 hr	no	20%
Paint Brush	2	stoves only	9,380 ft	no	Green Mountain	2.8 mi	860 ft	1.5 - 2 hr	no	38%
Renegade	1	stoves only	10,450 ft	no	Green Mountain	6.5 mi	1,880 ft	4 - 5 hr	no	69%
South Meadows	1	stoves only	9,380 ft	no	Green Mountain	2.8 mi	860 ft	1.5 - 2 hr	no	51%
Sunrise	1	stoves only	9,550 ft	no	Green Mountain	3.7 mi	900 ft	2 - 3 hr	no	54%
Sunset	1	stoves only	9,550 ft	no	Green Mountain	3.3 mi	850 ft	2 - 3 hr	no	50%
Timberline Group	1grp	yes	10,630 ft	no	Green Mountain	6.7 mi	1,990 ft	4 - 5 hr	no	60%
Tonahutu Horse/Group	1grp	stoves only	10,130 ft	yes	Green Mountain	6.2 mi	1,680 ft	3 - 4 hr	yes	64%
Tonahutu Meadows	2	stoves only	10,100 ft	no	Green Mountain	5.7 mi	1,510 ft	3 hr	no	54%
Upper Onahu	2	stoves only	9,600 ft	no	Onahu Creek	2.7 mi	860 ft	1 - 1.5 hr	no	8%

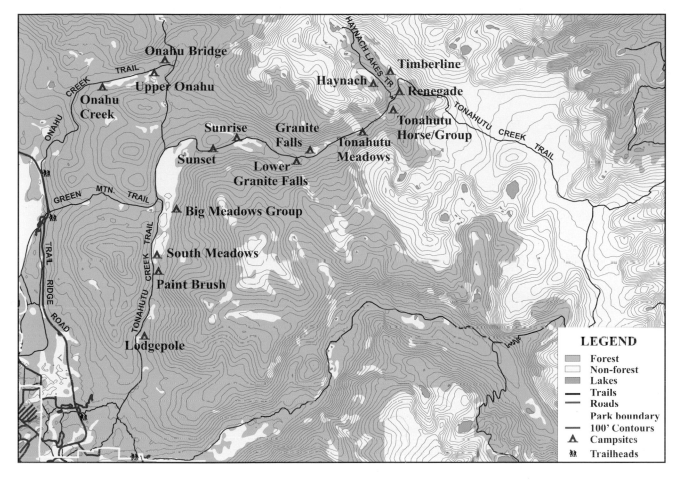

Tonahutu Area

The Tonahutu area is located in the western section of the Park. There are six trails in this area includ-

The Tonahutu Creek Trail travels along the western edge of Big Meadows.

ing: Tonahutu Creek, Onahu Creek, Green Mountain, Long Meadows, Onahu-Tonahutu Connector, and Haynach Lakes trails. Sixteen camping locations are found within this area with a total of 25 campsites. Three of these sites are group sites and two permit the use of livestock. Only two of the sites have toilet facilities. One of the sites permits the use of wood fires.

All of the rest allow camp stoves only. Elevations range from 9,380 feet at the Paint Brush and South Meadows campsites to 10,720 feet at the Haynach campsite.

Fishing is available in Tonahutu Creek and Haynach Lakes. Check with Park Service personnel to see if restrictions exist. Numerous peaks are found in this area. Some of these include: Mount Patterson (11,424'), Nisa Mountain (10,788'), Green Mountain (10,313'), Nakai Peak (12,216'), Sprague Mountain (12,713'), Gabletop Mountain (12,216'), Knobtop Mountain (12,831'), and Snowdrift Peak (12,274'). Most of these are found near the upper reaches of the Tonahutu Creek Trail.

Trailheads providing access to campsites in this area include: Onahu, Green Mountain, Kawuneeche VC, and Tonahutu trailheads. The distance from a trailhead to campsites ranges from 1.8 miles to 6.8 miles with hiking times ranging from 1 to 5 hours. Topographic maps that cover the area include the Grand Lake and McHenrys Peak quads.

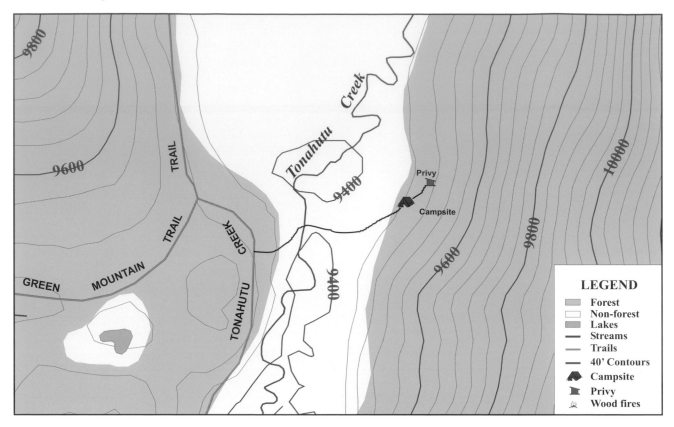

Big Meadows Group

Description:

The Big Meadows group campsite is located on the east side of Big Meadows in a stand of spruce trees. The campsite is situated at an elevation of 9,400 feet. The path to the site crosses Tonahutu Creek over a log foot bridge. A bear box is located near the campsite on the way into the site. There is a pit toilet (3 walls) northeast of the campsite. Water may be obtained from Tonahutu Creek. Wood and charcoal fires are not permitted here. Use camp stoves only. This site has room for 6 to 7 tents in a large bare area among the spruce trees and offers a pleasant atmosphere for group camping. The campsite is about 1000 feet from the Tonahutu Creek Trail. This together with the density of the trees provides plenty of privacy. The occupancy rate is about 67%.

Activities:

Fishing: Tonahutu Creek

Hiking: Green Mountain Trail, Tonahutu Creek Trail, Onahu-Tonahutu Connector Trail, Onahu Creek Trail

Peaks nearby: Mount Patterson, Nisa Mountain, Green Mountain

Scenic Features: Big Meadows, Granite Falls

Big Meadows Group campsite.

Directions:

The nearest access to this campsite is via the Green Mountain Trailhead. This trailhead is located on the east side of the road about three miles north of the Grand Lake Entrance. Take Trail Ridge Road for about 37.7 miles to the trailhead from the Beaver Meadows Entrance. Take the Green Mountain Trail for about 1.7 miles to its intersection with the Tonahutu Creek Trail. Turn right and travel about .1 miles to the campsite sign. Turn left and follow the path across Big Meadows to a log foot bridge. Cross the creek and continue to the other side of the meadow and the campsite. It takes about an hour to hike to this campsite.

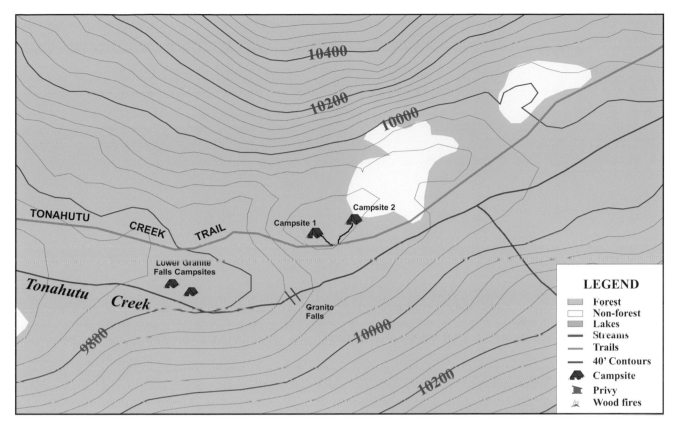

Granite Falls

Description:

The Granite Falls campsites are located about .2 miles above Granite Falls just north of the Tonahutu Creek Trail. The sites are situated at an elevation of 9,920 feet in a spruce/fir stand next to a wet meadow. There are two campsites with two separate paths leading to them. Campsite 1 is about 25 yards to the northwest from the trail. This site is level but somewhat rocky with a lot of protruding roots. Campsite 2 is nearest the meadow and is larger than campsite 1. The surface is much smoother and will accommodate 3 to 4 tents. There are no toilet facilities near these campsites. Water is available from Tonahutu Creek. Wood and charcoal fires are not permitted here. Use camp stoves only. These campsites are occupied about 51% of the time.

Activities:

Fishing: Tonahutu Creek

Hiking: Green Mountain Trail, Tonahutu Creek Trail, Onahu-Tonahutu Connector Trail

Peaks nearby: Mount Patterson, Snowdrift Peak, Nakai Peak

Scenic Features: Big Meadows, Granite Falls

Granite Falls campsite 2.

Directions:

The nearest access to this campsite is via the Green Mountain Trailhead. This trailhead is located on the east side of the road about three miles north of the Grand Lake Entrance. Take Trail Ridge Road for about 37.7 miles to the trailhead from the Beaver Meadows Entrance. Take the Green Mountain Trail for about 1.7 miles to its intersection with the Tonahutu Creek Trail. Turn left and travel north along the west edge of Big Meadows. Continue hiking on the Tonahutu Creek Trail for about 3.2 miles to the Granite Falls campsite sign. You will pass Sunset, Sunrise, and Lower Granite Falls campsites along the way. It takes about 3 hours to reach the Granite Falls campsites.

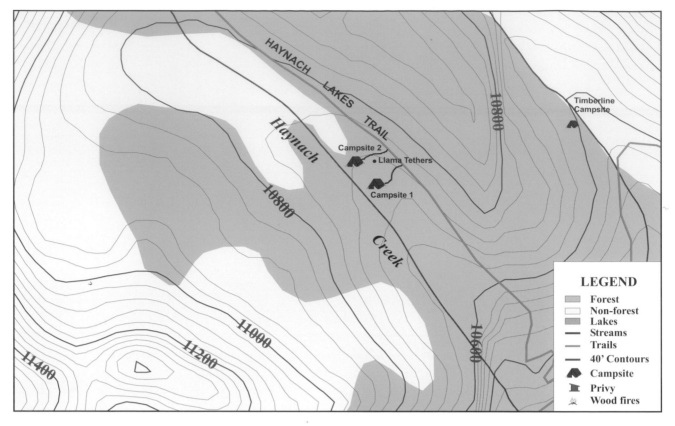

Haynach

Description:

   The Haynach campsites are located on a ridge west of the Haynach Lakes Trail and just east of Haynach Creek. There are two campsites situated at an elevation of 10,720 feet. Two paths provide access to the sites. The first path makes a short but steep climb to campsite 1. The second path leads to campsite 2. Campsite 1 lies underneath a large spruce tree and will accommodate 1 to 2 tents. Campsite 2 is about 50 to 60 yards north of campsite 1. Its primary tent pad is lined with wood chips. This site has room for 2 to 3 tents. Llama are permitted here with tethers located about 50 yards to the east. There are no toilet facilities near these campsites. Water is available from Haynach Creek. Wood and charcoal fires are not permitted here. Use camp stoves only. Occupancy rate is about 54%.

Activities:
Fishing: Tonahutu Creek, Haynach Lakes
Hiking: Green Mountain Trail, Tonahutu Creek Trail, Haynach Lakes Trail
Peaks nearby: Snowdrift Peak, Nakai Peak, Sprague Mountain, Gabletop Mountain, Knobtop Mountain
Scenic Features: Big Meadows, Granite Falls

Haynach campsite 2.

Directions:

   The nearest access to this campsite is via the Green Mountain Trailhead. This trailhead is located on the east side of the road about three miles north of the Grand Lake Entrance. Take Trail Ridge Road for about 37.7 miles to the trailhead from the Beaver Meadows Entrance. Take the Green Mountain Trail for about 1.7 miles to its intersection with the Tonahutu Creek Trail. Turn left and travel north along the west edge of Big Meadows. Continue hiking on the Tonahutu Creek Trail for about 4.7 miles to the Haynach campsite sign. Turn left on the Haynach Lakes Trail and travel about a half mile to the signs marking the paths to the campsites. Travel time is about 4 to 5 hours.

LEGEND

	Forest
	Non-forest
	Lakes
▬	Streams
—	Trails
—	40' Contours
◆	Campsite
⌷	Privy
♨	Wood fires

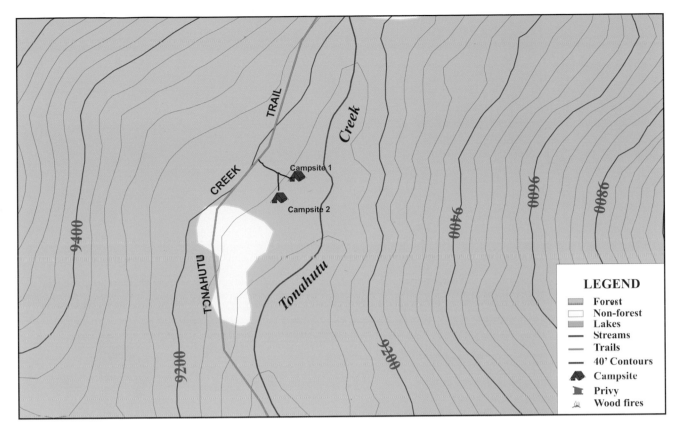

Lodgepole

Description:

The Lodgepole campsites are located in an open, almost park-like, stand of lodgepole pines just east of the Tonahutu Creek Trail. The sites are situated at an elevation of 9,150 feet between the trail and Tonahutu Creek. There are two campsites in a large area of bare ground under the widely spaced trees. Campsite 1 is off to the left and next to the creek. This site is level and has room for one tent. Campsite 2 is about 150 yards south of campsite 1 and is much larger. This campsite will accommodate 3 to 4 tents. There are no toilet facilities near these campsites. Water is available from Tonahutu Creek. Wood and charcoal fires are not permitted here. Use camp stoves only. The Lodgepole campsites are occupied only 22% of the time.

Activities:
Fishing: Tonahutu Creek
Hiking: Green Mountain Trail, Tonahutu Creek Trail,
Peaks nearby: Mount Patterson, Nisa Mountain,
   Green Mountain
Scenic Features: Big Meadows

Lodgepole campsite 1.

Directions:

The nearest access to this campsite is via the Kawuneeche Visitor Center Trailhead. This trailhead is located on the east side of the road just outside the Grand Lake Entrance. From the Beaver Meadows Entrance, take Trail Ridge Road for about 41 miles to the Kawuneeche Visitor Center. Take the Tonahutu SpurTrail from the south section of the parking lot for about .75 miles to its intersection with the Tonahutu Creek Trail. Turn left and travel about 1.35 miles to the campsite sign. Turn right in a open stand of lodgepole pine and travel a short distance to the campsites. It takes about an hour to an hour and a half to hike to Lodgepole from the visitor center.

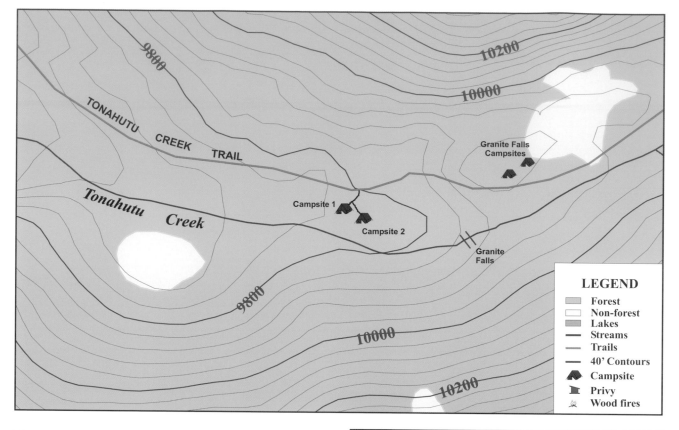

Lower Granite Falls

Description:

The Lower Granite Falls campsites are located about .1 miles below Granite Falls just south of the Tonahutu Creek Trail. The sites are situated at an elevation of 9,770 feet in a spruce/fir stand next to Tonahutu Creek. There are two campsites about 50 to 60 feet apart. Campsite 1 has a spruce tree growing in the middle of it. It is level and will accommodate 2 to 3 tents around the tree. There are a few roots protruding above the ground. Campsite 2 is to the left of campsite 1 and is smaller. This site is a little more rocky and has room for one tent. There are no toilet facilities near these campsites. Water is available from Tonahutu Creek. Wood and charcoal fires are not permitted here. Use camp stoves only. The occupancy rate is about 41%.

Activities:

Fishing: Tonahutu Creek

Hiking: Green Mountain Trail, Tonahutu Creek Trail, Onahu-Tonahutu Connector Trail

Peaks nearby: Mount Patterson, Snowdrift Peak, Nakai Peak

Scenic Features: Big Meadows, Granite Falls

Lower Granite Falls campsite 1.

Directions:

The nearest access to this campsite is via the Green Mountain Trailhead. This trailhead is located on the east side of the road about three miles north of the Grand Lake Entrance. Take Trail Ridge Road for about 37.7 miles to the trailhead from the Beaver Meadows Entrance. Take the Green Mountain Trail for about 1.7 miles to its intersection with the Tonahutu Creek Trail. Turn left and travel north along the west edge of Big Meadows. Continue hiking on the Tonahutu Creek Trail for about 2.9 miles to the Lower Granite Falls campsite sign. You will pass the Sunset and Sunrise campsites along the way. Turn right and travel about 100 feet down hill to the campsites. Travel time to Lower Granite Falls is 2 to 3 hours.

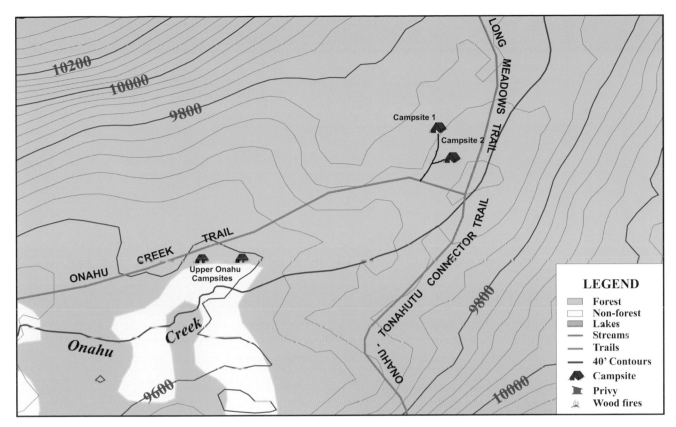

Onahu Bridge

Description:

The Onahu Bridge campsites are located just off the Onahu Creek Trail before it reaches a foot bridge across the creek at the end of the trail. The sites are situated at an elevation of 9,710 feet in a spruce/fir stand up stream from the foot bridge. There are two campsites that are quite close to each other. The path splits with campsite 1 off to the left. This campsite is well shaded with room for 4 to 5 tents. Campsite 2 is a short distance south of campsite 1. This site is long and narrow and more sunny than campsite 1. Campsite 2 will accommodate 2 to 3 tents. There are no toilet facilities near these campsites. Water is available from Onahu Creek. Wood and charcoal fires are not permitted here. Use camp stoves only. The Onahu Bridge campsites are rarely used. Their occupancy rate is about 13%.

Activities:

Fishing: Onahu Creek

Hiking: Onahu Creek Trail, Onahu-Tonahutu Connector Trail, Long Meadows Trail, Green Mountain Trail, Tonahutu Creek Trail,

Scenic Features: Big Meadows, Long Meadows

Onahu Bridge campsite 2.

Directions:

The nearest access to this campsite is via the Onahu Creek Trailhead. This trailhead is located on the east side of the road about 3.6 miles north of the Grand Lake Entrance. Take Trail Ridge Road for about 37.1 miles to the trailhead from the Beaver Meadows Entrance. Take the Onahu Creek Trail for about 2.8 miles to just before its intersection with the Long Meadows and Onahu-Tonahutu Connector trails. Turn left just before the foot bridge across the creek. It is a short distance back to the campsites. It takes about 1.5 to 2 hours to hike to the Onahu Bridge campsites.

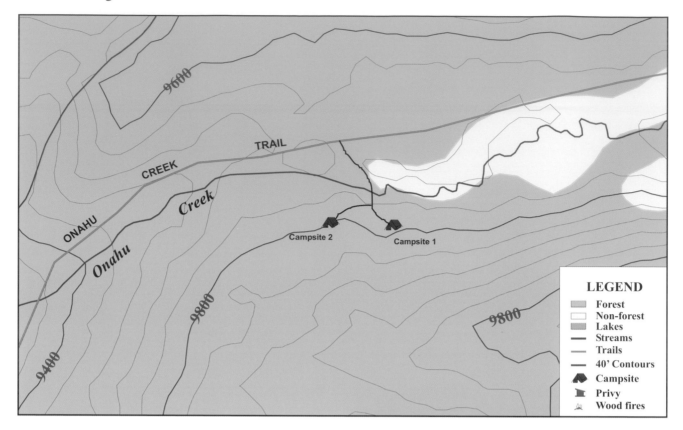

Onahu Creek

Description:

The Onahu Creek campsites are located south of the Onahu Creek Trail and Onahu Creek near the west end of a large meadow. The campsites are situated on a bench above Onahu Creek at an elevation of 9,570 feet. There are two campsites at this location with campsite 1 off to the left and campsite 2 to the right. Campsite 1 is fairly level with plenty of logs for sitting around the old camp stove. It has room for 2 to 3 tents. Campsite 2 is downstream from campsite 1. This campsite is more rocky and will accommodate one tent. There are no toilet facilities near these campsites. Water is available from Onahu Creek. Wood and charcoal fires are not permitted here. Use camp stoves only. These campsites are occupied about 20% of the time.

Activities:

Fishing: Onahu Creek
Hiking: Onahu Creek Trail, Onahu-Tonahutu Connector Trail, Long Meadows Trail, Green Mountain Trail, Tonahutu Creek Trail,
Scenic Features: Big Meadows, Long Meadows

Directions:

The nearest access to this campsite is via the Onahu Creek Trailhead. This trailhead is located on the east

Onahu Creek campsite 2.

side of the road about 3.6 miles north of the Grand Lake Entrance. Take Trail Ridge Road for about 37.1 miles to the trailhead from the Beaver Meadows Entrance. Take the Onahu Creek Trail for about 1.9 miles to the Onahu Creek campsite sign in a spruce and lodgepole pine forest. Turn right and cross Onahu Creek over a foot bridge near the west end of a large meadow. The path splits on a bench above the creek. It takes about 1 to 1.5 hours to hike to the Onahu Creek campsites.

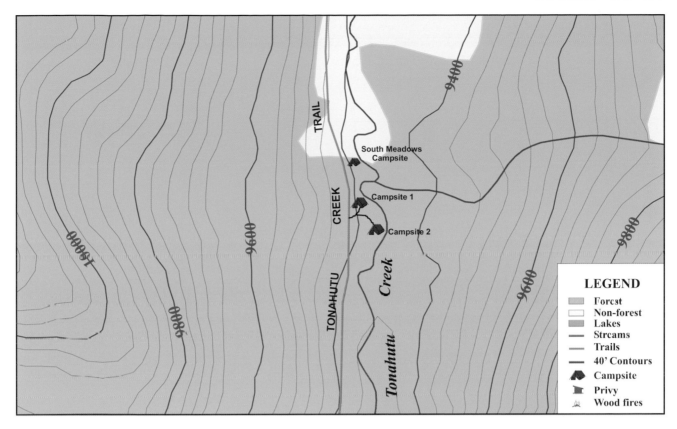

Paint Brush

Description:

The Paint Brush campsites are located about .1 miles south of Big Meadows and the South Meadows campsite in an open stand of lodgepole pine. There are two campsites situated at an elevation of 9,380 feet close to Tonahutu Creek. Campsite 1 is a fairly large bare area off to the left of the main path under some large lodgepole pines. It has a nice large log bench for sitting and will accommodate 1 to 2 tents. Campsite 2 is off to the right 100 to 200 yards on the edge of a small meadow. This campsite has room for one tent. There are no toilet facilities near these campsites. Water is available from Tonahutu Creek. Wood and charcoal fires are not permitted here. Use camp stoves only. The Paint Brush campsites have a 38% occupancy rate.

Activities:

Fishing: Tonahutu Creek

Hiking: Green Mountain Trail, Tonahutu Creek Trail, Onahu-Tonahutu Connector Trail, Onahu Creek Trail

Peaks nearby: Mount Patterson, Nisa Mountain, Green Mountain

Scenic Features: Big Meadows, Granite Falls

Paint Brush campsite 1.

Directions:

The nearest access to this campsite is via the Green Mountain Trailhead. This trailhead is located on the east side of the road about three miles north of the Grand Lake Entrance. Take Trail Ridge Road for about 37.7 miles to the trailhead from the Beaver Meadows Entrance. Take the Green Mountain Trail for about 1.7 miles to its intersection with the Tonahutu Creek Trail. Turn right and travel about 1.1 miles to the campsite sign. Turn left and follow the path about 100 feet to a split. Campsite 1 is to the left and campsite 2 is to the right. It takes about an 1.5 to 2 to hike to this campsite.

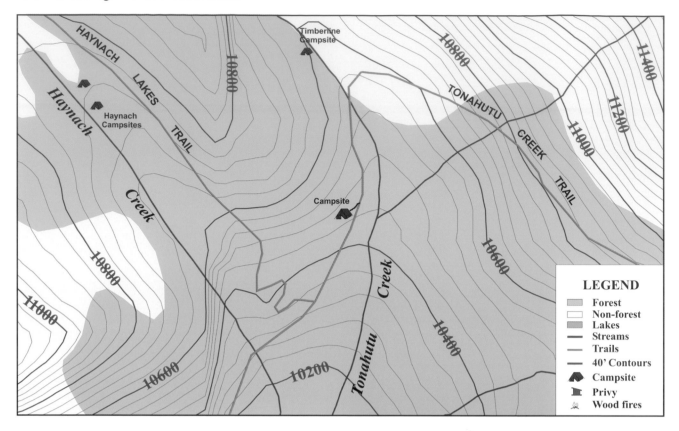

Renegade

Description:

The Renegade campsite is located in a dense spruce forest about 50 yards north of the Tonahutu Creek Trail. This site is situated at an elevation of 10,450 feet. The path to the campsite is about .1 miles beyond the Haynach Lakes Trail. This path travels north up the ridge for about 50 yards. The tent pad for this campsite is well defined and is lined with wood chips. There is room for one tent in this level area. There are no toilet facilities near this campsite. The dense forest keeps this campsite well shaded all day long. Water is available from Tonahutu Creek. Wood and charcoal fires are not permitted here. Use camp stoves only. The Renegade campsite is the most popular campsite in this area with an occupancy rate of 69%.

Activities:

Fishing: Tonahutu Creek, Haynach Lakes

Hiking: Green Mountain Trail, Tonahutu Creek Trail, Haynach Lakes Trail

Peaks nearby: Snowdrift Peak, Nakai Peak, Sprague Mountain, Gabletop Mountain, Knobtop Mountain

Scenic Features: Big Meadows, Granite Falls

Renegade campsite.

Directions:

The nearest access to this campsite is via the Green Mountain Trailhead. This trailhead is located on the east side of the road about three miles north of the Grand Lake Entrance. Take Trail Ridge Road for about 37.7 miles to the trailhead from the Beaver Meadows Entrance. Take the Green Mountain Trail for about 1.7 miles to its intersection with the Tonahutu Creek Trail. Turn left and travel north along the west edge of Big Meadows. Continue hiking on the Tonahutu Creek Trail for about 4.8 miles to the Renegade campsite sign (about a tenth mile past the Haynach Lake Trail). Turn left and climb the hill about 50 yards to the site. Travel time is about 4 to 5 hours.

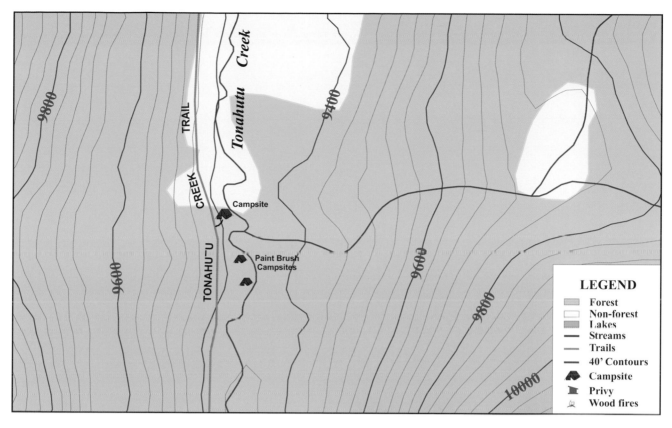

South Meadows

Description:

The South Meadows campsite is located near the south end of Big Meadows in an open stand of lodge-pole pine. The campsite is situated at an elevation of 9,380 feet close to Tonahutu Creek. It is well shaded by large lodgepole pine and spruce trees. The camp-site is a large bare area about ten feet above the creek. The area will accommodate 4 to 5 tents. This campsite has a parklike setting and offers great views of Big Meadows and the surrounding hills. There are no toi-let facilities near these campsites. Water is available from Tonahutu Creek. Wood and charcoal fires are not permitted here. Use camp stoves only. This beau-tiful campsite is occupied about 51% of the time.

Activities:

Fishing: Tonahutu Creek

Hiking: Green Mountain Trail, Tonahutu Creek Trail, Onahu-Tonahutu Connector Trail, Onahu Creek Trail

Peaks nearby: Mount Patterson, Nisa Mountain, Green Mountain

Scenic Features: Big Meadows, Granite Falls

South Meadows campsite 1.

Directions:

The nearest access to this campsite is via the Green Mountain Trailhead. This trailhead is located on the east side of the road about three miles north of the Grand Lake Entrance. Take Trail Ridge Road for about 37.7 miles to the trailhead from the Beaver Meadows En-trance. Take the Green Mountain Trail for about 1.7 miles to its intersection with the Tonahutu Creek Trail. Turn right and travel about one mile to the campsite sign. Turn left and follow the path about 100 feet to campsite. It takes about 1.5 to 2 hours to hike to this campsite.

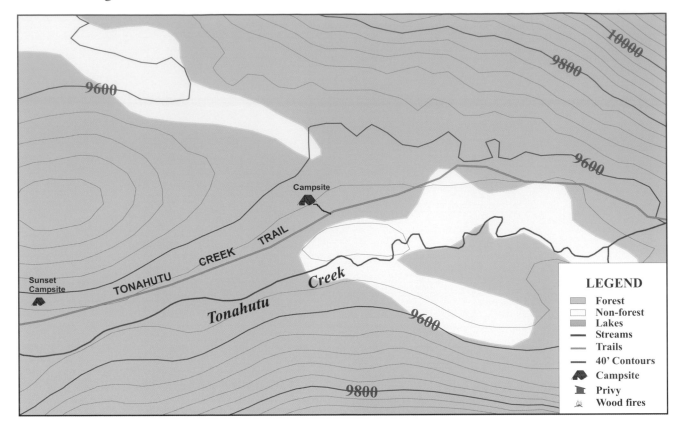

Sunrise

Description:

The Sunrise campsite is located north of the Tonahutu Creek Trail near a large meadow. The campsite is situated in a stand of spruce trees at an elevation of 9,550 feet. The path to the site makes a moderate climb for about 75 yards to the campsite. The site is a flat spot on the ridge next to a wet meadow to the east. The surface of the site is fairly smooth and will accommodate 1 to 2 tents. The trees here are dense making this campsite well shaded. There are no toilet facilities near these campsites. Water is available from Tonahutu Creek. Wood and charcoal fires are not permitted here. Use camp stoves only. The Sunrise campsite is occupied about 54% of the time.

Activities:

Fishing: Tonahutu Creek

Hiking: Green Mountain Trail, Tonahutu Creek Trail, Onahu-Tonahutu Connector Trail

Peaks nearby: Mount Patterson, Snowdrift Peak, Nakai Peak

Scenic Features: Big Meadows, Granite Falls

Directions:

The nearest access to this campsite is via the Green Mountain Trailhead. This trailhead is located on the

Sunrise campsite.

east side of the road about three miles north of the Grand Lake Entrance. Take Trail Ridge Road for about 37.7 miles to the trailhead from the Beaver Meadows Entrance. Take the Green Mountain Trail for about 1.7 miles to its intersection with the Tonahutu Creek Trail. Turn left and travel north along the west edge of Big Meadows. Continue hiking on the Tonahutu Creek Trail for about 2 miles to the Sunrise campsite sign. You will pass the Sunset campsite along the way. Turn left and travel about 75 yards up hill to the campsite. Travel time to the Sunrise campsite is 2 to 3 hours.

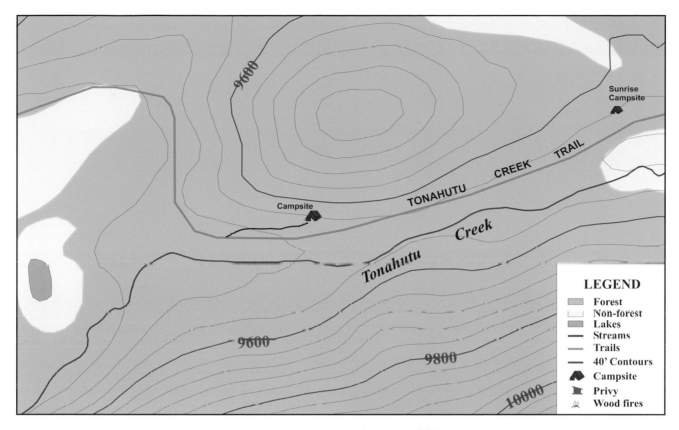

Sunset

Description:

The Sunset campsite is located north of the Tonahutu Creek Trail in a rocky area at the base of a south-facing slope. The campsite is situated in a stand of lodgepole pine and spruce trees at an elevation of 9,550 feet. The path to the site makes a slight climb for about 150 yards to the north east to the campsite. The site is a fairly large flat spot on the ridge above Tonahutu Creek. The surface of the site is fairly smooth and will accommodate 3 to 4 tents. The trees here are dense, making this campsite well shaded even though this is a south-facing slope. There are no toilet facilities near these campsites. Water is available from Tonahutu Creek. Wood and charcoal fires are not permitted here. Use camp stoves only. The Sunset campsite has an occupancy rate of about 50%.

Activities:

Fishing: Tonahutu Creek

Hiking: Green Mountain Trail, Tonahutu Creek Trail, Onahu-Tonahutu Connector Trail

Peaks nearby: Mount Patterson, Snowdrift Peak, Nakai Peak

Scenic Features: Big Meadows, Granite Falls

Sunset campsite.

Directions:

The nearest access to this campsite is via the Green Mountain Trailhead. This trailhead is located on the east side of the road about three miles north of the Grand Lake Entrance. Take Trail Ridge Road for about 37.7 miles to the trailhead from the Beaver Meadows Entrance. Take the Green Mountain Trail for about 1.7 miles to its intersection with the Tonahutu Creek Trail. Turn left and travel north along the west edge of Big Meadows. Continue hiking on the Tonahutu Creek Trail for about 1.6 miles to the Sunset campsite sign. Turn left and travel north east up the ridge. The campsite is about 150 yards off the trail. Travel time to the Sunset campsite is 2 to 3 hours.

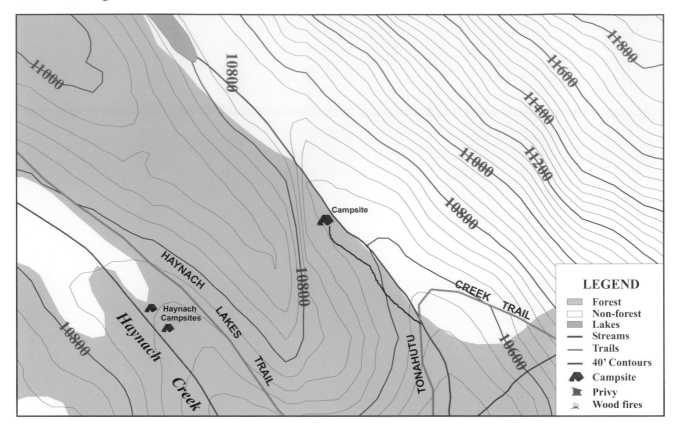

Timberline Group

Description:

The Timberline group campsite is located north west of the Tonahutu Creek Trail just below timberline. The site is situated in an open grassy area at an elevation of 10,630 feet. The path to the site begins just before the Tonahutu Creek Trail crosses the creek and parallels the stream for about 250 yards. Horses are not permitted on this path. This campsite is a nice level area next to a large rock. The site will accommodate 4 to 6 tents. There are no toilet facilities near this campsite. The campsite is sunny most of the day. Water is available from Tonahutu Creek. Wood and charcoal fires are not permitted here. Use camp stoves only. This group campsite is occupied about 60% of the time.

Activities:

Fishing: Tonahutu Creek, Haynach Lakes

Hiking: Green Mountain Trail, Tonahutu Creek Trail, Haynach Lakes Trail

Peaks nearby: Snowdrift Peak, Nakai Peak, Sprague Mountain, Gabletop Mountain, Knobtop Mountain

Scenic Features: Big Meadows, Granite Falls

Timberline group campsite.

Directions:

The nearest access to this campsite is via the Green Mountain Trailhead. This trailhead is located on the east side of the road about three miles north of the Grand Lake Entrance. Take Trail Ridge Road for about 37.7 miles to the trailhead from the Beaver Meadows Entrance. Take the Green Mountain Trail for about 1.7 miles to its intersection with the Tonahutu Creek Trail. Turn left and travel north along the west edge of Big Meadows. Continue hiking on the Tonahutu Creek Trail for about 5 miles to the Timberline campsite sign (about .3 miles past the Haynach Lake Trail). Turn left and follow the path for about 250 yards to the site. Travel time is about 4 to 5 hours.

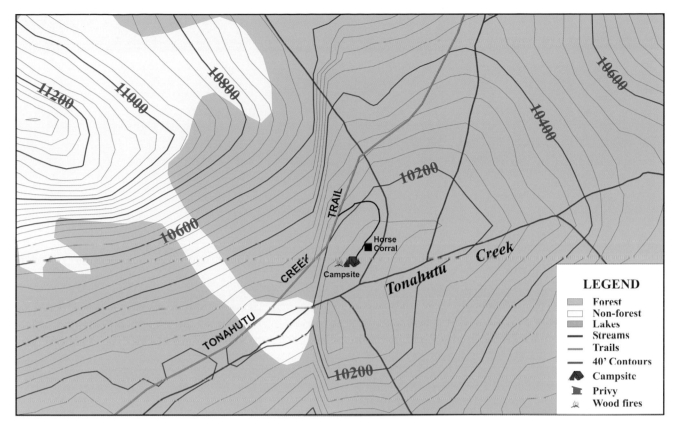

Tonahutu Group/Horse

Description:

The Tonahutu Group/Horse campsite is located south of the Tonahutu Creek Trail next to Tonahutu Creek. A wide path angles off to the right and down through the trees. It then bends back to the west to the campsite. The site is situated under some large spruce trees at an elevation of 10,130 feet. A large corral that will hold quite a few horses is located just east of the campsite. There is a pit toilet (3 walls) about 50 to 60 feet east of the corral. The campsite will accommodate 4 to 5 tents. Water is available from Tonahutu Creek. Wood fires are permitted at this campsite. Metal fire grates are provided at the site. Fires can only be built within these grates. Do not place rocks in or around your fire. Use only dead and down wood. This campsite is occupied about 64% of the time.

Activities:

Fishing: Tonahutu Creek, Haynach Lakes

Hiking: Green Mountain Trail, Tonahutu Creek Trail, Haynach Lakes Trail

Peaks nearby: Snowdrift Peak, Nakai Peak, Sprague Mountain, Gabletop Mountain, Knobtop Mountain

Scenic Features: Big Meadows, Granite Falls

Tonahutu horse corral.

Directions:

The nearest access to this campsite is via the Green Mountain Trailhead. This trailhead is located on the east side of the road about three miles north of the Grand Lake Entrance. Take Trail Ridge Road for about 37.7 miles to the trailhead from the Beaver Meadows Entrance. Take the Green Mountain Trail for about 1.7 miles to its intersection with the Tonahutu Creek Trail. Turn left and travel north along the west edge of Big Meadows. Continue hiking on the Tonahutu Creek Trail for about 4.5 miles to the Tonahutu Group/Horse campsite sign . Turn right and follow the wide path down through the trees to the site. Travel time is about 3 to 4 hours.

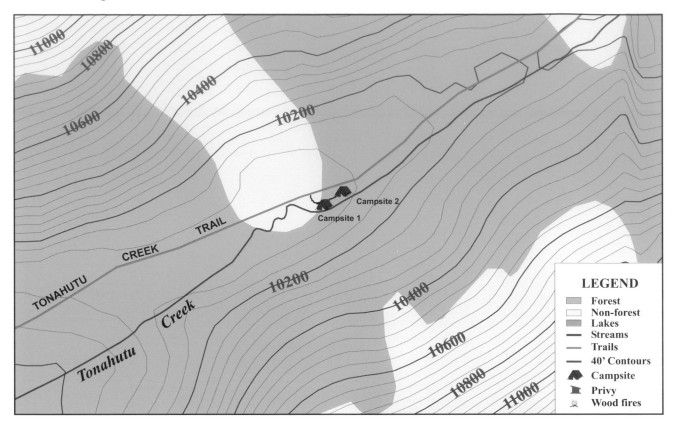

Map legend:

LEGEND
- Forest
- Non-forest
- Lakes
- Streams
- Trails
- 40' Contours
- Campsite
- Privy
- Wood fires

Tonahutu Meadows

Description:

The Tonahutu Meadows campsites are located in a dense stand of spruce trees south of the Tonahutu Creek Trail. There are two campsites situated at an elevation of 10,100 feet just inside the forest near the south east edge of the meadow. The path to the sites splits as you reach the trees. Campsite 1 is about 30 feet to the right of the split. This site is a level site under some large spruce and has room for 1 to 2 tents. Campsite 2 is off to the left about 200 feet and will also accommodate 1 to 2 tents. This campsite is a little more rocky than campsite 1. There are no toilet facilities near these campsites. Water is available from Tonahutu Creek. Wood and charcoal fires are not permitted here. Use camp stoves only. Tonahutu Meadows has an occupancy rate of about 54%.

Activities:

Fishing: Tonahutu Creek

Hiking: Green Mountain Trail, Tonahutu Creek Trail, Onahu-Tonahutu Connector Trail

Peaks nearby: Mount Patterson, Snowdrift Peak, Nakai Peak

Scenic Features: Big Meadows, Granite Falls

Tonahutu Meadows campsite 2.

Directions:

The nearest access to this campsite is via the Green Mountain Trailhead. This trailhead is located on the east side of the road about three miles north of the Grand Lake Entrance. Take Trail Ridge Road for about 37.7 miles to the trailhead from the Beaver Meadows Entrance. Take the Green Mountain Trail for about 1.7 miles to its intersection with the Tonahutu Creek Trail. Turn left and travel north along the west edge of Big Meadows. Continue hiking on the Tonahutu Creek Trail for about 4 miles to the Tonahutu Meadows campsite sign at the south east end of Tonahutu Meadows. Follow the path down hill across the meadow to the campsites. It takes about 3 hours to reach the campsites.

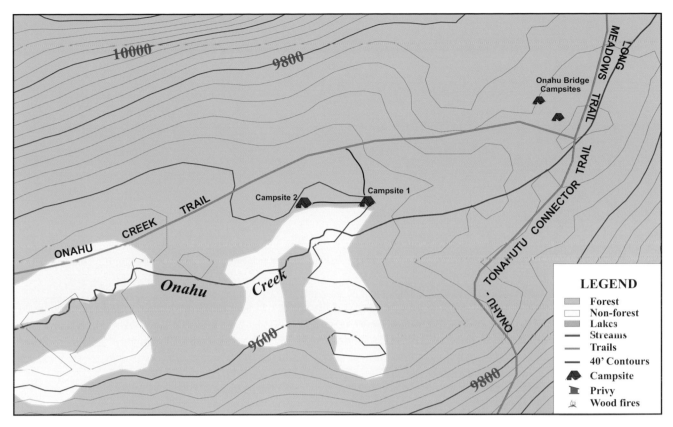

Upper Onahu

Description:

The Upper Onahu Creek campsites are located south of the Onahu Creek Trail and north of Onahu Creek near the north edge of a large meadow. The campsites are situated on a small bench above Onahu Creek at an elevation of 9,600 feet. There are two campsites at this location with campsite 1 directly south of the trail and campsite 2 to the right. Both sites are fairly sunny though surrounded by spruce and lodge-pole pines. Campsite 1 is fairly level and has room for 2 to 3 tents. Campsite 2 is downstream from campsite 1. The marker is behind a tree and not easy to see. It is a small bare spot that is not well defined. This camp-site will accommodate one tent. There are no toilet facilities near these campsites. Water is available from Onahu Creek that flows through the meadow. Wood and charcoal fires are not permitted here. Use camp stoves only. This campsite is the least used in this area with an occupancy rate of just 8%.

Activities:

Fishing: Onahu Creek

Hiking: Onahu Creek Trail, Onahu-Tonahutu Connector Trail, Long Meadows Trail, Green Mountain Trail, Tonahutu Creek Trail

Scenic Features: Big Meadows, Long Meadows

Upper Onahu campsite 1.

Directions:

The nearest access to this campsite is via the Onahu Creek Trailhead. This trailhead is located on the east side of the road about 3.6 miles north of the Grand Lake Entrance. Take Trail Ridge Road for about 37.1 miles to the trailhead from the Beaver Meadows Entrance. Take the Onahu Creek Trail for about 2.7 miles to the Upper Onahu Creek campsite sign in a spruce and lodgepole pine forest. Turn right and follow the path a short distance to campsite 1. Follow the edge of the bank above the meadow downstream to camp-site 2. It takes about 1 to 1.5 hours to hike to the Up-per Onahu Creek campsites.

Wild Basin Area Campsites

Campsite	No. of sites	Wood Fires	Elevation	Privy	Nearest Trailhead	Distance	Elevation Change	Travel Time	Stock	Use
Aspen Knoll	1	stoves only	9,300 ft	no	Wild Basin	2.2 mi	770 ft	1- 1.5 hr	llama	51%
Beaver Mill	1	stoves only	9,660 ft	no	Sandbeach Lake	2.9 mi	1,380 ft	2 - 3 hr	no	21%
Campers Creek	1	stoves only	9,240 ft	no	Sandbeach Lake	2.0 mi	940 ft	1- 1.5 hr	no	38%
Finch Lake	2+1grp	stoves only	9,930 ft	yes	Finch Lake	4.3 mi	1,900 ft	3 - 4 hr	yes	42%
Hole In The Wall	1	stoves only	9,160 ft	yes	Sandbeach Lake	1.8 mi	870 ft	1.5 hr	no	38%
Hunters Creek	1	stoves only	9,760 ft	no	Sandbeach Lake	3.2 mi	1,470 ft	2 - 3 hr	no	36%
North St Vrain	2	stoves only	9,530 ft	yes	Wild Basin	2.8 mi	1,010 ft	2 - 3 hr	no	65%
Ouzel Lake	1	stoves only	10,000 ft	yes	Wild Basin	5.0 mi	1,690 ft	3 - 4 hr	no	75%
Pear Creek	3	stoves only	10,480 ft	yes	Finch Lake	5.9 mi	2,510 ft	4 - 5 hr	no	27%
Pear Lake	1	stoves only	10,610 ft	yes	Finch Lake	6.3 mi	2,700 ft	4 - 5 hr	no	49%
Pine Ridge	2	stoves only	8,920 ft	yes	Wild Basin	1.5 mi	410 ft	1 hr	no	46%
Sandbeach Lake	4+1grp	stoves only	10,310 ft	yes	Sandbeach Lake	4.3 mi	2,110 ft	3 - 4 hr	no	45%
Siskin	1	stoves only	9,340 ft	no	Wild Basin	2.5 mi	840 ft	1.5 - 2 hr	no	52%
Tahosa	1	stoves only	9,130 ft	no	Wild Basin	1.8 mi	600 ft	1.5 hr	no	50%
Thunder Lake	4+1grp	stoves only	10,680 ft	yes	Wild Basin	5.5 mi	2,150 ft	4 - 5 hr	yes	57%
Upper Ouzel Creek	1	stoves only	10,655 ft	no	Wild Basin	6.0 mi	2,290 ft	5 hr	no	75%

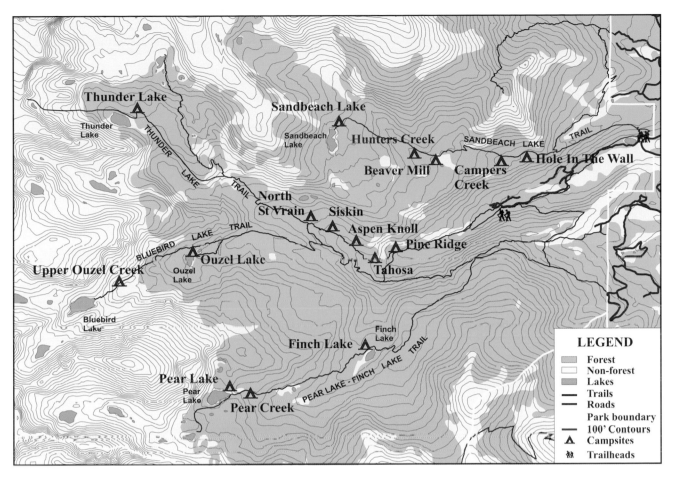

Wild Basin Area

The Wild Basin area is a very popular area located in the southeastern section of the Park. There are

Pagoda Mountain overlooks the expanse of Wild Basin.

eleven trails in this area including: Lookout Mountain, Sandbeach-Meeker Park, Sandbeach Lake, Thunder Lake, Finch Lake Cutoff, Allenspark, Finch Lake-Pear Lake, Lion Lakes, Bluebird Lake, Ouzel Lake, and North St Vrain Fire trails. Sixteen camping locations are found within this area with a total of 30 campsites. Three of these sites are group sites and three

permit the use of livestock. Nine of the sites have toilet facilities. Wood fires are not allowed at any of the campsites. You must use camp stoves only. Elevations range from 8,920 feet at the Pine Ridge campsites to 10,680 feet at the Thunder Lake campsites.

Many lakes and streams provide opportunities for fishing. Some are restricted to catch and release only. Check with Park Service personnel for the latest information. Numerous peaks are found in this area. Some of these include: Lookout Mtn. (10,715'), Tanima Peak (12,420'), Mt. Alice (13,310'), Ouzel Peak (12,716'), Copeland Mtn. (13,176'), Isolation Peak (13,318'), Elk Tooth (12,848'), and Ogalalla Peak (13,138').

Trailheads providing access to campsites in this area include: Sandbeach Lake, Wild Basin, Finch Lake, and Allenspark trailheads. Parking is limited due to the popularity of the area. An early arrival is advised. The distance from a trailhead to campsites ranges from 1.5 miles to 6.4 miles with hiking times ranging from 1 to 6 hours. Topographic maps that cover the area include the Allenspark and Isolation Peak quads.

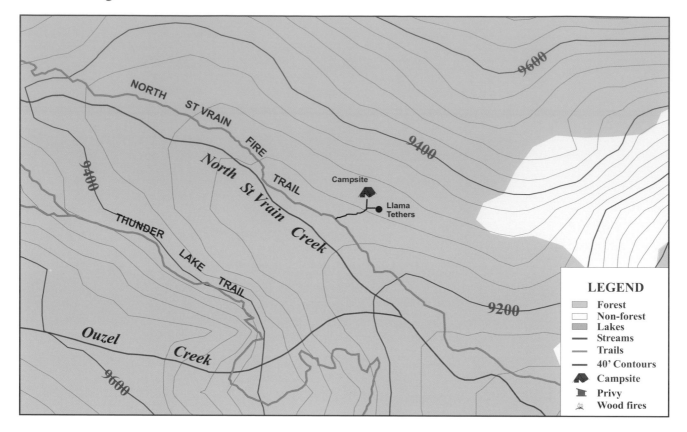

Aspen Knoll

Description:

The Aspen Knoll campsite is located in a stand of mixed conifers and aspen on a ridge north of the North St Vrain Fire Trail. The campsite is situated at an elevation of 9,300 feet. The path to the site leaves the trail and climbs the ridge to the north for about 100 yards. Llama are permitted at this campsite. Two tethering posts are located just to the right of the trail before reaching the campsite. The tent area is above and to the left of the tethering posts at the base of some large rocks. It is a well defined tent pad with room for 1 to 2 tents. There are no toilet facilities near this campsite. Water may be obtained from North St Vrain Creek below the trail. Wood and charcoal fires are not permitted here. Use camp stoves only. The occupancy rate for this campsite is about 51%.

Activities:

Fishing: North St Vrain Creek
Hiking: Thunder Lake Trail, North St Vrain Fire Trail, Bluebird Lake Trail
Scenic Features: Copeland Falls, Ouzel Falls, Calypso Cascades

Directions:

The nearest access to this campsite is via the Wild

Aspen Knoll campsite.

Basin Trailhead. Take Highway 7 south from Estes Park for about 10.8 miles to the Wild Basin Area turnoff (about 3.8 miles south of the Longs Peak access road). Turn right and follow the road for about .4 miles to the Wild Basin Entrance (just past the Wild Basin Lodge). Follow the narrow dirt road for about two miles to the Wild Basin Ranger Station and the trailhead. Take the Thunder Lake Trail for about 1.5 miles to the North St Vrain Trail intersection. There is a sign pointing the way to the campsites along this trail. Horses are not permitted on this trail. Follow this trail for about .7 miles to the campsite sign. Hiking time is about 1.5 hours.

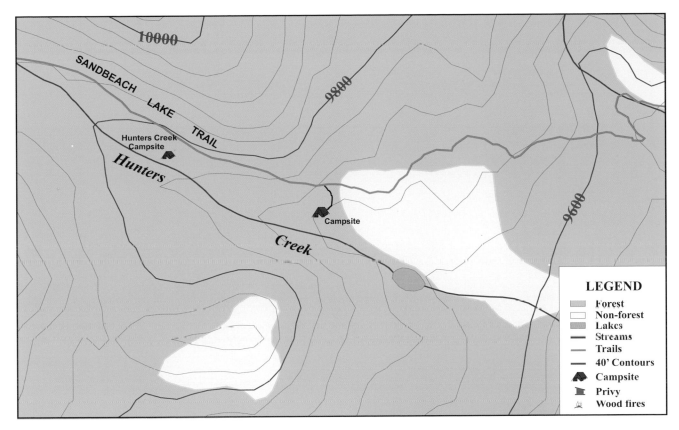

Beaver Mill

Description:

   The Beaver Mill campsite is located in a stand of lodgepole pine and spruce trees south of the Sandbeach Lake Trail. This site is situated at an elevation of 9,660 feet. The campsite is fairly level with a few rocks in it. It will accommodate 1 to 2 tents. This bare area is

surrounded by lodgepole pine and spruce trees and is well shaded. There are no toilet facilities near this campsite. Water may be obtained from Hunters Creek about 150 feet south of the site. Fishing is not permitted in the creek because of a Greenback Cutthroat recovery program. Wood and charcoal fires are not permitted here. Use camp stoves only. The Beaver Mill campsite has an occupancy rate of about 21%.

Activities:
Fishing: Sandbeach Lake
Hiking: Sandbeach Lake Trail, Sandbeach - Meeker Park Trail
Peaks nearby: Mount Orton, Horsetooth Peak, Lookout Mountain
Scenic Features: Sandbeach Lake

Beaver Mill campsite.

Directions:

   The nearest access to this campsite is via the Sandbeach Lake Trailhead. Take Highway 7 south from Estes Park for about 10.8 miles to the Wild Basin Area turnoff (about 3.8 miles south of the Longs Peak access road). Turn right and follow the road for about .4 miles to the Wild Basin Entrance (just past the Wild Basin Lodge). The trailhead is just north of the entrance station. Take the Sandbeach Lake Trail for about 2.9 miles to the campsite sign (just after passing through a stand of aspens). Turn left and follow the path downhill to the campsite. It takes about 2 to 3 hours to reach the campsite via this moderately strenuous trail.

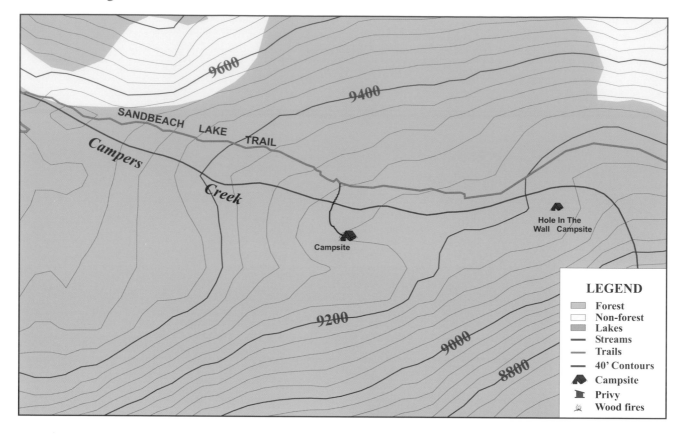

Campers Creek

Description:

The Campers Creek campsite is located in a dense stand of lodgepole pine and spruce trees south of the Sandbeach Lake Trail. This site is situated at an elevation of 9,240 feet. The path to the site crosses Campers Creek over a log foot bridge and then travels east for a hundred yards or so to the campsite. This campsite is a large bare area surrounded by lodgepole pine and spruce trees with a few trees in the middle. It is well shaded and has room for 2 to 3 tents. There are no toilet facilities near this campsite. Water may be obtained from Campers Creek north of the campsite. Wood and charcoal fires are not permitted here. Use camp stoves only. This campsite is occupied about 38% of the time.

Activities:

Fishing: Sandbeach Lake

Hiking: Sandbeach Lake Trail, Sandbeach - Meeker Park Trail

Peaks nearby: Mount Orton, Horsetooth Mountain, Lookout Mountain

Scenic Features: Sandbeach Lake

Campers Creek campsite.

Directions:

The nearest access to this campsite is via the Sandbeach Lake Trailhead. Take Highway 7 south from Estes Park for about 10.8 miles to the Wild Basin Area turnoff (about 3.8 miles south of the Longs Peak access road). Turn right and follow the road for about .4 miles to the Wild Basin Entrance (just past the Wild Basin Lodge). The trailhead is just north of the entrance station. Take the Sandbeach Lake Trail for about 2 miles to the campsite sign. Turn left and follow the path downhill across Campers Creek to the campsite. It takes about 1.5 hours to reach the campsite via this moderately strenuous trail.

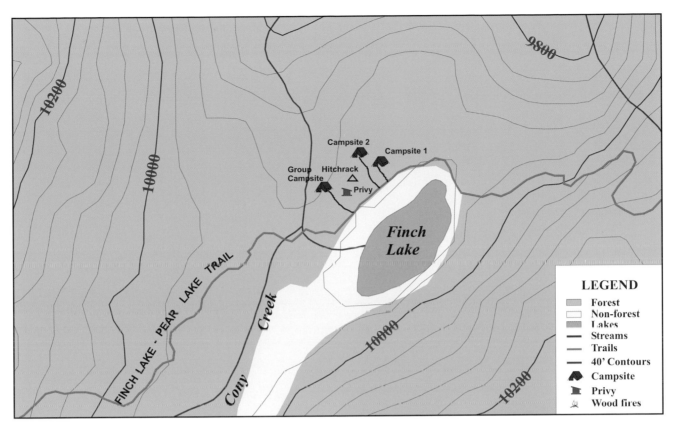

Finch Lake

Description:

The Finch Lake campsites are located in a lodgepole pine forest northwest of Finch Lake at an elevation of 9,930 feet. There are two individual campsites and one group/stock site at this location. Campsite 1 is a large, open area surrounded by lodgepole pine and spruce trees. This sunny site will accommodate 3 to 4 tents. The path to campsite 2 is a little farther west from the path to campsite 1. This site is farther away from the lake but more shaded than campsite 1. The level tent pad has room for two tents. The group/stock site is farther west from the individual sites. This campsite is a large bare area under a dense canopy of spruce and lodgepole. It will accommodate 6 to 8 tents. An outhouse privy and hitchrack are located near this campsite. Water may be obtained from the lake or Cony Creek. Wood and charcoal fires are not permitted here. Use camp stoves only. Occupancy rate is about 42%.

Activities:

Fishing: Cony Creek, Pear Lake

Hiking: Finch Lake-Pear Lake Trail, Finch Lake
   Cutoff Trail

Scenic Features: Finch Lake, Pear Lake

Finch Lake campsite 1.

Directions:

The nearest access to this campsite is via the Finch Lake Trailhead. Take Highway 7 south from Estes Park for about 10.8 miles to the Wild Basin Area turnoff (about 3.8 miles south of the Longs Peak access road). Turn right and follow the road for about .4 miles to the Wild Basin Entrance (just past the Wild Basin Lodge). Follow the narrow dirt road for about 1.8 miles to the Finch Lake Trailhead on the left side of the road. Take the Finch Lake Cutoff Trail for about 2.3 miles to its intersection with the Finch Lake - Pear Lake and Allenspark trails. Turn left and travel another 2 miles to Finch Lake and the campsites. It takes 3 to 4 hours of moderately strenuous hiking to reach these campsites.

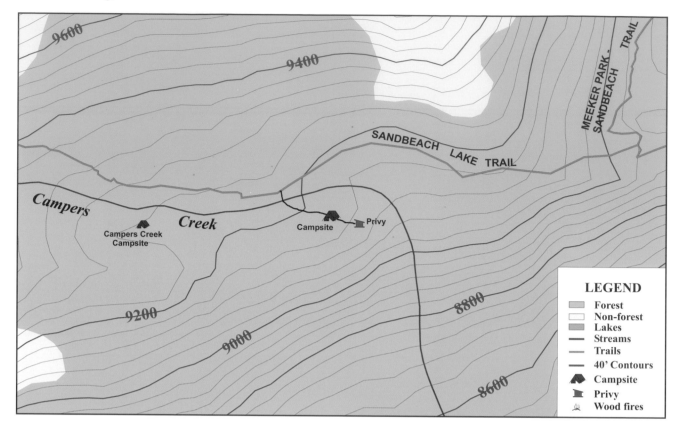

Hole In The Wall

Description:

  The Hole In The Wall campsite is located in a dense stand of lodgepole pine and spruce trees south of the Sandbeach Lake Trail. This site is situated at an elevation of 9,160 feet. The path to the site crosses Campers Creek over a log foot bridge and then travels southeast for 300 to 400 yards or so to the campsite. Red arrowheads on the trees mark the way to the campsite. This campsite is well shaded and has room for 2 to 3 tents. The dense forest and distance from the trail makes this campsite well isolated from the traffic on the Sandbeach Lake Trail. There is a pit toilet south east of the campsite. Water may be obtained from Campers Creek north of the campsite. Wood and charcoal fires are not permitted here. Use camp stoves only. The occupancy rate for this campsite is about 38%.

Activities:

Fishing: Sandbeach Lake

Hiking: Sandbeach Lake Trail, Sandbeach - Meeker Park Trail

Peaks nearby: Mount Orton, Horsetooth Mountain, Lookout Mountain

Scenic Features: Sandbeach Lake

Hole In The Wall campsite.

Directions:

  The nearest access to this campsite is via the Sandbeach Lake Trailhead. Take Highway 7 south from Estes Park for about 10.8 miles to the Wild Basin Area turnoff (about 3.8 miles south of the Longs Peak access road). Turn right and follow the road for about .4 miles to the Wild Basin Entrance (just past the Wild Basin Lodge). The trailhead is just north of the entrance station. Take the Sandbeach Lake Trail for about 1.8 miles to the campsite sign. Turn left and follow the path downhill across Campers Creek about 300 to 400 yards to the campsite. It takes about 1.5 hours to reach this campsite via this moderately strenuous trail.

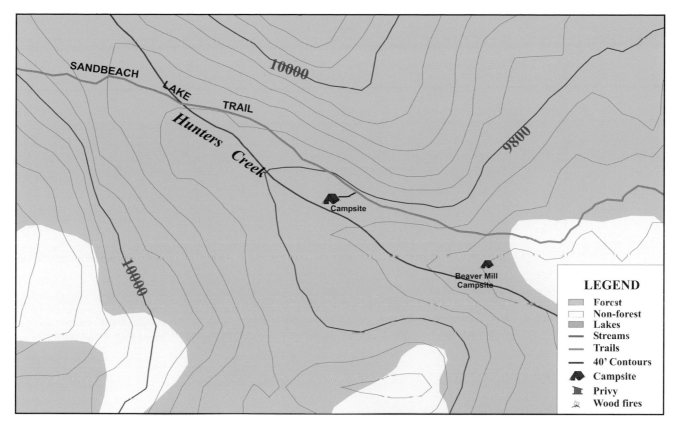

Hunters Creek

Description:

The Hunters Creek campsite is located in a dense stand of lodgepole pine and spruce trees south of the Sandbeach Lake Trail. This site is situated at an elevation of 9,760 feet. The campsite has a level, smooth surface and will accommodate 2 to 3 tents. This site is  surrounded by lodgepole pine and spruce trees and is well shaded. There are no toilet facilities near this campsite. Water may be obtained from Hunters Creek south of the campsite beyond some large rocks. Fishing is not permitted in the creek because of a Greenback Cutthroat recovery program. Wood and charcoal fires are not permitted here. Use camp stoves only. The Hunters Creek campsite has an occupancy rate of about 36%.

Activities:

Fishing: Sandbeach Lake

Hiking: Sandbeach Lake Trail, Sandbeach - Meeker Park Trail

Peaks nearby: Mount Orton, Horsetooth Mountain, Lookout Mountain

Scenic Features: Sandbeach Lake

Hunters Creek campsite.

Directions:

The nearest access to this campsite is via the Sandbeach Lake Trailhead. Take Highway 7 south from Estes Park for about 10.8 miles to the Wild Basin Area turnoff (about 3.8 miles south of the Longs Peak access road). Turn right and follow the road for about .4 miles to the Wild Basin Entrance (just past the Wild Basin Lodge). The trailhead is just north of the entrance station. Take the Sandbeach Lake Trail for about 3.2 miles to the campsite sign (about .2 miles before the trail crosses Hunters Creek). Turn left and follow the level path about 100 yards to the campsite. It takes about 2 to 3 hours to reach this campsite via this moderately strenuous trail.

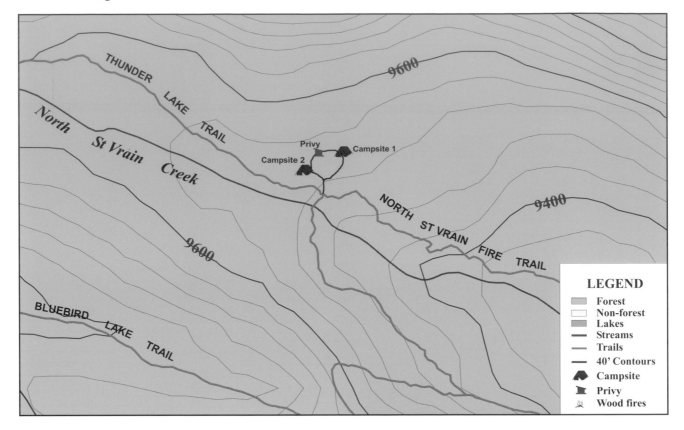

North St Vrain

Description:

The North St Vrain campsites are located in a stand of spruce and lodgepole pine on a ridge north of the intersection of the Thunder Lake and North St Vrain Fire trails. The campsites are situated at an elevation of 9,530 feet. There are two campsites at this location. The path to the sites branches to the left and right soon after leaving the trail. Campsite 1 is to the right. This campsite has a large "T" shaped tent pad with room for 3 to 4 tents. Campsite 2 (off to the left) has two large tent pads and will accommodate 2 to 3 tents. There is a pit toilet on a path between the campsites. Water may be obtained from North St Vrain Creek below the trail. Wood and charcoal fires are not permitted here. Use camp stoves only. These campsites are occupied about 65% of the time.

Activities:

Fishing: North St Vrain Creek

Hiking: Thunder Lake Trail, North St Vrain Fire Trail, Bluebird Lake Trail, Lion Lakes Trail

Peaks nearby: Mount Orton

Scenic Features: Copeland Falls, Ouzel Falls, Calypso Cascades

North St Vrain campsite 2.

Directions:

The nearest access to this campsite is via the Wild Basin Trailhead. Take Highway 7 south from Estes Park for about 10.8 miles to the Wild Basin Area turnoff (about 3.8 miles south of the Longs Peak access road). Turn right and follow the road for about .4 miles to the Wild Basin Entrance (just past the Wild Basin Lodge). Follow the narrow dirt road for about two miles to the Wild Basin Ranger Station and the trailhead. Take the Thunder Lake Trail for about 1.5 miles to the North St Vrain Trail intersection. There is a sign pointing the way to the campsites along this trail. Horses are not permitted on this trail. Follow this trail for about 1.3 miles to the campsite sign. Hiking time is about 2 to 3 hours.

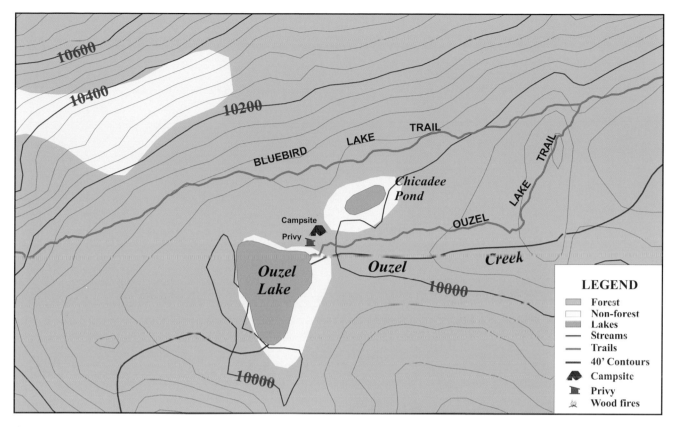

Ouzel Lake

Description:

The Ouzel Lake campsite is located on a flat bench north of the outlet end of Ouzel Lake. The campsite is situated about 50 yards north of the trail at an elevation of 10,000 feet. There are two well marked tent pads that are smooth and level. These tent pads will accommodate 2 to 3 tents. There is an outhouse just south and west of the campsite. Water may be obtained from Ouzel Lake or Ouzel Creek. Wood and charcoal fires are not permitted here. Use camp stoves only. This is a very beautiful spot to camp. Fishing in Ouzel Lake and Ouzel Creek above Ouzel Falls is by catch and release methods only. The campsite is one of the more popular campsites in this area with a 75% occupancy rate.

Activities:

Fishing: Ouzel Lake, Ouzel Creek

Hiking: Thunder Lake Trail, Bluebird Lake Trail, Ouzel Lake Trail

Peaks nearby: Mahana Peak, Ouzel Peak, Copeland Mountain

Scenic Features: Copeland Falls, Ouzel Falls, Calypso Cascades, Ouzel Lake

Ouzel Lake campsite.

Directions:

The nearest access to this campsite is via the Wild Basin Trailhead. Take Highway 7 south from Estes Park for about 10.8 miles to the Wild Basin Area turnoff (about 3.8 miles south of the Longs Peak access road). Turn right and follow the road for about .4 miles to the Wild Basin Entrance (just past the Wild Basin Lodge). Follow the narrow dirt road for about 2 miles to the Wild Basin Ranger Station and the trailhead. Take the Thunder Lake Trail for about 3.2 miles to the Bluebird Lake Trail intersection. Turn left and hike about 1.4 miles to the Ouzel Lake Trail. This trail travels downhill for about a half mile to Ouzel Lake. The campsite is on a bench above the east end of the lake, just beyond the outhouse. Hiking time is about 3 to 4 hours.

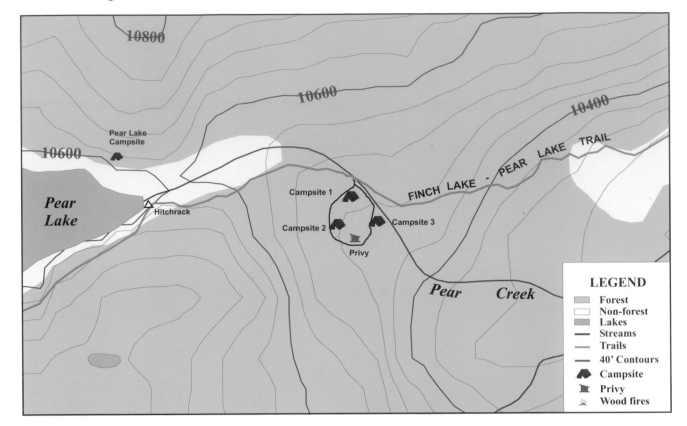

Pear Creek

Description:

The Pear Creek campsites are located in a dense spruce forest just south of Pear Creek at an elevation of 10,480 feet. There are three individual campsites at this location. A loop path connects the campsites. Campsite 1 is a short distance from the creek. The ground here is soft but not as level as the other sites. This site will accommodate 2 to 3 tents. Campsite 2 is south and west of campsite 1 along the loop path. This well shaded site has room for three tents under the spruce canopy. Campsite 3 is east along the creek a few hundred yards. This level site will accommodate 3 to 4 tents in a bare area among the spruce trees. A pit toilet is located between campsites 2 and 3. Water may be obtained from Pear Creek. Wood and charcoal fires are not permitted here. Use camp stoves only. The Pear Creek campsites are occupied about 27% of the time.

Activities:

Fishing: Cony Creek, Pear Lake, Hutcheson Lakes
Hiking: Finch Lake-Pear Lake Trail, Finch Lake Cutoff Trail
Peaks nearby: Copeland Mountain, Elk Tooth, Ogallala Peak
Scenic Features: Finch Lake, Pear Lake

A camper prepares to go fishing at Pear Creek campsite 1.

Directions:

The nearest access to this campsite is via the Finch Lake Trailhead. Take Highway 7 south from Estes Park for about 10.8 miles to the Wild Basin Area turnoff (about 3.8 miles south of the Longs Peak access road). Turn right and follow the road for about .4 miles to the Wild Basin Entrance (just past the Wild Basin Lodge). Follow the narrow dirt road for about 1.8 miles to the Finch Lake Trailhead on the left side of the road. Take the Finch Lake Cutoff Trail for about 2.3 miles to its intersection with the Finch Lake - Pear Lake and Allenspark trails. Turn left and travel 3.6 miles to the campsites. The path to the campsites is on the south side of Pear Creek. Hiking time is 4 to 5 hours.

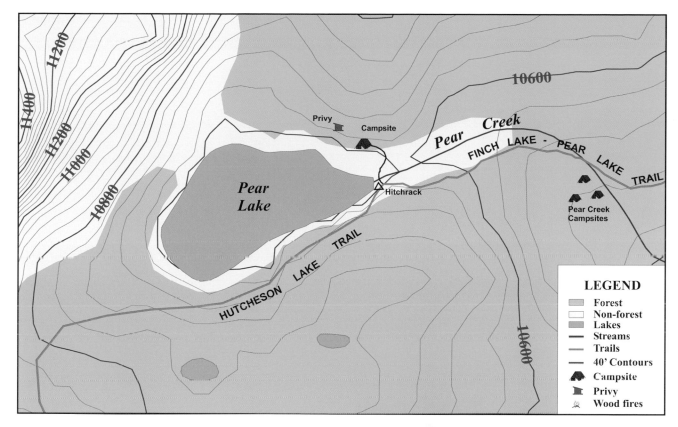

Pear Lake

Description:

The Pear Lake campsite is located in an open area behind some spruce trees on a bench above the northeast end of Pear Lake. The site is situated at an elevation of 10,610 feet. The path to the campsite leaves the trail near a horse hitchrack and crosses Pear Creek over a log foot bridge. It climbs the bench north of Pear Lake. The path turns west and travels about 100 yards to the campsite. This level site lies beside a small snowfield and has a great view of the lake below. The campsite has room for one tent. A pit toilet is located west of the campsite. Water may be obtained from Pear Creek or Pear Lake. Wood and charcoal fires are not permitted here. Use camp stoves only. This campsite is occupied about half of the time (49%).

Activities:

Fishing: Cony Creek, Pear Lake, Hutcheson Lakes
Hiking: Finch Lake-Pear Lake Trail, Finch Lake Cutoff Trail
Peaks nearby: Copeland Mountain, Elk Tooth, Ogallala Peak
Scenic Features: Finch Lake, Pear Lake

Directions:

The nearest access to this campsite is via the Finch

Pear Lake campsite.

Lake Trailhead. Take Highway 7 south from Estes Park for about 10.8 miles to the Wild Basin Area turnoff (about 3.8 miles south of the Longs Peak access road). Turn right and follow the road for about .4 miles to the Wild Basin Entrance (just past the Wild Basin Lodge). Follow the narrow dirt road for about 1.8 miles to the Finch Lake Trailhead on the left side of the road. Take the Finch Lake Cutoff Trail for about 2.3 miles to its intersection with the Finch Lake - Pear Lake and Allenspark trails. Turn left and travel 4 miles to the campsite. The path to the campsite crosses Pear Creek and climbs a bench above the lake. Hiking time is 4 to 5 hours.

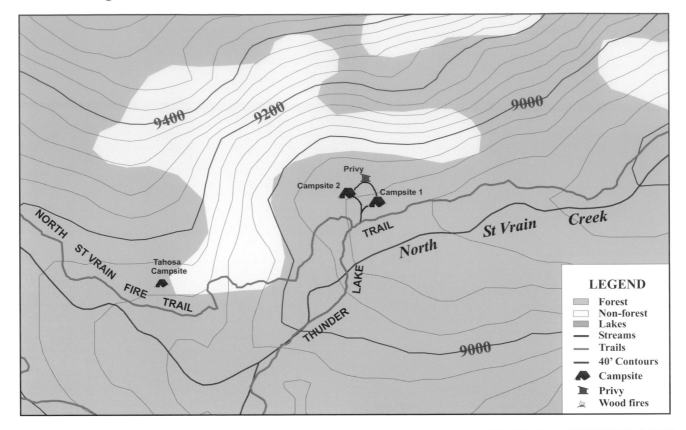

Pine Ridge

Description:

The Pine Ridge campsites are located in a stand of lodgepole pines on a ridge north of the Thunder Lake Trail. There are two campsites situated at an elevation of 8,920 feet. The path to the site leaves the trail and climbs the ridge to the north for about 100 yards. Campsite 1 is to the right. A long narrow tent pad is lined with lodgepole pines. This smooth, level site will accommodate two tents. Campsite 2 is to the left and is just beyond the ridge. This campsite is a large flat area under mature lodgepole pines. It is large enough to accommodate 3 to 4 tents. There is a pit toilet on a path between the campsites. Water may be obtained from North St Vrain Creek below the trail. Wood and charcoal fires are not permitted here. Use camp stoves only. These easy access campsites have an occupancy rate of about 46%.

Activities:

Fishing: North St Vrain Creek

Hiking: Thunder Lake Trail, North St Vrain Fire Trail, Finch Lake-Pear Lake Trail

Scenic Features: Copeland Falls, Ouzel Falls, Calypso Cascades

Pine Ridge campsite 1.

Directions:

The nearest access to this campsite is via the Wild Basin Trailhead. Take Highway 7 south from Estes Park for about 10.8 miles to the Wild Basin Area turnoff (about 3.8 miles south of the Longs Peak access road). Turn right and follow the road for about .4 miles to the Wild Basin Entrance (just past the Wild Basin Lodge). Follow the narrow dirt road for about two miles to the Wild Basin Ranger Station and the trailhead. Take the Thunder Lake Trail for about 1.5 miles to the campsite sign just before the North St Vrain Fire Trail and the bridge across North St Vrain Creek. Turn right and climb the ridge for about 100 yards to the campsites. It takes about an hour of easy hiking to reach these campsites.

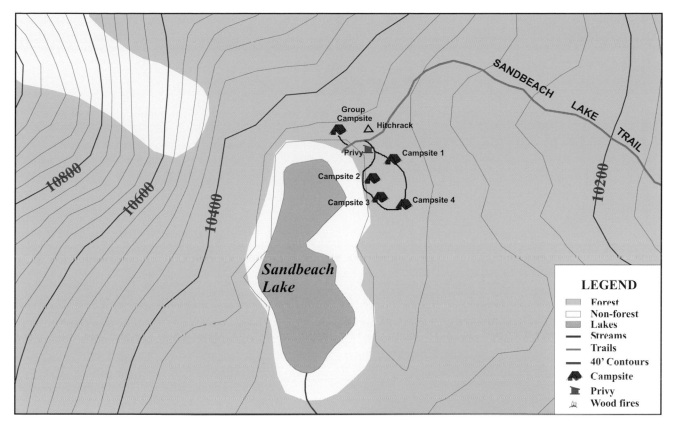

Sandbeach Lake

Description:

The Sandbeach Lake campsites are located in a dense stand of spruce trees on the northeast side of Sandbeach Lake. There are four individual sites and one group site situated at an elevation of 10,310 feet. The group campsite is off to the right beyond a horse hitchrack under a dense canopy of spruce. This large area has room for 4 to 5 tents and is isolated from the individual campsites. The individual sites are south of the trail just off the eastern shore of the lake inside the trees. These sites are level and more open than the group site with room for 1 to 3 tents. Campsites 2 and 3 are beach-front property with nice views of the lake. There is an outhouse just south of the trail where it ends. Water is available from the lake or inlet streams west of the lake. Wood and charcoal fires are not permitted here. Use camp stoves only. The occupancy rate for these campsites is about 45%.

Activities:
Fishing: Sandbeach Lake
Hiking: Sandbeach Lake Trail, Sandbeach - Meeker
   Park Trail
Peaks nearby: Mount Orton, Horsetooth Mountain,
   Lookout Mountain
Scenic Features: Sandbeach Lake

Sandbeach Lake campsite 3.

Directions:

The nearest access to this campsite is via the Sandbeach Lake Trailhead. Take Highway 7 south from Estes Park for about 10.8 miles to the Wild Basin Area turnoff (about 3.8 miles south of the Longs Peak access road). Turn right and follow the road for about .4 miles to the Wild Basin Entrance (just past the Wild Basin Lodge). The trailhead is just north of the entrance station. Take the Sandbeach Lake Trail for about 4.3 miles to Sandbeach Lake. The group campsite is to the right of the trail beyond the hitchrack while the individual sites are to the left, south of the trail and east of the lake.   It takes about 3 to 4 hours to reach these campsites via this moderately strenuous trail.

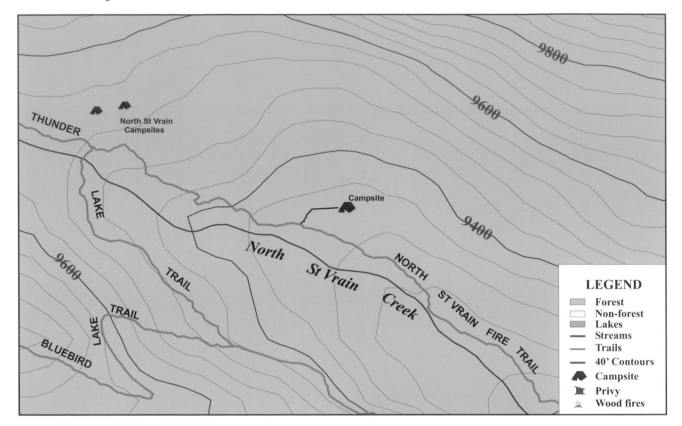

Siskin

Description:

The Siskin campsite is located in a stand of lodge-pole pine and spruce on a ridge north of the North St Vrain Fire Trail. The campsite is situated at an elevation of 9,340 feet. The path to the site leaves the trail and makes a gentle climb up the ridge to the northeast, almost paralleling the trail for about 75 yards. This campsite is well shaded by the dense forest. There are two distinct areas for pitching your tent. They are fairly level and have a smooth surface. Together, they will accommodate 2 to 3 tents. The dense forest provides good privacy from the little used North St Vrain Fire Trail. There are no toilet facilities near this campsite. Water may be obtained from North St Vrain Creek below the trail. Wood and charcoal fires are not permitted here. Use camp stoves only. Occupancy rate is 52%.

Activities:

Fishing: North St Vrain Creek
Hiking: Thunder Lake Trail, North St Vrain Fire Trail, Bluebird Lake Trail
Scenic Features: Copeland Falls, Ouzel Falls, Calypso Cascades

Siskin campsite.

Directions:

The nearest access to this campsite is via the Wild Basin Trailhead. Take Highway 7 south from Estes Park for about 10.8 miles to the Wild Basin Area turnoff (about 3.8 miles south of the Longs Peak access road). Turn right and follow the road for about .4 miles to the Wild Basin Entrance (just past the Wild Basin Lodge). Follow the narrow dirt road for about two miles to the Wild Basin Ranger Station and the trailhead. Take the Thunder Lake Trail for about 1.5 miles to the North St Vrain Trail intersection. There is a sign pointing the way to the campsites along this trail. Horses are not permitted on this trail. Follow this trail for about a mile to the campsite sign. Hiking time is about 1.5 to 2 hours.

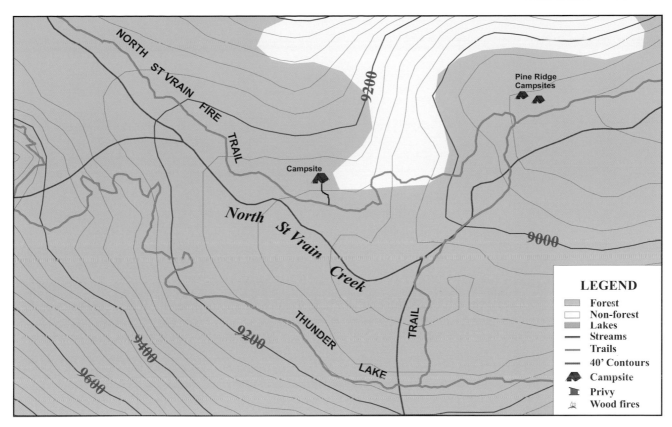

Tahosa

Description:

The Tahosa campsite is located in a stand of spruce and lodgepole pines on a ridge north of the North St Vrain Fire Trail. The campsite is situated at the edge of a small, rocky bluff at an elevation of 9,130 feet. The path to the site leaves the trail and climbs the ridge to the north for about 200 yards. This path is marked with red arrowheads on the trees and logs lining its edges. The campsite is a large bare area surrounded by lodgepole pine trees. It is a level area that has room for 2 to 3 tents. There are no toilet facilities near this campsite. Water may be obtained from North St Vrain Creek below the trail. Wood and charcoal fires are not permitted here. Use camp stoves only. This campsite is occupied about 50% of the time.

Activities:

Fishing: North St Vrain Creek

Hiking: Thunder Lake Trail, North St Vrain Fire Trail, Bluebird Lake Trail

Scenic Features: Copeland Falls, Ouzel Falls, Calypso Cascades

Directions:

The nearest access to this campsite is via the Wild Basin Trailhead. Take Highway 7 south from Estes Park

Tahosa campsite.

for about 10.8 miles to the Wild Basin Area turnoff (about 3.8 miles south of the Longs Peak access road). Turn right and follow the road for about .4 miles to the Wild Basin Entrance (just past the Wild Basin Lodge). Follow the narrow dirt road for about two miles to the Wild Basin Ranger Station and the trailhead. Take the Thunder Lake Trail for about 1.5 miles to the North St Vrain Trail intersection. There is a sign pointing the way to the campsites along this trail. Horses are not permitted on this trail. Follow this trail for about .3 miles to the campsite sign. Hiking time is about 1.5 hours.

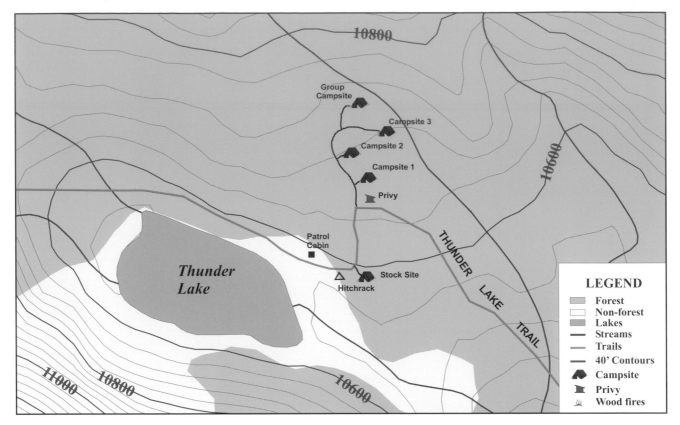

Thunder Lake

Description:

The Thunder Lake campsites are located in a stand of spruce northeast of Thunder Lake at an elevation of 10.680 feet. There are four individual sites, including a stock site, and one group site at this location. The group campsite and three individual sites are to the north of the trail while the stock site is to the south. Campsites 1, 2, and 3 are located east of a path that travels along a small stream. These campsites have well marked tent pads that will each accommodate 2 to 4 tents. The group site is north of the individual sites and has room for 6 to 8 tents. An outhouse is located where the path to the northern sites begins. The stock site is south of the trail that leads past Thunder Lake. There is a hitchrack across the trail from the site. This site has room for 2 to 3 tents. Water may be obtained from the small stream west of the campsites. Wood and charcoal fires are not permitted here. Use camp stoves only. Thunder Lake has an occupancy rate of about 57%.

Activities:

Fishing: Thunder Lake
Hiking: Thunder Lake Trail, Lion Lakes Trail
Peaks nearby: Pilot Mtn., Tanima Peak, Mt. Alice
Scenic Features: Thunder Lake, Lion Lakes

Thunder Lake campsite 3.

Directions:

The nearest access to this campsite is via the Wild Basin Trailhead. Take Highway 7 south from Estes Park for about 10.8 miles to the Wild Basin Area turnoff (about 3.8 miles south of the Longs Peak access road). Turn right and follow the road for about .4 miles to the Wild Basin Entrance (just past the Wild Basin Lodge). Follow the narrow dirt road for about two miles to the Wild Basin Ranger Station and the trailhead. Take the Thunder Lake Trail for about 1.5 miles to the North St Vrain Trail intersection. Take the North St Vrain Fire Trail for 1.3 miles to it intersection with the Thunder Lake Trail again. Continue northwest on the Thunder Lake Trail for 2.7 miles to the sites. Hiking time is 4 to 5 hours.

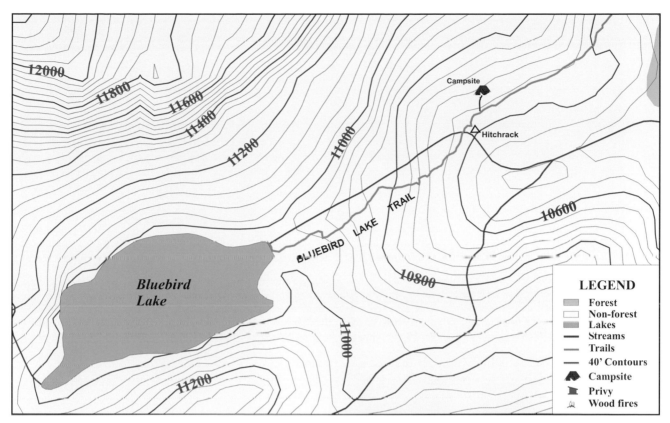

Upper Ouzel Creek

Description:

The Upper Ouzel Creek campsite is located on a bench north of the Bluebird Lake Trail above a small meadow. There is a horse hitchrack just below the path to the campsite. This campsite is situated at an elevation of 10,655 feet. It is a moderate climb over the path to the campsite. The tent pad is very smooth and level. It is in the open but surrounded on three sides by spruce trees. The open side offers a great view of the valley below. This campsite sees plenty of sunshine during the day. There are no toilet facilities near this campsite. Water may be obtained from Ouzel Creek. Wood and charcoal fires are not permitted here. Use camp stoves only. This campsite is about .4 miles below Bluebird Lake. Occupancy rate is about 75%.

Activities:

Fishing: Ouzel Lake, Ouzel Creek

Hiking: Thunder Lake Trail, Bluebird Lake Trail, Ouzel Lake Trail

Peaks nearby: Mahana Peak, Ouzel Peak, Copeland Mountain

Scenic Features: Copeland Falls, Ouzel Falls, Calypso Cascades, Ouzel Lake, Bluebird Lake

Upper Ouzel Creek campsite.

Directions:

The nearest access to this campsite is via the Wild Basin Trailhead. Take Highway 7 south from Estes Park for about 10.8 miles to the Wild Basin Area turnoff (about 3.8 miles south of the Longs Peak access road). Turn right and follow the road for about .4 miles to the Wild Basin Entrance (just past the Wild Basin Lodge). Follow the narrow dirt road for about two miles to the Wild Basin Ranger Station and the trailhead. Take the Thunder Lake Trail for about 3.2 miles to the Bluebird Lake Trail intersection. Turn left and hike about 1.4 miles to the Ouzel Lake Trail. Continue west for another 1.4 miles to a meadow. The campsite lies on a bench above this meadow to the north. Hiking time is about five hours.

Ouzel Falls is a popular destination for day hikers in the Wild Basin area.

Cross-country Zones

Cross-country zones are some of the least accessible and least travelled areas of the Park. There are twenty three cross-country zones scattered in every section of the Park. The total area occupied by these zones is about 34,794 acres, about 13% of the total area of Rocky Mountain National Park. They range in size from 455 to 5,890 acres. All of the cross-country zones are below treeline and are heavily forested. The terrain is generally moderate (8 to 25 percent slope) to steep (greater than 25 percent, usually 30 to 60 percent) in slope. Most of the forests have significant amounts of deadfall making travel and navigation more difficult. Backcountry campers who wish to experience the solitude and challenge offered by these areas should be highly skilled in navigating by map and compass and be very proficient in the use of Leave No Trace camping and hiking techniques. There are no established campsites, no toilet facilities, or established trails. You should plan on longer travel times to reach your destination within a cross-country zone. Usage of the cross-country zones is very low compared to developed campsites. The most popular zone is the Hunters Creek zone followed closely by the Ptarmigan Creek and Upper North Inlet zones. These cross-country zones average about 27 to 28 percent use during the heaviest camping season. The least used zone is the Columbine Creek zone with only one night in 1999.

Livestock are not permitted in any of the cross-country zones. Fires are not allowed. Carry a portable stove for cooking. No more than seven people can be in a camping party. The following rules and guidelines apply to cross-country zone campers:

- Camp within the boundaries of the cross-country zone

- Be out of sight and sound of any other camping party

- Camp at least 200 feet (70 steps) from any water source

- Move your camp at least one mile (1.6 kilometers) each day

- Stay no more than two nights in any one cross-country zone

- Camp below treeline and out of meadows

- Practice Leave No Trace camping techniques

Cache La Poudre

The Cache La Poudre zone, located in the north west section of the Park, is a long narrow area of about 2,476 acres covering the moderately steep ridge to the east of the Cache La Poudre River. The zone is forested with Englemann spruce, subalpine fir, and lodgepole pine. Three groups are permitted in this zone at one time. Elevations range from 9,900' to 11,500'. Water is available from the Poudre River just outside the zone. Access is via the Poudre River Trail. Topographic maps that cover the area include the Comanche Peak and Trail Ridge quads.

Cascade Creek flows through the lower portion of the Cascade Creek cross-country zone.

Cascade Creek

The Cascade Creek zone is an area of 1,580 acres located in the northwest section of the Park, north of the Mummy Pass Trail and west of Mirror Lake. The vegetation here is a mix of spruce, fir, and lodgepole pine with wet meadows along Cascade Creek. Two groups are permitted in this zone at any one time. Elevations range from 9,800' on the west to 11,500' at the tundra interface on the north. Most of the zone is of moderate steepness descending to Cascade Creek. Water is available from Cascade Creek. Access to this area is via Mummy Pass Trail and the Mirror Lake Trail near the Koenig campsite. This area is covered by the Comanche Peak quad.

Chiquita Creek

The Chiquita Creek zone is an area of 794 acres located about .35 miles north of the Endovalley Picnic area. Only one group is permitted in this zone at a time. Fifty to sixty percent of the area is steep with elevations ranging from 9,200' to 11,300'. It is densely forested with spruce, fir, and lodgepole pine. Water is available from Chiquita Creek and a small feeder stream. This zone may be accessed by following Chiquita Creek from the Endovalley Picnic area. The Trail Ridge quad includes all of this zone.

Columbine Creek

The Columbine Creek zone is the largest cross-country zone in the Park (5,890 acres). It is located east of the Colorado River in the southwest corner of the Park. The vegetation here is predominantly lodgepole pine with spruce and fir occupying the higher elevations. The terrain here is moderate to mostly steep with elevations ranging from 8,500' to 11,500' in the southeast section of the zone. Access to this area is available from the East Shore Trail near Columbine

Beautiful Columbine Bay is the jumping off point for entry into the Columbine Creek cross-country zone.

Creek. There is a trail along the creek that is no longer maintained. Water is available from Columbine and Pole creeks. This zone is covered by the Shadow Mountain and Isolation Peak quads. Up to four parties may camp in this zone at one time.

Cony Creek

The Cony Creek zone is an area of 455 acres located about .3 miles southeast of Peak Lake in the Wild Basin area of the Park. One group is allowed to camp in this area of spruce and fir at any one time. Water is available from Cony Creek that runs through the northern part of the zone. Eighty percent of the area is of moderate slope with elevations ranging from

The Cony Creek cross-country zone is southeast of Pear Lake.

10,300' to 11,200'. There are some rocky areas scattered throughout the zone. Access is via the Finch Lake-Pear Lake Trail near Pear Lake. The topographic features of this area are shown on the Isolation Peak and Allenspark quads.

Cow Creek

The Cow Creek zone, in the northeast section of the Park, covers an area of 1,392 acres northwest of Bridal Veil Falls. Dark Mountain is located in the center of the area. Vegetation in the area includes: spruce, fir, lodgepole pine, and limber pine. Two groups are permitted in this area at one time. Elevations range from 9,000' near the falls to 11,200' near treeline in the northwest section of the zone. All of the terrain is moderate to steep in slope. Water is available from Cow Creek. Access to this zone may be made from the Cow Creek, Dark Mountain, and Black Canyon trails. The Estes Park quad shows topographic features for this zone.

Echo Creek

The Echo Creek zone is an area of spruce, fir, and lodgepole pine (1,602 acres) located southeast of Grand Lake and south of the East Inlet Trail. This zone will accommodate up to two groups at a time. The area straddles the east and west sides of Echo Creek with elevations ranging from 9,100' in the east to 11,100' in the southeast section of the zone. Most of the terrain is moderate to steep in slope with some level ground along Echo Creek. Water is available from Echo Creek. Access is from the East Inlet Trail. This area is covered by the Shadow Mountain quad.

Hague Creek

The Hague Creek zone is an area of 1,872 acres located south of Hague Creek and east of the Poudre

River in the northwest section of the Park. This zone will accommodate up to five groups at any one time. It is forested with primarily spruce and fir. There are some wet meadows around Hague Creek as it crosses the eastern portion of the zone. Elevations range from 9,900' at the northwest end to 11,400' on the north slope of Flatiron Mountain. Most of the terrain is moderate to steep in slope. Water is available from Hague Creek. Access to this zone is via the Mummy Pass Trail and Hague Creek Meadow. Topographic features are displayed in the Comanche Peak and Trail Ridge quads.

Hayden Gorge

Hayden Gorge zone is a 617 acres area including the steep valley containing Hayden Creek south of Forest Canyon. This zone is forested with spruce and fir. The sides of the gorge are very steep with the most level ground along the creek. Elevations range from 9,900' in the northeast section to 11,400' below Terra Tomah Mountain in the southwest. Water is available from Hayden Creek. Access to this zone requires a great deal of cross-country travel, none of which is easy. It either involves travel through dense forest or across long stretches of tundra and down rocky slopes. Only one group is permitted in this area at a time. This zone requires four quads to cover access. These include: Fall River Pass, Trail Ridge, Grand Lake, and McHenrys Peak.

Hunters Creek

The Hunters Creek zone is an area of about 820 acres located north of Sandbeach Lake and south of Pagoda Mountain in the Wild Basin area. The area is vegetated with mostly spruce and fir with some willows in the northwest and limber pine in the northeast. Regulations permit only one group in this zone at a time. Elevations range from 9,900' in the southeast section to 11,600' in the northwest section south of Pagoda Mountain. The terrain in this zone is mostly moderate in slope with steep areas in the northeast and below the slopes of Mount Orton. Water is available from Hunters Creek. Access is available via the Sandbeach Lake Trail. The Allenspark quad provides topographic information for this zone.

Lower Forest Canyon

The Lower Forest Canyon zone contains 3,356 acres of mostly spruce and fir with some aspen and limber pine in the lower elevations. It is a boot-shaped area surrounding the Big Thompson River from Hayden Creek to just upstream of "The Pool". Four groups are permitted in this zone at one time.

The Hunters Creek cross-country zone lie just north of Sandbeach Lake.

Elevations range from 9,100' at the southeast edge of the zone to 11,300' on the northeast slopes of Stones Peak. Eighty percent of the zone is in steep terrain. The only reasonably level areas are along the Big Thompson River and Spruce Creek. Water can be found in Hayden Creek, Lost Brook, Big Thompson River, Spruce Creek, and Hidden River. The best access is via the Fern Lake Trail. Topographic quads covering this area include the Trail Ridge and McHenrys Peak quads.

Mosquito Creek

The Mosquito Creek zone is an area of 455 acres located about .2 miles east of the Grand Ditch Trail. The area consists of about 75% spruce-fir forest, 20% rock, and 5% wet meadow. Just one group at a time is permitted in this zone. This is a high elevation zone with elevations ranging from 10,400' along the eastern edge to 11,400' in the southwest. The slope of this terrain is mostly moderate to steep. Water is available from Mosquito and Opposition creeks. Access is via the Grand Ditch Trail. Topographic information is provided by the Mount Ritchtofen and Fall River Pass quads.

Mount Dickinson

The Mount Dickinson zone lies between the North Boundary Trail on the east and Mount Dickinson on the west. The area contains 700 acres of spruce-fir forest. The terrain here is moderate to steep with the steepest in the center of the zone and the west end toward Mount Dickinson. Elevations range from 9,400' near the northeast boundary to 11,300' on the east slopes of Mount Dickinson. Water is available from a small stream near the north edge of the zone. Access to the area is via the North Boundary Trail.

The Estes Park quad provides topographic information for this zone.

Mount Enentah

The Mount Enentah zone is an area of 774 acres located around Mount Enentah and south in the southwest section of the Park. Only one group at a time can camp in this predominantly lodgepole pine forest. The moderately steep terrain in this zone has elevations ranging from 9,800' in the north to 11,500' in the southeast portion of the zone. The terrain is steepest on the north and east slopes of Mount Enentah. There is no available water in this zone. Access to this zone can be made via the North Inlet Trail on the north and the East Inlet Trail on the south. It requires over a mile of cross-country travel through dense forest. Topographic information is provided on the Grand Lake and Shadow Mountain quads.

Mount Patterson

The Mount Patterson zone is a "C" shaped area of 2,162 acres that surrounds Mount Patterson on the north, west, and south. It is located east of Tonahutu Creek in the western portion of the Park. Park regulations permit three groups in this zone at a time. This area is heavily forested with spruce, fir, and lodgepole pine. Elevations range from 9,700' in the southeast section of the zone to 11,400' around Mount Patterson. The terrain in this zone is moderate to steep in slope with the steepest areas west of Mount Patterson. Water is available from a few feeder streams that flow into Tonahutu and North Inlet creeks. Access

You are more likely to observe more secretive wildlife in the cross-country zones.

to this area is from the Tonahutu Creek Trail on the west and the North Inlet Trail on the south. The Grand Lake quad provides topographic information for this zone.

Nakai Peak

The Nakai Peak zone contains 696 acres of spruce, fir, and lodgepole pine. It is located between Nakai

Large meadow near the Nakai Peak cross-country zone.

Peak on the north and the Tonahutu Creek Trail on the south. This high elevation zone has elevations ranging from 10,000' along the southern edge to 11,400' on the southwest slope of Nakai Peak. The slopes of the terrain in this zone are moderate to steep. One group is permitted in this zone at a time. Water is available from a small pond in the north part of the zone and the stream that flows south from it. Access is via the Tonahutu Creek Trail to the south of the zone. The topographic character of this zone is shown on the Grand Lake quad.

North Inlet

The North Inlet zone is an area of 1,900 acres that is located north of the North Inlet Trail and south and east of Mount Patterson. This zone is situated in the southwest portion of the Park. Vegetation in this zone includes spruce, fir, and lodgepole pine forest, wet meadows, and alpine tundra. Elevations range from 9,700' along the south edge of the zone to 11,400' on the slopes of Mount Patterson. Most of the terrain is moderate in slope with some level, rolling ground in the wet areas along small streams. Four parties are allowed to camp in this zone at any one time. Water is available from small feeder streams flowing into North Inlet Creek and some scattered small ponds. Access to this zone is via the North Inlet Trail. Topographic information is contained on the Grand Lake and McHenrys Peak quads.

Onahu Creek

The Onahu Creek zone is a heavily forested area of 1,636 acres located east of Long Meadows on the west side of the Park. Vegetation in this zone consists of mainly spruce and fir with a few pockets of

Long Meadows lies west of the Onahu Creek zone. The Long Meadows Trail provides access to this cross-country zone.

lodgepole pine. The area also contains some wet meadows and areas of rock. Elevations range from 9,900' near the southwest edge of the zone to 11,200' near its eastern border. The terrain in this zone is moderately steep with about 5% being level to rolling. Water is available from Onahu Creek and some of its tributaries. Only one group at a time is permitted to camp in this zone. Access is via the Long Meadows Trail from the Timber Lake Trail on the north and the Onahu Trail on the south. The Grand Lake quad provides topographic information for this zone.

Ptarmigan Creek

The Ptarmigan Creek zone is a forested area of 567 acres located in a steep valley containing Ptarmigan Creek. This zone is situated in the southwest section of the Park. One party is allowed to camp in this zone at a time. The vegetation is mostly spruce and fir with some wet meadows in the northern part of the zone. The area west of Bench Lake is rocky. Elevations range from 10,100' in the south to 11,300' south of Ptarmigan Lake. The sides of the valley are steep with level, rolling terrain in the bottom near the creek. Water is available from Bench Lake and Ptarmigan Creek. Access is from the North Inlet Trail along Ptarmigan Creek. The McHenrys Peak quad contains map information for exploring this zone.

Ptarmigan Mountain

The Ptarmigan Mountain zone is an area of 1,278 acres of predominately spruce-fir forest located between the North Inlet Trail and Ptarmigan Mountain. The zone is located southwest of Pettingell Lake in the southwest portion of the Park. Sixty percent of the terrain in this area is steep with elevations ranging from 9,600' in the southwest part of the zone to 11,500' in

the east. The most level ground is located north of Pettingell Lake. Water is available from small feeder streams that drain into North Inlet Creek and Pettingell Lake. Access is via the North Inlet Trail. This area is covered by the Grand Lake and McHenrys Peak quads.

South Cache La Poudre

The South Cache La Poudre zone lies along the northern boundary of the Park. This 622 acre zone contains the valley surrounding the South Fork Cache La Poudre River (no fishing allowed). Vegetation in this zone consists of spruce-fir forest with some limber pines on the north edge and some small wet meadows. Elevations range from 9,400' at the northeast end to 11,300' at its closest point to the Mummy Pass Trail. The sides of the valley are steep with the steepest slopes above treeline. One party is allowed to camp here at one time. Water is available from the river or from small ponds in the southwest section of the zone. Access can be made from the Mummy Pass Trail on the north and west and the Stormy Peaks Trail on the south and east. Topographic information is available on the Comanche Peak and Pingree Park quads.

Upper Forest Canyon

The Upper Forest Canyon zone is a 2,205 acres strip about a mile wide centered on the Big Thompson River. It begins about 1.5 miles east of Forest Canyon Pass and continues southeast for about 3.5 miles. This

This meadow in the bottom of Forest Canyon is just west of the Upper Forest Canyon cross-country zone.

is a very dense spruce-fir forest with considerable deadfall. Elevations range from 9,400' near the eastern end of the zone to 11,000' at the northwest edge. Most of the terrain is moderately steep with the steepest being the north side of the canyon. Three groups may camp in this zone at the same time. Water is available from the Big Thompson River and several small streams flowing into it. The best access is via the Milner Pass-Fall River Pass Trail near Forest Canyon Pass. Topographic maps that cover this zone include the Fall River Pass and Trail Ridge quads.

Upper North Inlet

The Upper North Inlet zone is a forested area of 945 acres that lies east of Lake Nanita, including the steep valley containing North Inlet Creek. This zone is located in the southwest portion of the Park. The

The Upper North Inlet cross-country zone lies in this valley below the North Inlet Trail.

vegetation is predominately spruce-fir forest with some wet meadow near Lake Solitude. Park regulations permit two groups to camp in this zone at one time. Elevations range from 9,700' near Lake Solitude to 11,200' along the northeast edge of the zone. Most of the terrain is steep with level, rolling ground along North Inlet Creek. Water is available from Lake Solitude and North Inlet Creek. Access is via the Lake Nanita Trail and along North Inlet Creek. Topographic maps that include this zone are the McHenrys Peak and Isolation Peak quads.

Cross-country Zones

Zone	No. parties	Area (acres)	Elevations (feet)	Terrain Slopes	Nearest Trail
Cache La Poudre	3	2,476	9,900 - 11,500	moderate	Poudre River
Cascade Creek	2	1,580	9,800 - 11,500	moderate	Mummy Pass / Mirror Lake
Chiquita Creek	1	794	9,200 - 11,300	steep	Endovalley Picnic area
Columbine Creek	4	5,890	8,500 - 11,500	steep	East Shore
Cony Creek	1	455	10,300 - 11,200	moderate	Finch Lake - Pear Lake
Cow Creek	2	1,392	9,000 - 11,200	steep	Cow Creek / Dark Mountain
Echo Creek	2	1,602	9,100 - 11,100	steep	East Inlet
Hague Creek	5	1,872	9,900 - 11,400	moderate	Mummy Pass
Hayden Gorge	1	617	9,900 - 11,400	steep	Utc
Hunters Creek	1	820	9,900 - 11,600	moderate	Sandbeach Lake
Lower Forest Canyon	4	3,356	9,100 - 11,300	steep	Fern Lake
Mosquito Creek	1	455	10,400 - 11,400	moderate	Grand Ditch
Mount Dickinson	2	700	9,400 - 11,300	moderate	North Boundary
Mount Enentah	1	774	9,800 - 11,500	moderate	East Inlet / North Inlet
Mount Patterson	3	2,162	9,700 - 11,400	moderate	Tonahutu Creek / North Inlet
Nakai Peak	1	696	10,000 - 11,400	steep	Tonahutu Creek
North Inlet	4	1,900	9,700 - 11,400	moderate	North Inlet
Onahu Creek	1	1,636	9,900 - 11,200	moderate	Long Meadows
Ptarmigan Creek	1	567	10,100 - 11,300	moderate	North Inlet
Ptarmigan Mountain	2	1,278	9,600 - 11,500	steep	North Inlet
South Cache La Poudre	1	622	9,400 - 11,300	steep	Mummy Pass / Stormy Peaks
Upper Forest Canyon	3	2,205	9,400 - 11,000	moderate	Milner Pass - Fall River Pass
Upper North Inlet	2	945	9,700 - 11,200	steep	Lake Nanita

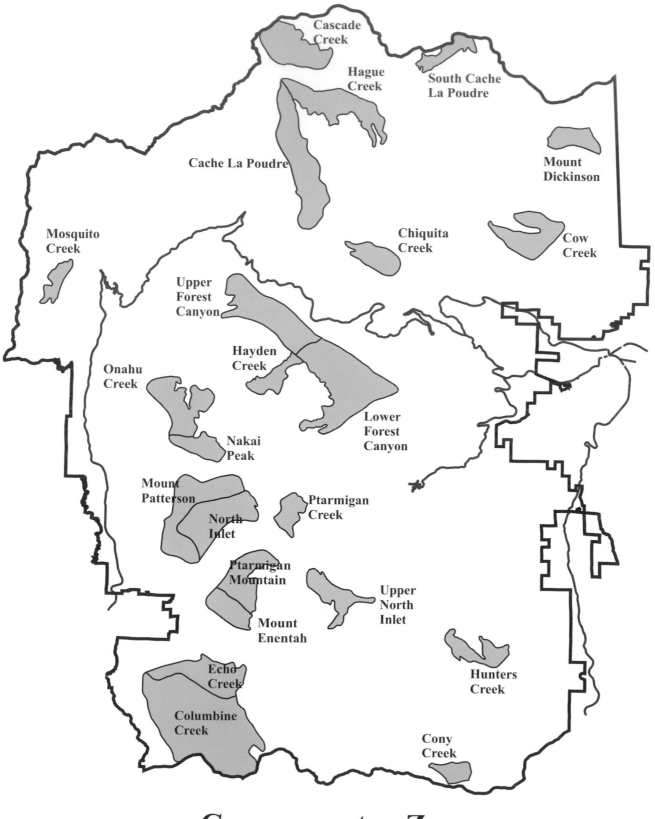

Cross-country Zones

Camping With Livestock

Livestock, in Rocky Mountain National Park, are defined as horses or ponies and pack animals. Horses, burros, mules, and llama are considered pack animals. No other animal may be used as packstock. There are ten campsites in the Park that permit the use of any type of livestock and three additional sites that allow the use of llama only. Stock sites are located in the North Fork (Lost Meadow and Bighorn Mountain), Mummy Range (Lawn Lake), Bear Lake (Ute Meadow - llama only), Wild Basin (Aspen Knoll - llama only, Thunder Lake, and Finch Lake), North Inlet (North Inlet Group), Tonahutu (Tonahutu Group and Haynach - llama only), Never Summer Range (Ditch Camp), and Hague Creek (Hague Creek and Koenig) areas. Six of these campsites are individual sites (Lawn Lake, Ute Meadow, Aspen Knoll, Thunder Lake, Haynach, and Koenig) and seven are group sites (Finch Lake, Ditch Camp, Hague Creek, Lost Meadow, Bighorn Mountain, North Inlet Group, and Tonahutu Group).

Horses must be securely tied to hitchracks while camping in stock sites such as here at Bighorn Mountain stock site.

Party size is limited to six people and eight stock (one pack stock per three people and saddle stock) for individual sites. Group stock sites permit up to twelve people and sixteen stock. You must have at least eight people in your party to make reservations for group stock sites. Unreserved group sites, however, are available to smaller parties within five days of your planned trip.

Hitchracks are provided at most of the stock sites. The Tonahutu Group and North Inlet Group sites have large corrals. Tethering posts are provided at the llama only campsites as well as at the Bighorn Mountain Group/Stock site. Highlining, hobbling, loose herding,

Llama tethering posts at the Ute Meadow campsite.

temporary corrals or any other means of confinement are strictly prohibited. Hitchracks are generally well away from the tent areas.

Grazing is not permitted anywhere in the Park. Only certified weed-free feed may be used to feed livestock while within Rocky Mountain National Park. Pelleted feed or hay cubes work best for feeding your stock while in the backcountry. Backcountry campers using livestock are expected to clean up after their stock. This includes packing out unused feed, spreading manure, and filling in holes caused by pawing. As with backpackers, all campers who use stock should learn and practice Leave No Trace techniques for minimizing the impact of using livestock in the backcountry. Always stay on maintained trails to help prevent vegetation, soil erosion, and trail

Horses unloading area at Wild Basin.

braiding. When approaching other users of the backcountry, make your presence known to give them time to clear the trail.

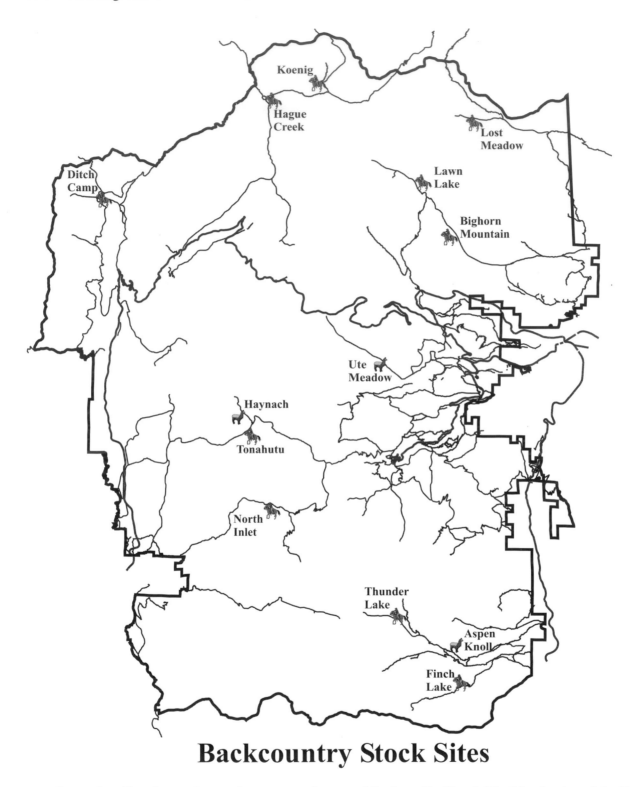

Backcountry Stock Sites

Several trailheads can be used to access these campsites. These include: Never Summer and Colorado River trailheads (Dutch Camp), Corral Creek Trailhead (Hague Creek and Koenig), Wild Basin Trailhead (Thunder Lake, Aspen Knoll, Finch Lake), Green Mountain Trailhead (Tonahutu, Haynach), North Inlet Trailhead (North Inlet), Lawn Lake Trailhead (Lawn Lake, Bighorn Mountain), Upper Beaver Meadows Trailhead (Ute Meadow), and the Dunraven Trailhead (Lost Meadow). About 20% of the trails in the Park are not open to stock use. Most are well signed. Some trails may be temporarily closed due to conditions. Check with park personnel before planning your trip.

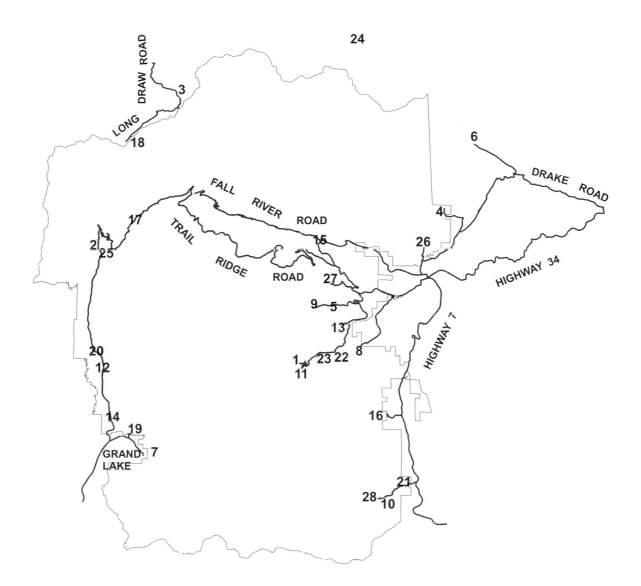

Trailheads

1 Bear Lake
2 Colorado River
3 Corral Creek
4 Cow Creek
5 Cub Lake
6 Dunraven
7 East Inlet
8 East Portal
9 Fern Lake
10 Finch Lake
11 Glacier Gorge Junction
12 Green Mountain
13 Hollowell Park
14 Kawuneeche VC
15 Lawn Lake

16 Longs Peak
17 Milner Pass
18 Never Summer
19 North Inlet
20 Onahu
21 Sandbeach Lake
22 Sprague Lake
23 Storm Pass
24 Stormy Peaks
25 Timber Lake
26 Twin Owls
27 Upper Beaver Meadows
28 Wild Basin

Index